Frances Mabel Robinson

Irish history for English readers

from the earliest times to the close of the year 1885

Frances Mabel Robinson

Irish history for English readers

from the earliest times to the close of the year 1885

ISBN/EAN: 9783744739986

Printed in Europe, USA, Canada, Australia, Japan

Cover: Foto ©ninafisch / pixelio.de

More available books at **www.hansebooks.com**

No. 62 *25 Cts.*

Copyright, 1885,
by HARPER & BROTHERS

MARCH 12, 1886

Subscription Price
per Year, 52 Numbers, $15

Extra   Entered at the Post-Office at New York, as Second-class Mail Matter

IRISH HISTORY
FOR ENGLISH READERS

*FROM THE EARLIEST TIMES
TO THE CLOSE OF THE YEAR 1885*

By WM. STEPHENSON GREGG

Books you may hold readily in your hand are the most useful, after all
DR. JOHNSON

NEW YORK
HARPER & BROTHERS, PUBLISHERS
1886

HARPER'S HANDY SERIES.

Latest Issues.

NO.		CENTS.
27.	SELF-DOOMED. A Novel. By B. L. Farjeon	25
28.	MALTHUS AND HIS WORK. By James Bonar, M.A.	25
29.	THE DARK HOUSE. A Novel. By G. Manville Fenn	25
30.	THE GHOST'S TOUCH, and Other Stories. By Wilkie Collins	25
31.	THE ROYAL MAIL. By James Wilson Hyde. Illustrated	25
32.	THE SACRED NUGGET. A Novel. By B. L. Farjeon	25
33.	PRIMUS IN INDIS. A Romance. By M. J. Colquhoun	25
34.	MUSICAL HISTORY. By G. A. Macfarren	25
35.	IN QUARTERS WITH THE 25TH DRAGOONS. By J. S. Winter	25
36.	GOBLIN GOLD. A Novel. By May Crommelin	25
37.	THE WANDERINGS OF ULYSSES. By Prof. C. Witt. Translated by Frances Younghusband	25
38.	A BARREN TITLE. A Novel. By T. W. Speight	25
39.	US: AN OLD-FASHIONED STORY. By Mrs. Molesworth. Ill'd.	25
40.	OUNCES OF PREVENTION. By Titus Munson Coan, A.M., M.D.	25
41.	HALF-WAY. An Anglo-French Romance	25
42.	CHRISTMAS ANGEL. A Novel. By B. L. Farjeon. Illustrated	25
43.	MRS. DYMOND. A Novel. By Miss Thackeray	25
44.	THE BACHELOR VICAR OF NEWFORTH. A Novel. By Mrs. J. Harcourt-Roe	25
45.	IN THE MIDDLE WATCH. A Novel. By W. Clark Russell	25
46.	TIRESIAS, AND OTHER POEMS. By Alfred, Lord Tennyson	25
47.	LAST DAYS AT APSWICH. A Novel	25
48.	CABIN AND GONDOLA. By Charlotte Dunning	30
49.	LESTER'S SECRET. A Novel. By Mary Cecil Hay	30
50.	A MAN OF HONOR. A Novel. By J. S. Winter. Illustrated	25
51.	STORIES OF PROVENCE. From the French of Alphonse Daudet. By S. L. Lee	25
52.	'TWIXT LOVE AND DUTY. A Novel. By Tighe Hopkins	25
53.	A PLEA FOR THE CONSTITUTION, &c. By George Bancroft	25
54.	FORTUNE'S WHEEL. A Novel. By Alex. Innes Shand	25
55.	LORD BEACONSFIELD'S CORRESPONDENCE WITH HIS SISTER—1832–1852	25
56.	MAULEVERER'S MILLIONS. A Yorkshire Romance. By T. Wemyss Reid	25
57.	WHAT DOES HISTORY TEACH? Two Edinburgh Lectures. By John Stuart Blackie	25
58.	THE LAST OF THE MAC ALLISTERS. A Novel. By Mrs. Amelia E. Barr.	25
59.	CAVALRY LIFE. Sketches and Stories. By J. S. Winter	25
60.	MOVEMENTS OF RELIGIOUS THOUGHT IN BRITAIN DURING THE NINETEENTH CENTURY. By John Tulloch, D.D., LL.D.	25
61.	HURRISH: A STUDY. By the Hon. Emily Lawless	25
62.	IRISH HISTORY FOR ENGLISH READERS. By Wm. Stephenson Gregg.	25

Other volumes in preparation.

☞ HARPER & BROTHERS *will send any of the above works by mail, postage prepaid, to any part of the United States or Canada, on receipt of the price.*

CONTENTS.

CHAP.		PAGE
I.	THE AGE OF LEGENDS,	3
II.	ST. PATRICK AND HIS TIMES,	8
III.	THE RISE AND FALL OF HOLINESS AND LEARNING,	12
IV.	THE INVASION.	17
V.	THREE CENTURIES OF NORMAN RULE,	21
VI.	THE GERALDINES,	25
VII.	HOW SHANE O'NEILL HELD ULSTER,	32
VIII.	THE DESMOND REBELLION,	40
IX.	ELIZABETH'S WAR WITH HUGH O'NEILL,	46
X.	THE PLANTATION OF ULSTER,	52
XI.	THE CIVIL WAR OF 1641,	57
XII.	THE PLANTATION OF CROMWELL,	65
XIII.	THE RESTORATION,	69
XIV.	THE REVOLUTION,	77
XV.	THE TREATY OF LIMERICK,	83
XVI.	THE PENAL CODE,	86
XVII.	THE COMMERCIAL RESTRAINTS,	91
XVIII.	THE LAND DIFFICULTIES,	94
XIX.	WOOD'S HALFPENCE,	99
XX.	THE PATRIOT PARTY,	101
XXI.	THE VOLUNTEERS,	107
XXII.	GRATTAN'S PARLIAMENT,	111
XXIII.	THE UNITED IRISHMEN,	115

CONTENTS.

CHAP.		PAGE
XXIV.—"Ninety-eight,"		119
XXV.—The Prospect of Union,		122
XXVI.—The Act of Union,		128
XXVII.—The Peace of 1815,		133
XXVIII.—Emancipation,		138
XXIX.—The Repeal Year,		144
XXX.—The Famine,		147
XXXI.—Young Ireland,		156
XXXII.—The Land,		160
XXXIII.—Fenianism,		166
XXXIV.—Lopping the Upas Tree,		172
XXXV.—The Home Rule Movement,		178
XXXVI.—The Land League,		182
XXXVII.—The Land Act,		191
XXXVIII.—Ireland Under the Crimes Act,		195
XXXIX.—The Elections of 1885,		201
Table of Dates,		208
List of Authorities,		215

IRISH HISTORY
FOR ENGLISH READERS.

CHAPTER I.

THE AGE OF LEGENDS.

It is perhaps because there is so little that is pleasant in their modern history that the Irish cherish the traditions of olden times so deeply. We profess to know but little of the history of Britain before the Roman conquest, but Irish legends and mythology go back to two thousand three hundred and seventy nine-years before the Christian era: or thirty years before the flood, and two hundred years earlier than the supposed date of the building of Memphis.

Such early dates are naturally of no historic value, and refer to legendary events and legendary personages, but the fact that the gods and heroes of those bygone days are remembered proves that Ireland had reached a degree of civilization very rarely attained so early in the world's history.

The legends tell us that Queen Keasair and her followers came to Ireland from the east of Europe about 2,380 years before Christ, and that the Keasaireans were driven from the island by Partolān three hundred years later; but the monks, taking advantage of the intermediate deluge, say that the Keasaireans were destroyed by the flood. Be this as it may, only one of the Keasaireans has left any impress on Irish history—that one is Fintan, the salmon god, the patron of poets and historians, who duly reappeared from time to time as long as any belief in fairies continued.

When the Keasaireans were drowned in the deluge,

Fintan escaped by taking the form of a salmon, until the receding waters left him high and dry on Tara Hill, when he resumed his humanity. It was he who related the history of Ireland to St. Patrick, and some legends tell us that it is to Fintan that we owe our knowledge of these early times, he having visibly appeared to the bards for their enlightenment. Others say that Amergin, the Druid, collected the materials for this early history, but as he did not live till a thousand years after the Keasaireans, he may have been very glad of a little help from Fintan in his researches.

After the destruction of the Keasaireans, Partolán and his followers came to the island. These invaders came from some civilized country, and brought with them a knowledge of sowing and reaping and other agricultural arts, and began cultivating the island. But this was already owned by a savage race of giants called the Formorians, who, though they themselves cared nothing for the land, grudged the use of it to others, and exterminated the unlucky race of Partolán. The fate of those unhappy invaders seems to have remained unknown in the distant country whence they came, for Partolán was followed by his cousin Nemed, who, with his five sons, headed a large party of invaders, and landed on the coast of Leinster. The Nemedians fared no better than their forerunners; the Formorians gave them battle and conquered them, with such terrible slaughter that only three of their chiefs escaped. These were Briotan, who settled in Britain and became the ancestor of the British gods, Semeon Brac and Ibath, who escaped to the east of Europe. The descendants of both these latter were destined to return to Ireland; the children of Semeon Brac as the Firbolgs, and those of Ibath as the Tuatha-de Danān (people of the fairies), the last and greatest race of Irish gods. The Firbolgs were not deities; still, in the time of their last king, Eocha-Mac-Erc, Ireland was in a position almost without parallel in her history, for, say the bards, "Good were the days of the sovereignty of Mac-Erc, there was no wet or tempestuous weather in Erin, neither was there any unfruitful year."

This happy state of things was, however, brought to a

THE AGE OF LEGENDS.

close by the Tuatha-de Danān, the descendants of Ibath, and therefore, like the Firbolgs, of Nemedian descent.

These heroes landed on Wexford coast, and then, having burnt their fleet to cut off their retreat, they wrapped themselves in the black cloud of invisibility, and drifted like a mighty mist to the Iron Mountains on the borders of Leitrim. The Firbolgs were assembled on the neighboring plains of Sligo, and there, for six days, waged the uneven fight between gods and men. At last the brave Mac-Erc fell on the coast near Ballysadare, where a mound of earth still marks the grave of the last of the Firbolg kings. His people were reduced to the condition of a subject race, and the Tuatha-de Danān believed themselves masters of the soil. But the Formorians, though absentees, were still in possession, and yearly, after harvest-time, sent agents to sweep away the produce of the land, and the Tuatha-de Danān in their turn became a crushed and broken people, till they were freed from their bondage by Lu-Lam-Finn, a prince of mixed Formorian and de Danān descent, and from that time till the Scoto-Milesian invasion the de Danān people owned the land. Nor, say the legends, did they then utterly abandon it; but, drawing around them that cloak of misty darkness which had helped them to victory at their invasion, they retired to the mountains, whence from time to time they appear in the guise of Ban-Shees, for the Shees and Tuatha-de Danān are alike the people of the fairies.

The story of Ireland before the Milesian invasion is purely mythological, but it is probable that an invasion from the Spanish peninsula really took place about 1,000 years before Christ, when Solomon was king of Israel, and about 300 years before the foundation of Rome.

Milesius, or Miles, though a native of Spain was probably of Phoenecian descent, and from him and his wife, Scotia, all the royal and noble families in Ireland claim to be descended. A peaceable colonization of Ireland was attempted during the lifetime of Milesius by his brother Ith, who was slain by the Tuatha-de Danān, and in revenge for this deed the eight sons of Milesius set out to conquer the country.

Many and terrible were the adventures of that invasion, in which five out of the eight sons of Milesius lost their lives, but at length Heber, Herēmon, and Amergin landed on different parts of the coast, and, attacking the Tuatha-de Danān from all sides, managed to subdue them.

Amergin, being a Druid, could not reign, so Heber and Herēmon arranged to divide the country between them, but being unable to come to any agreement, they met for a decisive battle at Gaeshill, in King's County, where Heber and many of his followers were killed, and from then till the date of the Norman invasion the descendants of Herē-mon ruled the island in an unbroken line of 197 Scoto-Milesian kings.

The first of these with whom we need concern ourselves is Ollav Fohla, the founder of that famous code known as the Brehon laws. These were administered by the Brehons or judges, and, having been revised by St. Patrick, were obeyed by Christian Ireland; it was decreed by Edward III. that no English subject should be tried by Brehon law, but its authority was recognized by the native Irish until the middle of the seventeenth century. Ollav Fohla was succeeded by a line of five or six and twenty kings, and then a ruling queen—Macha. The date of her accession (299 B. C.) is important, for Tiherna, the great Irish historian of the eleventh century, held it to be the earliest authentic date in Irish history, and Macha is also noteworthy as the founder of the city of Armagh, the capital of Ulster throughout the heroic ages.

In these early days Ireland was divided into four or five provinces, each governed by its own Ard-Righ, or head king, who had many petty kings or chieftains reigning under him. The latest and best known division of Ireland was into the five provinces of Ulster, Leinster, Munster, Connaught, and Meath, and the kings of these provinces were perpetually contending for the supremacy. In very early times the king of Ulster usually was victorious, but about the year seventy of our era the king of Meath became Ard-Righ of all Erin, and held his court at Tara. The eldest son of the reigning king was usually elected *Tanist*, or heir, but any member of the five royal families of Ireland might be chosen during the lifetime of the king. But Meath did not gain or maintain the supremacy without a struggle, and the petty chieftains were in a state of perpetual warfare with one another. The island, thus weakened by internal dissensions, would doubtless have fallen an easy prey to invaders from Rome, Gaul, Britain, and Caledonia, had not a volunteer army been raised from among the nobles of the whole of Ireland for the defence of the country from foreign foes. These Fianna-Erin, or Fenians, were in many respects the equivalent to King Arthur's knights: chivalrous, courageous, pure. The "heroes of Erin" were the idols of the people upon whom they were quartered during the six winter months. In the summer they lived by hunting and fishing, and after a time they exacted as a right the whole of the wild game and large fish of the country. In return for their privileges, they performed both in times of peace and war all the duties of police, and in internal warfare they espoused the cause of the chieftain by whose people they were maintained. Thus Munster Fenians fought against the Fenians of Meath in the early days of their society, but as the organization grew in power and extent, they banded themselves together and held all Ireland in a state of subjection or fear. The need for such an organization, too, was passing away; Ireland was yearly growing more united, and the supremacy of the Tara king was more and more generally acknowledged. The power of Rome, and the consequent fear of Roman invasion, was waning, and the Fenians, abusing their power, had become an oppressive burden to the country, till, in the year 281, the king of Tara headed the populace in a revolt against the Fianna, who from that time gradually faded away. The supremacy of Tara now became undisputed, and the power of Ireland grew in extent till, in the time of Niall Mōr, the invasions of the Scotic marauders were a terror to the neighboring coasts of Britain, Gaul, and Caledonia.

CHAPTER II.

ST. PATRICK AND HIS TIMES.

AFTER many successful raids in Gaul and Britain, Niall Mōr, in the tenth year of his reign (388) invaded Gaul, and at the close of a successful campaign in Brittany returned to Erin, bringing with him "thousands of Christian captives," among whom was a lad of sixteen named Succoth, who from his noble birth was called Patricius. The young Patrick was sold into slavery, and was employed as a shepherd, till after seven years of captivity a prophetic dream inspired him to escape. But in the happy Breton home, which he reached after many perils, the vision of heathen Erin distressed his soul, and a second prophetic dream bade him prepare himself for the evangelization of Erin. Breaking free from all earthly ties, he took the monastic habit of Tours, and seven years later he went to Rome; but he eventually joined the barefooted Augustines, and was in their monastery at Auxenre when the news of the death of St. Paladius reached him. He then went to Rome and offered to succeed Paladius as missionary to Erin, and having been consecrated archbishop he, with a company of twenty priests, set out on his mission in 432. There were already a few Christians in Ireland; five unsuccessful missions had prepared the ground for St. Patrick's success, but the mass of the people still adhered to some form of heathenism of which little trace remains. There is proof that the fire and sun were worshipped, but, curiously enough, the race which after the introduction of Christianity became the most devout in Europe seems to have been singularly irreligious in pagan times. We find no trace of intense devotion to the gods or of ascetic qualities, and the influence of the Druids seems to have been moral rather than spiritual. The legends, too, are devoid of religious feeling, and the virtues of the people—uprightness, truth, courage, justice, chivalry, and hospitality—are purely moral. In the age of St. Patrick the Irish or Scotti had attained to a considerable degree of civilization: the laws were just and were justly administered; death was the punishment for murder, theft, and rape, but the families of the injured person might accept in atonement a fine or *eric*, whose amount was fixed by the Brehons. The law of inheritance was that known as gavelkind. All the sons inherited in equal shares, but except where there were no sons the daughters did not inherit. The land belonged to the nations or tribes that dwelt upon it, and was divided into three classes—common lands on which the whole clan had the right of pasturage, lands set apart for the benefit of the chief, and lands cultivated by individual members of the tribe, and for which the cultivators paid tribute, and the tenure of such land was hereditary. Seven kinds of grain were grown, but the people were in the main pastoral, and lived chiefly off the flesh and milk of their beasts.

The sea-board inhabitants had acquired great skill in ship-building, and in the manufacture of weapons the Scotti nearly equalled the Romans, whose influence in Britain and Gaul was very beneficial to Erin. Among other arts learned from the Romans was that of building with the aid of mortar, and the presence of mortar in their construction proves the Irish round towers to have been built after the Roman colonization of Britain. The purpose of these round towers is not known. Some antiquarians hold them to be Christian belfries, but they were probably connected with heathen rites of fire worship. There are in Ireland, as in England, many cromlechs and other Druidic remains of early temples and tombs built before the use of mortar was introduced; among these are funeral piles so vast, and composed of such huge blocks of stone, that they can only be compared to the Egyptian pyramids.

Stone and mortar were used only for buildings intended to last for ever; dwelling-houses were of wrought wood, usually oak, and consisted for the most part of one apartment with a dome-shaped roof, in the middle of which there was a space for the smoke to escape. But long before the days of St. Patrick, the houses of the great nobles contained seven or eight rooms, besides separate halls for feasting and for the various members of the chieftain's family.

The under-dress of both sexes and all classes consisted of a tight-fitting garment—stocking, trouser, and vest in one. Over this, men of the upper class wore a long mantle, and women full-plaited skirts reaching below the knee; the dress itself was usually the dark color of the wool of a black sheep, and was trimmed with bands of bright dyed cloth, but color was an indication of rank, and yellow was probably the royal, as it was the favorite color of the early Irish. Shoes were merely a leather sandal tied across with a lacing of ribbon. The head-dress of the men was the pointed Phrygean cap; married women wore a linen coif, and girls their own hair braided in long plaits. Even in early times the goldsmithry of the Irish was very beautiful.

The custom of fosterage was universal, and the respect and veneration paid to the foster parents continued through life.

Fishing, shooting, riding, and the arts of agriculture and war, formed the basis of every Irishman's education; but the sons of noble houses were well instructed in the history of their country, and in music, singing, and verse-making. They were also taught to read and write the Celtic character, which consisted of an alphabet of seventeen letters named after the seventeen trees indigenous to Erin.

Girls were, of course, taught the domestic arts of spinning, weaving, cooking; but this last was a simple matter, for fish, flesh, and bread, all baked in the ashes, butter, milk, honey, and herbs, among which watercress and shamrock were the favorites, formed the diet of the Scotti, and their only strong drink was ale.

So long as the summer lasted life was passed chiefly out of doors, but the winter evenings were beguiled with feasting and carousing, with chess and draughts, music, and the recitation of poems. The bards, accompanied by

ST. PATRICK AND HIS TIMES.

their harp-bearers, went from place to place singing the old legends, but also making such free use of their tongues in the invention of scandals and libels that from time to time they were punished by wholesale banishment.

Such were the Scotti when Patrick came amongst them —a people in no sense barbarous; warlike, but not cruel, and civilized enough to have framed a code of laws which, in a modified form, sufficed their posterity till the seventeenth century; a people devoted to the virtues of honesty, justice, and hospitality; a moral, poetic, and imaginative people, who were but loosely bound to the religion he was to bid them cast aside.

The years of Patrick's captivity now stood him in good stead; he knew the language and the customs of the people he was to evangelize. During the fifteen years that had passed since his escape he had thought and prayed much over this mission. Harshness he knew must fail with this brave nation, who, easy to lead, were impossible to drive, and he resolved never to wound innocent prejudice or denounce harmless customs. His tact and knowledge, too, led him to address himself first to the chieftains, and at the outset of his mission he won the Leinster princes over to his side. These Leinster converts were made by twos and threes, but as the fame of the new faith spread converts came in by the thousand, and after fifteen years' evangelization the saint had to go over to Britain to bring over more clergy. He returned with thirty bishops, and then set to work preparing some of the native Christians for ordination, founding schools for their instruction in church doctrine and history and the Latin tongue. The conversion of Ireland was thus completed in the lifetime of the saint who is said to have died in his monastery at Saul at the age of 120 years (A.D. 253). The church which he founded soon became rich and powerful, and during the fifth and sixth centuries Ireland produced so many holy men and women that it was called "The Isle of Saints," and an old author tells us that "it was enough to be an Irishman, or even to have been in Ireland, to be considered holy."

CHAPTER III.

THE RISE AND FALL OF HOLINESS AND LEARNING.

UNTIL the close of the eighth century Christian Ireland was far more peaceful and prosperous than heathen Ireland had ever been. There were, it is true, wars between the different provinces, but not nearly to the same extent as in pagan times when war had been the occupation of the young nobles' courage and physical strength, the qualities they aspired to. But now a new ideal had been raised, and the youth of Ireland imitated no longer the prowess of their forefathers, but an outcast God who had died a shameful death. The crown of martyrdom was not granted to these Irish saints, for almost alone among nations the conversion of Ireland had been bloodless. But though they could not die for their Master, the best and noblest in the land devoted their lives entirely to His service, and the better to accomplish this many of them retired to monasteries, where their time was passed in prayer, contemplation, learning, and good works, and also in the cultivation of the arts of building, sculpture, goldsmithry, and the illumination of manuscripts. Wars, invasions, and rebellions have swept over Ireland since those days, yet much of the art of the sixth, seventh, and eighth centuries remains to us. The churches of this early period are small, but very numerous, and near together. Of the date of the round towers antiquaries are not agreed, but the beautifully sculptured stone crosses of which some few still remain, were undoubtedly the work of the Scotic monks. The ornamentation of these, of the illuminated manuscripts, and of the jewelled shrines and book covers of this period, all have the same characteristics, and are quite unlike the work of any other age and people, excepting the Anglo-Saxons, who were the pupils of these Irish monks. For beauty of design and minuteness of execution the Celtic manuscripts have never been excelled, and that they were very highly prized is proved by their having been kept in metal cases exquisitely wrought in gold, silver, and precious stones; but, after the Danish invasion, the cases proved a greater danger than defence, for the Northmen stole the books for the sake of their precious coverings, and in many cases the manuscripts were wantonly destroyed, though in others they were contemptuously returned to their owners. One of the best known, and finest of these manuscripts, is the Book of Kells, now preserved in Trinity College, Dublin. It is attributed to St. Columba, a prince of the O'Donnell family, born in the year 521, and who, in the course of his life of 77 years, wrote and illuminated nearly 300 volumes, but who is still more widely known and honored as the apostle of the northern Picts. The prosperity of Erin, and its fame as a seat of learning and piety, increased yearly, till it was looked upon by the neighboring countries as a school for the education of their young nobles, but at the close of the eighth century an invasion of the Danes put an end to Ireland's prosperity

English history tells us who were the Danes, and what the terror occasioned by their invasions. Under this comprehensive title of Danes we include the Finn Galls or "White Strangers" of Norway, as well as the Duvh or Black Galls of Denmark, with whom they often made common cause.

Emigration was a necessity to Scandinavia—the poor, cold land could not support the fast increasing population, and the Northmen were driven for very lack of food at home to seek a livelihood elsewhere. Ireland and England both became the victims of their dauntless, pitiless courage: next they desolated the coasts of France and Spain, and at last carried their enterprise along the shores of the Mediterranean Sea.

No nation seems to have been able to withstand them; their magnificent barbaric strength, their boundless ferocity, and their undaunted courage made them the conquerors of all whom they attacked.

In England, in Normandy, and later in Italy, they established themselves and founded dynasties and settlements. With such an enemy Scotia of the eighth century was little fitted to contend.

Had the old Fenian warriors still been in existence, and the whole island risen under their command against the invaders, the history of Ireland might have been different; but a country weakened by the clan system, so fatal to any spirit of nationality, and given over to the peaceful rule of monks and priests, was a certain prey to the determined Northmen, whose hosts were no sooner killed off by the despairing natives than they were replaced by fresh armies from the apparently unlimited resources of the Scandinavian population.

Danish warfare was carried on without thought of mercy. The invaders wished the island for their own possession, and were careless as to the fate of the natives; indeed, their ideas of the destiny of subject races seem to have run almost exclusively on the lines of extermination.

The Irish made a desperate fight against the invaders, but after much bloodshed on both sides they were vanquished. It had been better for them had they slunk tamely into the bogs and morasses, for the Danes, in revenge for the losses they had received, took every opportunity of degrading the natives. Danish soldiers were quartered on every Irish family, and the cast-off garments of the invaders was the only clothing permitted to Irishmen even of the highest class. This savage supremacy could only be maintained in an ignorant and disunited country, and knowing this the Danes prohibited the teaching of reading, writing, or any military art, and forbade public assemblies of any kind whatever. Church services, of course, came within this prohibition, and the clergy, being the best educated and most influential class, were the special objects of the hatred of the Northmen.

For twelve years this miserable state of things endured, then Malachi, king of Meath, succeeded in driving the invaders from the country, but under pretext of peaceable colonization a number of Finn Galls obtained leave to settle on the east coast, where they founded the cities of Strangford, Carlingford, and Wexford, and once possessed of these landing places the Northmen came over in greater numbers than before their expulsion. The early settlers resented these invasions almost as bitterly as the Scotti with whom they formed alliances, but these naturalized colonists were almost powerless against the hosts that repeatedly descended like swarms of locusts upon the unhappy island. War followed war, disaster succeeded to disaster, colleges, monasteries, even churches had almost ceased to exist, and under the blighting influences of war and anarchy the country sank into a state of barbarism. The native chieftains finding that resistance led to nothing but outrage, submitted for the most part to the Danish dominion, and paid tribute to the invader. Among those who were in this inglorious position were the petty princes of South Munster, of the Dalcassian and Eoghanite families. But when Brian Dal-Cas succeeded his father in 954 he determined never to pay tribute, and for long he carried on a solitary guerilla warfare against the Danes of Limerick and Waterford. He met with some success, and persuaded his brother Mahon to join him in giving battle to the Danes at Sulcoit, in Tipperary. To the surprise of all, the Danes were beaten, and Limerick fell into the hands of Mahon, who was murdered at the instigation of the Danish chieftain of the city. To avenge this wrong, Brian renewed the war, and after some fighting became king of the whole of Munster. He was then joined by Malachi, king of Meath, and Ard-Righ of Erin, and the allied armies routed the Danes from Dublin city. But Brian, like Alfred of England, was something more than a successful general: he was a great ruler. Personally ambitious, he had resolved to die Ard-Righ of Erin, although he did not belong to those families who alone claimed the right to reign. By each of his several marriages he connected himself with the various reigning families in Ireland, and the marriages of his children were all planned with the same view. But he did not let his own gain blind him to the good of the country; he revised the laws and enacted new ones; he forced the Danes to restore the church property they had destroyed, he re-established schools, raised fortresses, built and mended roads, constructed bridges, and returned those lands which the Danes had usurped to their rightful owners. He also decreed that all branches of the Scoto-Milesian race should take as a surname the name of the founder or some illustrious member of their clan, with the prefix O' or Mac, the son or descendant of. Thus the descendants of Niall became O'Neill, of Concobar or Coner O'Connor, and of Brian himself O'Brien. Brian, having married for his third wife Gormley, sister to Maelmurra, king of Leinster, and having united his daughter to the Danish king of Dublin, felt himself strong enough to depose Malachi and declare himself Ard-Righ of Erin, and he then demanded and obtained tribute from the Ulster kings. His victorious wars with the Danes had been expensive, and to raise revenue he revived the obsolete tribute of cattle, which centuries ago had been levied upon Leinster. This Boromean tribute, deriving its name from "Bo," a cow, had been exacted in revenge for a wrong done by the Leinster king, and even in early times had been very irregularly paid, but its re-enactment after a lapse of 322 years was an oppression that neither King Maelmurra nor his sister, Brian's wife, could forgive, and which brought forth more serious results than Brian's nickname of "Boiroimhe" or Boru. For long the fire smoldered, but at length an insulting word from Brian caused it to burst into flame, and determined on revenge the Leinster king allied himself with the Danes, and sent an express to Denmark for an army. Twelve thousand Danes and four thousand Norsemen obeyed the summons, and these, with the Leinstermen and the Danes of Dublin, made a formidable army. But Brian, though eighty years old, had still strength to organize an army, and between Munster, Connaught, and Meath he raised a force of 30,000 men. He was past fighting, and the command was entrusted to his eldest son, but throughout the march the old leader headed his people, and when the armies met at Clontarf he exhorted his troops to remember that theirs was the cause of freedom and fatherland, and then in a tent near by he stood watching the conflict. From eight in the morning till five in the afternoon of Good Friday of the year 1014 the battle raged, but after a loss of 10,000 men, including the traitorous

Maelmurra, the Danes and Leinster men were utterly routed. But Brian did not survive that day; he and four of his sons and his young grandson fell with 7000 of their troops, and the Munster tribe that Brian raised from obscurity he almost exterminated by his wars, for of all the brave host that left Munster only 850 men returned. Brian's son Donagh, succeeded him as king of Munster, but the Ard-Righ-ship was claimed by Malachi II., who ruled over Ireland for nine years. But the sacred line of the Ard-Righs had been broken; Brian's success inspired many a petty prince to contend for the supremacy, and after the death of Malachi II. no Irish king ever held undisputed sway. The law that might is right became more and more recognized, and the strength of the country was exhausted by petty wars till, in 1172, the troubled and disunited country fell an easy prey to the ambition of Henry II. of England.

CHAPTER IV.

THE INVASION.

THE invasion of Ireland by the Normans was the natural outcome of their conquest of Britain. The Danes, who had already done so much to ruin the prosperity of Erin, were now to make another attempt on her liberty by the circuitous route of Normandy and Britain. Henry, duke of Anjou and Normandy, and king of England, resolved to add Ireland to the list of his unwieldy possessions, and the island was in a state to tempt the invader. The centuries of strife against the Danes, and the anarchy and self-seeking which had followed Brian's usurpation of the Ard-Righship had destroyed all spirit of nationality, for each chief struggling to be master saw in his neighbors only rivals and possible enemies. The country was in that demoralized and disorganized condition which is the inevitable outcome of prolonged civil war. Learning had declined, and Christianity shared the common moral degradation. The national Church was in schism from the Church of Rome, both as to the observance of Easter and in permitting the marriage of the secular clergy—indeed, the marriage bond was of the loosest. Henry II. was too astute a personage to fail to take advantage of this degeneration; dismal accounts of the heretical condition of the Irish Church reached England through the Danish settlers, who, acknowledging the supremacy of Rome, received their orders not from the Irish but the English archbishop. So, armed with an account of Irish heresy, Henry sought the papal sanction to invade the island. In those days the Pope was commonly held to be the suzerain of all islands, and acting on this prerogative Adrian IV. issued a bull authorizing Henry to undertake the conquest "to enlarge the bounds of the Church, to restrain the progress of vices, to correct the manners of its people, to plant virtue and to increase the Christian religion, to subject the people to laws, to extirpate vicious customs, and to enforce the payment of Peter's pence." But the Norman barons were found to be so strongly opposed to the project that the bull was laid aside, and for a time the scheme was abandoned.

At the time of Henry's accession, Turlogh O'Connor was Ard-Righ of Erin, and at his death, in 1166, was succeeded by his son Roderic O'Connor, the last Milesian king of Ireland. The prince of Leinster was Dermid M'Murrough, and Breffny was governed by O'Rourke. Unhappily for Ireland, Dermid fell in love with O'Rourke's wife, and persuaded her to elope with him. To avenge this outrage and recover the woman, O'Rourke declared war on Leinster, and the Ard-Righ took up his quarrel. Dermid tried in vain to raise an army; lax as was the marriage bond in Ireland, the Leinstermen refused to fight for a licentious old man of sixty, who had eloped with a woman already past her fortieth year. But Dermid, thus driven to bay, did not hesitate to fly to Henry and ask help of the dreaded Normans, nor to offer to pay for their services by doing homage for his kingdom. Henry was then in Aquitaine, and was too much engaged in a French war to grant any assistance beyond letters to certain Norman nobles in England, authorizing them to take up Dermid's cause. Thus accredited, the Leinster king went to Britain, and, by bribes and promises, persuaded Richard Clare, earl of

Pembroke, and a group of Norman-Welsh barons, to espouse his cause. Of these Norman-Welsh noblemen, the most conspicuous were Maurice Fitz Gerald, founder of the family of Fitz Gerald, Robert Fitz Stephen, Raymond le Gros, and Hervey Montmorres. The fortunes of these gentlemen were of the kind that may be bettered but cannot be made worse, and for various bribes and considerations they agreed to raise armies, and invade Ireland in the following spring. In the meantime, Dermid retired to his monastery at Fells, where in May, the news was brought him that the Norman fleet was on the Wexford coast. The invaders were commanded by Fitz Stephen, who for years had been a state prisoner in Wales, and who had been released only on promise to go to Ireland and never return thence. He and Dermid laid siege to the Danish town of Wexford; they took it, and then began devastating the surrounding country; but by this time O'Connor, who had raised a formidable army, forced the invaders to come to terms, and a treaty was drawn up by which Wexford was given to Fitz Stephen, and Leinster restored to Dermid, on condition of his doing homage to O'Connor and promising never again to call the Normans to his aid. But the treaty was no sooner signed than Fitz Stephen's half-brother, Fitz Gerald, landed in Wexford in command of a large force, and Dermid, after very little hesitation, broke the conditions of his treaty by joining the invaders and leading them to Dublin. In August of this same year, Richard Clare (nicknamed Strongbow) also fulfilled his promise of coming to Dermid's aid; he had been bribed to come over by promises of the hand of Dermid's beautiful daughter Eva, and of succession to the throne of Leinster after Dermid's death; but, the Irish kings being elected by their clans from certain families, Dermid had no power to dispose of his crown, which could not be inherited by a foreigner. So long as the Normans confined their devastations to the Danish towns and the east coast, O'Connor ignored their ill-conduct, but when they marched toward Meath, he sent a message to Dermid, telling him that if he persisted in violating the treaty, the head of his son Arthur, who was held as hostage, should pay for it. The amiable parent replied that he was indifferent to his son's fate, and should act as he pleased. Poor Arthur's end is unknown, but the winter soon terminated the hostilities, and in the spring Dermid died miserably, "as his sins deserved." Strongbow now found how he had been tricked; he asserted his claim to the throne of Leinster, but every Irishman rose up against him, and, after many defeats, of which the most famous is that of Thurles, where 1,700 Normans fell, Strongbow and the remnant of his army were blockaded in Wexford and Waterford.

The news that Strongbow was contending for the crown of Leinster awakened Henry to the fact that the earl was making war on his own account, probably with the intention of setting up an independent kingdom in Ireland. He therefore commanded all the Normans to return to England at once, and he severely upbraided Strongbow for the devastation he had caused; but a promise to put all the places he held in Ireland into the king's power ensured the earl's pardon, and Henry now produced the bull of Adrian, set sail for Ireland, and on St. Luke's day in October, 1171, this last and greatest Norman force landed at Waterford. The Fitz Geralds, Fitz Stephens, and other Norman-Welsh settlers hastened to do homage to their sovereign, and the southern Irish chiefs, tired of war, divided by petty strifes, alarmed by the strength of the invading force, and overawed by the papal bull, followed their example. M'Carthy, king of Cork, was the first to come in, and then one by one all the surrounding princes made their submission; but Roderic O'Connor and Henry tacitly agreed to let each other alone, and the O'Neills and O'Donnels of Ulster then, and for many hundred years, refused to bend the knee to a foreign prince.

Henry at once set to work on a social reformation; he tried to establish the feudal land system and the Roman method of government, and his papal bull brought the clergy to his side; but this work of organization was brought to an abrupt close by a summons from the papal legate commanding him to render an account of Becket's murder, so in April, 1172, he left Ireland, leaving Strongbow governor. The greater part of Leinster and Munster he divided between about ten Anglo-Norman families, but these grants of land were purely nominal, and in many cases the settlers were unable to dislodge the clans already in possession. This weak and wavering Norman power extended only to the *Pale*, a district whose boundaries varied with the relative strength of Norman and Celt, but which was supposed to include the counties of Dublin, Kildare, Meath, and Uriel or Louth, and the cities and neighborhoods of Cork, Waterford, and Limerick; but till the time of James I. the English power was seldom great enough to keep all these districts, much less to subdue the outlying country.

CHAPTER V.

THREE CENTURIES OF NORMAN RULE.

The Normans had subdued the "proud Saxon" by a course of rigorous oppression, and they thought to govern the Celts by the same means. The inhabitants of Britain had yielded to their Norman invaders just as their predecessors had already submitted to the conquering Roman and Dane. But the invasion of Ireland was carried out in a very different manner, and produced very different results.

The Anglo-Saxons had been thoroughly conquered, and had been forced to entire submission. There was no doubt as to which was the victorious race. The dominant Northmen had enforced their legislation on the natives, and were powerful enough to carry out their policy. There had been no intermission in the administration of this iron Norman rule; no moment when rebellion had had a chance of success. There was a resident king and a court, and after a few generations the Normans had grown to consider England their own country; common interests had grown up between the two races, till the Anglo-Saxons and the Normans gradually lost their antagonistic and distinct nationality, and formed together the English nation.

But in Ireland matters were very different; the Norman invasion had only resulted in a partial conquest of the eastern and southern provinces, and for a period of more than four hundred years the western and northern parts of the island failed to make even a nominal submission. The country was in a perpetual state of strife—first the English and then the Irish gaining some advantage, for there were two distinct powers in Ireland, two codes of law, two rival interests, two, and in later times three, hostile races.

The Norman lords settled down in the Pale with the intention of quickly becoming masters of the whole island. Henry had presented them with vast estates, but to obtain these was quite another matter. In the first place, the Irish did not understand what was expected of them. The feudal system of land tenure was incomprehensible to them. The land of Ireland had always belonged to the people—the territory of Leinster to the Leinstermen, of Munster to the Munster clans. The kings could not give away or sell any part of it, nor did Irish conquerors take the lands of the clans they overcame; the same people went on living on their old estates, only they were ruled over and paid tribute to the conquering chief. Individual property in land was no more dreamed of than property in light or air. The Normans had other ideas; where they could they dispossessed the natives, and took the land for their own. They bought and sold it at pleasure, sometimes allowing the natives to become tenants-at-will, but the Irish naturally resisted the new order of things, and lost no opportunity of harrowing and turning out the new-comers.

Then arose the difficulty of laws. The Irish were governed by Brehon laws, which must have seemed ridiculously mild to the Normans. But as Irishmen who murdered Englishmen were tried by English law and hanged, and Englishmen who murdered Irishmen were tried by Brehon law and let off with a fine, both races learned that there may be a considerable difference between law and justice.

Still, despite the differences of race and law, despite the

irritations caused by the forays of the Norman barons, despite the brutal retaliation of the natives, despite the hatred which the two peoples at first felt for one another, the Normans gradually adopted the manners and customs of the Irish, and that fusion of races which had had so happy an effect in England began to be enacted across the water. But the proportion of colonists was here much smaller, the Irish learned little from the Norman though these swiftly "degenerated" into "mere Irish," and it was clear that if left to themselves, the "Irish enemy" would soon absorb the settlers.

This was, indeed, a terrible disaster, for by this degeneration the "kings of England and lords of Ireland" were in danger of losing what little power they had in Ireland. And it was, therefore, deemed necessary to stimulate the old race hatred in order to keep the two peoples apart. For this end a law was passed in the reign of Edward III. known as the statute of Kilkenny, by which it was made high treason for the colonists to marry with, bring up, foster, or stand sponsor to any of the Irish; and any Englishman using an Irish name, wearing an Irish dress, speaking the Irish language, following the Irish custom of growing his mustache, or of riding without a saddle, had all his possessions sold in atonement for the crime, or, if he were a poor man, was condemned to imprisonment for life; and it was also made criminal for English settlers to be governed by Brehon law.

These laws did not increase the love of the two peoples, and their obvious injustice was not calculated to make either natives or settlers a law-abiding people. But the Irish had not even the choice of being ruled by English law, for only the five royal families of the O'Neills, the O'Connors, the O'Briens, the O'Melaghlins, and the M'Murroughs (now Kavanaghs), commonly known as the, "five bloods," were allowed to plead in an English court. Had the Pale been a hard and fast line, the two nations might perhaps have gone on pretty comfortably, the English within the Pale and the Irish without, but the barons of the Pale were a set of lawless marauders and half their subsistence was drawn from forays across the borders, which forays were followed by risings of the surrounding Irish clans, who sometimes drove the settlers back into the very walls of Dublin. To suppress these incursions, the hateful customs of "Coyne and Livery," or free quarters, was resorted to. Nothing breeds ill-will so quickly as this abuse; from time to time it has been resorted to by the governors of Ireland, and has invariably produced misery, hatred, and rebellion. The custom was originally Irish, for the Fenian heroes of the olden times lived during the six winter months at free quarters on the people: but so unbearable was felt the obligation to maintain even the friend and protector that the nation had risen in revolt and overthrown the Fenian power. But who shall describe the burden, the hateful charge which was now laid upon each family? A soldier to pay and lodge, food to be found for him and his horse; a stranger and an enemy, always in the best seat by the hearth, always watching and spying on the unhappy household. Every one was in the same case, each household had its unwelcome guest to feed and care for. There he was, policeman, soldier, master, spy; a being of such superior race that if he married the daughter or stood sponsor to the baby of his unwilling host, he must die for his sin; or if he followed the customs or spoke the language of those who gave him food and shelter, all he had was taken from him or he was thrown into prison for life. He dared not love the people he lived with, dared not speak to them, or live otherwise than an enemy—a hateful life for him and them.

In many cases the soldiers proved their superiority by laying waste the little farms, despoiling the gardens, and ill-treating the natives; but in others, despite the threatened imprisonment and traitors' death, they grew moustachios, rode without saddles, learned to speak Erse, and were even sufficiently depraved to marry the women. But many of the baser sort of Irish thinking it but lost labor to work to keep the enemy, and caring nothing for a home whose comfort and privacy were destroyed by the presence of an unfriendly stranger, nor for land whose produce was too often ruined by the malice or rough horse play of the soldiers, threw up their homes, left their land waste, and took to an idle life of begging by the road side. Still, as time went on, the laws became less and less strictly obeyed; saddles which wore out were not replaced, and first one, then another spoke Erse, or forgot to shave his upper lip, till in the time of Henry VI. the statute of Kilkenny had to be re-enforced, and a new law passed actually rewarding any Englishman who beheaded any "mere Irishman whom he met going to or coming from robbing or stealing." It is probable that the Irishmen did not publicly announce when they were on a robbing expedition, so it is difficult to understand how the English could be aware of their intentions, and the Irishman, moreover, had no chance of proving his innocence, as the execution took place on the spot, and it is likely that many private quarrels were legally revenged in this manner, for, in addition to getting rid of his enemy, the murderer made a comfortable little sum of money, levied in fines of pence and farthings on the district in which the execution took place.

It has often been stated that religious differences are the chief causes of the misunderstanding between English and Irish, yet never was there more oppression, race-hatred, and ill-will than in the centuries before the Reformation, when all professed the same creed; but so great was the mutual dislike that each people built and worshipped in their own churches, erected and retired to their own monasteries as exclusively as though some great difference of faith kept them apart, yet though this carefully fostered race-hatred and a constant influx of new settlers, kept most of the colonists from "degenerating," certain of the Anglo-Norman families threw in their lot with the natives, and by the time of Henry VII. had become "more Irish than the Irish."

CHAPTER VI.

THE GERALDINES.

NEVER, since the invasion, had the power of England been so weak in Ireland as it became at the time of the accession of Henry VII. The Wars of the Roses, followed by the short and turbulent reigns of Edward V. and Richard III., had, during the last four reigns, given the English enough to do without thinking much about Irish affairs. The Pale was now reduced to Dublin, Meath, Louth, and Kildare, and the "Irish enemy" extorted tribute from the settlers.

Still, at the beginning of his reign, Henry VII. paid little attention to the state of Ireland, though the inhabitants were more disunited than ever. There were Yorkists and Lancastrians among both the old Irish and the colonists. There were old Irish who cared for neither red rose nor white; old Irish who acknowldged the English king, and old Irish who ignored his very existence; Anglo-Irish, as the original settlers were now called, who hated the old Irish; new settlers, who hated both old and Anglo-Irish, and Anglo-Irish who were more Irish than the Irish. Of these last none had more thoroughly "degenerated" than the great family of Fitzgerald, decendants of that Fitz Gerald who landed at Waterford soon after the treaty between Dermid M'Murrough and Roderic O'Connor. The Fitzgeralds had now two peerages in the family—the earldom of Desmond and that of Kildare. They and the Butlers were the most influential of the Anglo-Irish families. The Butlers were Lancastrians, both branches of the Fitzgeralds Yorkists, and at the time of Henry VII.'s accession Gerald Fitzgerald, earl of Kildare, was governor of Ireland. Henry was far too wise to depose Kildare, he restored to Thomas Butler, earl of Ormonde, those lands of which he had been deprived under Edward IV., but otherwise took little notice of the Butlers; of their support he was pretty sure, but the Yorkist Fitzgeralds needed conciliation. Henry felt that their favor would greatly strengthen his power in Ireland, yet he had so little faith in Kildare's loyalty that in 1486 he invited him to pay a visit to London. This honor Kildare prudently declined; he knew that such visits were apt to end in free lodgings in the Tower of London, and moreover he had designs of his own.

The mysterious fate of the child-king, Edward V., and his brother, the duke of York, left the people uncertain as to what had become of them. Many refused to believe they had been murdered in the Tower, and were willing to receive any prince who should declare that he was the true king. There was, also, Prince Edward, earl of Warwick, who was the Yorkist heir to the throne. Edward was reported to be kept a close prisoner in the Tower, but no one had seen him there who could say whether he really were there or no.

It was easy to persuade a people as remote from London as the Irish that the prince was not a prisoner, and for this purpose Lambert Simnel, the son of an Oxford bootmaker, a boy about the young prince's age, was trained to act the part of earl of Warwick, and was then taken to Ireland in that character. The people were delighted with him. The young prince was so regal, so gracious, and so charming that the masses received him without a wavering or doubt, but it is difficult to believe that Kildare and the other nobles of the Pale were equally convinced; they may have been deceived by the urbanity of the cobbler's son, but if so they cannot have made very searching inquiries into his past.

In vain Henry exhibited the real Edward in London; the English who saw him believed, but the Irish rebels thought the unseen English prisoner the impostor, not the courteous youth whose manners were so regally convincing. Margaret, duchess of Burgundy, sister of Edward IV., and aunt to the real earl of Warwick, was the chief promoter of the plot, and sent over 2,000 German veterans to assist the rebels. Their aid was little needed in Ireland, for the Yorkist nobles and all the people of the Pale were wild about the little prince, who was solemnly crowned king in the presence of Kildare and other nobles, lay and ecclesiastical.

The crown, an iron one, was taken from the head of the statue of the Blessed Virgin, near Dame's Gate, and when the ceremony was over the new king was placed on the shoulders of a gigantic Anglo-Irishman, named D'Arcy, and carried in triumph to Dublin Castle. Henry treated this rebellion, usurpation, and coronation with wise contempt; the whole thing was a bubble that must quickly burst: but Simnel's adherents, not satisfied with his Irish success, now determined to win for him the English crown. We must, in justice to them, remember that most of his adherents firmly believed him to be the earl of Warwick, and also that within the last twenty years the English crown had been won five times by violence, and that Edward Plantagenet, earl of Warwick, really had a sort of claim to the throne. Simnel, with his German and Anglo-Irish army, embarked for Lancashire, where they were met by the English and utterly defeated, with the loss of half their number, and Ireland's king, with humiliating lenience, was made the royal scullion. Kildare and the other rebels wrote to crave the king's pardon, which was immediately granted: he even retained Kildare as lord deputy; and, indeed, throughout the whole affair Henry's good sense was admirable. Those of the rebels who had been killed in battle were gone beyond punishment, and the best penalty that could be inflicted on the survivors was to make them see what contemptible fools they had been. He did not even permit them the dignity of suffering. The exposure of this plot, and the ridiculous part the rebels had been made to play should have sickened the Anglo-Irish of imprisoned princes, but when five years later the duchess of Burgundy sent over a supposed duke of York, he also was welcomed as the rightful heir. It must be conceded that this new claimant for the throne was more mysterious than the son of the Oxford shoemaker. He is supposed to have been a native of Tourney, in Flanders, named Peter Osbeck, but is better known as Perkin Warbeck, and he really resembled Edward IV. so greatly that many persons believed him to have been a natural son of that monarch. In the meantime, Kildare had been deposed from the deputyship, and Fitzsimons, archbishop of Dublin, reigned in his stead. It could never be proved against Kildare that he took part in the Warbeck rebellion, but many members of the Fitzgerald family, including the earl of Desmond, openly declared for the pretender, who with the aid of Desmond laid siege to Waterford.

Henry was now really alarmed at the state of Ireland,

for he himself was not sure whether or no Warbeck were the duke of York—so he sent over Sir Edward Poyning with a force to quell the rebellion. This was soon done, and Poyning then assembled a Parliament, wherein the odious statute of Kilkenny was re-enforced, save only that part relating to the use of the Irish language and the custom of riding without a saddle, both of which were now so general that it was hopeless to try to prevent them. Here, too, was passed the famous act called after the deputy, "Poyning's Law," and which was not repealed till 1782. Poyning's act provided that henceforward no parliament should be held in Ireland "until the chief governor and council had certified to the king, under the great seal, as well the causes and considerations as the acts they designed to pass, and till the same should be approved by the king and council." An act passed by the Irish parliament could not in future become law till it had been sent to and approved by the English privy council, whose members might revise and alter it as they thought fit; it was then returned to the Irish house, and here it might receive *no further alteration*. The bills often returned altered beyond all recognition, yet they must be passed exactly as they came from England, or altogether rejected. Thus was the Irish parliament reduced to a nullity. Bills of attainder were also passed at this time against the earl of Kildare, his brother James, and others suspected of sympathy with Warbeck. Desmond had already made his submission, and had left his son in London as a hostage for good behavior, but Kildare was sent to an English prison, and his wife, overwhelmed with grief and horror at the ghastly fate she feared for her husband, died. Her fears were groundless, for when Kildare was at length allowed to plead before the king, the simplicity and straight-forwardness of his manner won for him the friendship of Henry, who saw at once that such a man would be as useful as a friend as he had been dangerous as an enemy.

A long string of indictments were brought against the Geraldine, and many witnesses were called to prove his iniquities. One of the most serious charges was that, to revenge himself on the archbishop of Cashel, who was a supporter of the Butlers, he had set fire to the cathedral. Kildare disarmed his enemies by naively pleading that "he would never have done it had he not thought the archbishop was within." There was a general laugh at this novel plea, and Henry, saying the earl needed time to prepare his defence, gave him leave to choose his own counsel. "I doubt if I will be allowed to choose the good fellow I wish to select," said Kildare, thoughtfully. The king, nothing suspecting, gave him his hand in token of good faith. "Marry," cried the irrepressible rebel, "I can see no better man in England than your highness, and I will choose no other." Like many reserved persons, Henry was more shy than proud, and, to the surprise of the assembled court, was delighted with the shameless earl of Kildare. It was easy to see which way the tide was setting. The Butlers, earl Ormonde, and the aggrieved archbishop whose cathedral had been burned in the hope that he was within, were desperate. Was this traitor to escape through sheer impudence? "All Ireland could not govern the earl of Kildare," they cried. "Then," said the king, "the earl of Kildare shall govern all Ireland;" and true to his word, Henry sent him back as lord deputy, with increased power and the new title of lord lieutenant, and with Elizabeth St. John, Henry's cousin, for a wife. This policy answered well; the authority of the crown was maintained within the Pale as it had not been for two generations, and Kildare lost no opportunity of repressing the native chiefs and Irish rebels. He had become more English than the English. Among the many petty wars carried on under him was one which, though it began in a private quarrel between the Fitzgeralds and Ulick Mac William (Bourke), developed into a terrible struggle between the tribes of the northeast and those of the southwest. The battle of Knocktow turned the scale in favor of the Fitzgeralds, and showed the Irish that henceforward the side of England would be the side of victory.

In 1509 Henry VII. died, and was succeeded by his son Henry VIII. The young king, satisfied with the management of the Pale, left it in the hands of Kildare, and when, four years later, the deputy died, his son Gerald was appointed in his stead. The young earl did not profit by his father's experience; his conduct was so extraordinary that three times he was deposed and sent to London, the last time in 1534, when his rivals, the Butlers, accused him with apparent truth of such arbitrary and senseless acts of injustice and cruelty that they can only be accounted for by madness. When the earl left Dublin, his son Thomas was chosen to continue the government. A less suitable appointment could hardly have been made; Thomas was only twenty years of age, inexperienced, brave, headstrong, passionately attached to his father, whose deposition he resented hotly. The earl, well aware of his son's character, implored him to be prudent, but he might as well have pleaded with the raging sea, for soon after he reached England his son was deceived by a false report that the earl had been beheaded. Without waiting to inquire into the truth of the rumor, Thomas, mad with grief and rage, presented himself, at the head of a hundred and forty followers, before the council. Striding up to the council table he threw down his sword of office, and in a loud voice declared war against Henry VIII., king of England. The lad, for he was nothing more, was thoroughly in earnest—the entreaties of his friends that he would beg pardon for his rashness were of no avail; in his anger he feared neither the death he must bring upon himself, or the ruin he had called down on his relations. He and his hotheaded followers laid waste the district of Fingal, and besieged Dublin Castle, whither archbishop Allen, his father's great enemy, had fled. The prelate soon escaped, and embarked on a vessel which unfortunately stranded at Clontarf, where the archbishop fell into the hands of the insurgents and was slain, and for this sacrilege Thomas was excommunicated. The earl, hearing of his son's miseries, died in London of a broken heart, and young Fitzgerald, hunted by the royal army into the fastnesses of Munster, surrendered himself on condition that his life should be spared. He now heard how he had been deceived, and willingly went to London to crave the king's pardon—a sadder and a wiser man.

To celebrate his forgiveness and the close of the insurrection, the English general, Gray, who had married Kildare's sister, invited Thomas's five uncles to a banquet, and while they were feasting they were all treacherously seized, taken to London, and thrown into the Tower, where, to their dismay, they found their pardoned nephew a prisoner like themselves. They were kept prisoners till the following year, when all six were hanged as traitors at Tyburn, and the Kildare estates declared forfeited. But a younger brother of Thomas was saved by his aunt from the vengeance of Henry VIII., and in the time of Queen Mary, he recovered the title and part of the estates of the earl of Kildare.

CHAPTER VII.

HOW SHANE O'NEILL HELD ULSTER.

THE power of England greatly increased in Ireland during the reigns of Henry VII. and Henry VIII. The Pale was enlarged, and its inhabitants no longer paid tribute to the native kings. Round the Border the Celtic chiefs were resigning their lands, and getting them back under letters patent with new titles, and the outlying leaders began to inquire what was gained by this. They learned in reply, that if they held the land by English law their "title" would be recognized by the English king, who would not give it to others, as he would do in the event of conquest if they held it by Brehon law; and also that by English law the land would belong to the chief himself, that his children would inherit it, that he could sell it, and evict his clansmen, or force their obedience by threats of eviction—in fact, that tribute would be rent, and the land, instead of belonging to the people, would become the property of the chieftain. Property has such great attractions that we cannot wonder that the idea of owning the land was pleasant to the Irish chiefs. They persuaded themselves that it was quite unnecessary to explain the change to the clansmen, who need know nothing about their new position till it was too old a tale to quarrel over. The O'Neills had never yet submitted to the English power, but in the time of Henry VIII. Lame Con, who was then "The O'Neill," resigned his people's lands, and received them back with the title of earl of Tirowen or Tyrone, while his eldest, though base-born, son Matthew was declared his heir, and created baron of Dungannon. Con did not explain to his clansmen how he had wronged them, but his eldest legitimate son Shane, or John, took the matter into his own hands. He was indignant that Matthew was made heir, though illegitimacy did not affect the Irish law of inheritance, but there was some doubt as to his being Con's son at all. But beyond this sense of wrong and thwarted ambition, young O'Neill had a genuine hatred of the new order of things, and scorned the brand new letters patent title of earl of Tyrone. It was enough for him to be The O'Neill, king of Ulster, as his ancestors had been well nigh 2,000 years. So long had the O'Neill's held the land for the people by right of the sword, and while he had a voice in the matter so they should keep it. Shane was not the man to keep his views to himself; he told the clansmen how they were being cheated, and by sheer force of will he brought round his father to his side, so that Matthew, trembling for his inheritance, had the old man imprisoned in Dublin. But the clansmen, fearing to lose their lands, had the offensive Matthew murdered with Shane's connivance, and when soon afterwards Con died, Shane was elected "The O'Neill."

The territory of the O'Connors and the O'Moores—the counties of Leix and Offaly, now Queen's County and King's County—were at this time confiscated by Henry VIII. O'Moore and O'Connor were seized and sent prisoners to England, their tribes ejected, and English settlers "planted" on their land. This was the first attempt at forfeiture that had been made for centuries; but from this time confiscation became the ruling passion of the English sovereigns, and in succession nearly all Ireland has been planted several times. When either soldiers or nobles or illegitimate children had a claim on an English ruler which it was impossible to satisfy at home, a piece of Irish land was taken and liberally bestowed on the claimant, on condition of his planting it with English subjects. No one cared what became of the outcasts, who made desperate resistance to the injustice.

The plantation of Leix and Offaly was but the thin end of the wedge, and O'Neill was wise enough to perceive that it was the beginning of the end, but he determined that while he lived Ulster should not be planted. He saw, too, that the weakness of the Irish was chiefly owing to their divisions, and he resolved to subdue all the Ulster chiefs to his power and reduce them to their former tributary condition. His correspondence with them on this subject was short and to the point. "Send me the tribute you owe me, or else——" he wrote to The O'Donnell, who, nothing daunted, replied in the same style, "I owe you no tribute, and if I did——" The chiefs carried out their unspoken threat, and after much bloodshed Shane was the victor. But O'Neill was not the only person who knew that in their divisions lay the weakness of the Irish. The English of the Pale knew it too, and efforts were made to disunite the northern chiefs and make them rivals of proud John. For this purpose O'Reilly was made earl of Breffny and baron of Cavan; and Calvagh O'Donnell was offered the earldom of Tyrconnel, and letters sent by Sussex telling the countess that Elizabeth was about to send her costly presents. O'Neill saw the turn affairs were taking, and cut the rivalry short by first invading Breffny and then taking the earl and countess of Tyrconnel prisoners. This affair is the darkest stain on O'Neill's by no means spotless character. His wife was Calvagh O'Donnell's daughter by a former marriage. Her mother being dead, O'Donnell had married the countess of Argyll, who probably betrayed her husband to O'Neill, for she immediately became his mistress. O'Neill's wife died of shame and grief at the treatment of herself and her imprisoned father.

The other Ulster chiefs were now terrified into submission, and O'Neill fancied that, with a little help, he could free all Ireland from the English yoke. Accordingly, he sent word to the king of France that with five or six thousand men he could free the country from the English. The French made no response; but, on the other hand, Sussex returned from England with the intention of wasting and plundering Tyrone. His troops, however, were defeated by O'Neill, and fresh supplies of men had to be sent from England; but meanwhile, to maintain the war, the Anglo-Norman earls of Kildare, Desmond, Ormonde, Thomond, and Clanrickarde enlisted in the English service. Even against this force O'Neill was a powerful adversary; he could muster 7,000 men in the field, and Elizabeth began to fear that she would lose Ireland as her sister had lost Calais, for Sussex was no match for his adversary in military tactics. He had, however, the advantage in treachery, and when he found that his arms made no impression on the Ulster troops, he wrote to inform Elizabeth that he had arranged with one Neil Gray to assassinate O'Neill. Elizabeth made no remonstrance, neither did she recall the deputy, but at the last moment Gray drew back; thus the plot failed. Still treachery was the cheapest and easiest way of getting rid of the obnoxious Ulsterman, and Sussex was unwilling to abandon so brilliant a scheme. His next effort took the form of a present. Through the agency of one John Smith, he sent O'Neill a present of poisoned wine, but either the drug was less potent or the O'Neill household less heavy drinkers than Sussex fancied, for though every one was made ill by the harmful stuff, not one person died. But John Smith was never discovered or brought to justice, O'Neill being easily persuaded to "forget the matter." Still peace was not made between Elizabeth and O'Neill till the earl of Kildare, who, through family connections, had great influence with his kinsman, persuaded him to make his submission; and Elizabeth, acting on her own discretion, invited him to visit her at the English Court. Sussex raised all sorts of obstacles to the visit, but the chief had set his heart on the plan, and was not to be balked. He had resolved to go in regal state, and show the English what an Irish king was like; he knew very well how an English deputy looked, and felt much contempt for the court costume of the period. His suite of forty gallow-glasses were dressed in no provincial imitation of the London mode, but wore their native saffron shirts, made of many yards of yellow linen, furry short coats, and sandalled shoes or brogues. Their hair they wore long behind and curled on to the shoulders, and cut in front to cover the forehead with a fringe or "glib." None of them—not even Shane himself—spoke English, so all negotiations had to be carried on through an interpreter. But the natural grace of the chief's manner and his shrewdness gained him the queen's good graces; so that, though she kept him in London longer than he wished, when at length, in May, 1562, he was allowed to return to Dublin, he expressed himself well pleased with the visit. Ulster was still in an unsettled state; the chiefs were jealous of O'Neill's influence, and the English of the Pale did their utmost to foster the feeling: Shane punished all insubordination by laying waste the land of the offenders, and the English government having broken their pledges to him, he considered himself freed from his share in the bargain, so Ulster drifted once more into a state of war. Elizabeth again invited the "rebel" to London, but he, remembering the difficulty he had had in persuading her to let him leave, courteously but firmly declined, saying that the state of his country was such that he could not leave it, but that he would be pleased to receive the English ambassador at his house at Benburb. Here the English were hospitably received, and O'Neill signed articles of peace.

He was now the unrivalled in Tyrone, and governed the country with justice and vigor; he encouraged all kinds of husbandry and wheat growing; and if a robbery were committed he forced restitution, or if this were impossible, reimbursed the loser from his own resources. But at last, by an act of treachery, he brought about his own ruin. The Scottish settlers had always been his firm adherents and the enemies of the English, but now to please his new friends he turned against his old allies, made war on them and defeated them with great slaughter. Thus he alienated his truest friends, and his interests and those of England were too opposite for there to be any lasting peace between them, for both Elizabeth and O'Neill wanted Ireland. In 1564, Sussex was recalled and when shortly afterward Sir Henry Sidney was sent in his place he found the Pale invaded and Ulster at war with the English settlers. Sidney played upon O'Neill's unpopularity, and induced the

Ulster chiefs to join his army. Even Shane's old friend, Hugh O'Donnell. who by the death of Calvagh, had become earl of Tyrconnel, turned against him, and the united army marched through and wasted Tyrone. Shane in extremity, with the English on one side and the injured Scotch on the other, knew not which way to turn. He thought of throwing himself on the mercy of the English, but his retainers, mindful of the repeated attempts to assassinate him, and remembering the fate of the Fitzgeralds, advised him rather to trust the Scottish settlers. They willingly consented to receive him and his retainers, and taking this opportunity to revenge O'Neill's treachery, prepared a great banquet for the fugitives, and then barring the doors of the dining hall they fell upon the Ulstermen and slew them to a man.

Such was the end of Shane O'Neill. He had connived at the murder of his half-brother, and stolen the wife of the man who was at once his father-in-law and his friend, and he turned against his truest allies when he believed it would serve his purpose. But in judging him we must compare him with others of his time, with Henry VIII., with Mary, with Elizabeth, and we shall see he was no worse, if no better than his age. On the other hand, poor, ignorant, and badly armed, he kept his country for his own people against the forces of a great power, and his sword held the rooftree over many families in defiance of the fire-arms of England. At his death, Elizabeth thought the time had come for the colonization or plantation of Ulster.

Sidney had been recalled, but he now returned to Ireland and called a parliament in Dublin. To this assembly Englishmen who had never seen their counties and boroughs were "returned" without election, and mayors and sheriffs elected themselves. This was one of the first acts of the Protestant ascendancy, for until this time the Reformation had been little more than a name in Ireland, for though during the reign of Mary English Protestants had fled in great numbers to Papist Ireland, where religious persecution was unknown, these refugees had had no influence on the natives. Protestant services had to be performed in Latin, as the ministers spoke no Irish and the people understood no English. Protestantism and reformation meant to the Irish England and oppression, and the new creed had for them but few attractions. But now new means of enlightening the idolatrous Papists were to be tried—life, temporal and eternal, were to be offered to the convert, and a violent and eternal death dealt out to the unregenerate. Seldom, indeed, has religion held out such double advantages; henceforth, in Ireland, straight was the gate and narrow the way that led to eternal damnation, yet many there were who entered in thereat; indeed, up to the time of James I., not sixty Irish accepted the Protestant salvation offered on such advantageous terms. Sidney's scandalous parliament had been got together for the special purpose of confiscating Tyrone, and only such men were sent to it as were supposed to favor the project. An act was accordingly passed attainting of high treason the late Shane O'Neill, suppressing the name O'Neill, and annexing the territory of Tyrone to the royal possessions. Protestant settlers were to be imported and Protestant schools established by law, and an old and feeble member of the O'Neill family, named Tirlough Lynnogh, was appointed to the earldom of Tyrone. By this same parliament Sidney now carried measures for his favorite scheme of local government. Sir Edward Fitton was created president of Connaught, and to Sir John Perrot was entrusted the government of Munster.

Elizabeth felt it would be useless to attempt to plant the whole island at once, but she hoped little by little to compass its colonization, and a scheme was proposed for sending over one able-bodied emigrant from every two English villages. But at first the queen began in a small way by giving Ards and Down in the territory of Tyrone to the natural son of her secretary, Sir Thomas Smith. At this news the whole country was in an uproar. Young Smith began in a high-handed manner, turning out the clansmen, who made desperate resistance, and the young man was killed in an eviction fray. Elizabeth now thought that plantation would answer better if carried out on a larger scale, and the earl of Essex had Clannaboy and Ferney presented to him if he could clear them of the rebels.

Brian, Hugh, and old Tirlough O'Neill all rose against him, and Essex sought the help of Con O'Donnell, whom he afterward betrayed. At last Brian O'Neill made peace with Essex, who treacherously murdered him, his wife, and his two hundred retainers at a banquet. Frightened by this treachery the other chieftains could not for some time be induced to make their submission, and their resistance had been so desperate, and the English losses so great, that for that time the plantation of Ulster was abandoned. In the meantime Fitton was committing all kinds of atrocities in Connaught. Men were hanged and beheaded, stripped naked and buried alive in the bogs for no other crime than that they were Papists. The practice of coign and livery, so rightly condemned by the English when resorted to by the natives, was revived, but it had the immediate effect of producing rebellion, and the government were obliged to recall Fitton.

In Munster, things were better under Sir John Perrot, who, though cruelly severe, was perfectly impartial, and governed English and Irish with the same degree of rigor, and gained thereby the lasting gratitude of the subject race.

While he was governor of Munster, Elizabeth made her most serious attempt to plant. A company of English gentlemen was formed to colonize the counties of Cork, Limerick, and Kerry. They tried to turn out the owners, and a desperate and bloody war ensued. Of these planters, Sir Peter Carew has immortalized his name by his fiendish cruelty; among other barbarities, he slew the whole family of the Butlers, not even sparing the child of three years old. The Geraldines, the M'Carthys, and Ormonde's brothers now united for self-defence. The standard of revolt was raised by Sir James Fitzmaurice Fitzgerald, cousin to the earl of Desmond, who, with his brother John, was at that time a prisoner in the Tower of London.

Sidney marched his forces through Tipperary, Waterford, and Limerick, burning villages, blowing up castles, and hanging garrisons. The Irish, on their side, fought with such savage fierceness that government, exhausted by the struggle, disavowed any intention of planting, and once more the confiscation scheme was abandoned.

CHAPTER VIII.

THE DESMOND REBELLION.

WHEN, after two years of hiding in the Kerry hills, James Fitzmaurice Fitzgerald was pardoned, he prudently retired to the Continent, and the rebellion being quelled, the earl of Desmond and his brother Sir John Geraldine were released from the Tower, wherein they had been imprisoned six years. But even now Elizabeth did not intend the earl to escape; she could not prove any acts of disloyalty against him, but she distrusted him, and this feeling was no doubt fostered by his hereditary rival the earl of Ormonde, head of the Butler family, who lived in London, and was a favorite of the queen. Elizabeth therefore ordered that when the earl disembarked in Dublin he should be seized and imprisoned in the Castle. But somehow Desmond got wind of this plot, and fled from Dublin on a swift horse, and after five days and nights of peril he arrived at his castle in Munster a less loyal man than he set out from London. By nature Desmond was frank, courageous, and honorable—and had he been well treated, would probably have proved a loyal subject. Six years before this time he and Ormonde had had a dispute about some property, and the queen had graciously granted him permission to explain his case in London. On his arrival both he and his brother John, who accompanied him, had been imprisoned in the Tower, where they were kept for six years, and it was during this time that the unsuccessful attempt to plant Munster had been made, and that James Fitzmaurice had rebelled. It is strange that the earl made no rebellious effort on his return to Munster, but he was of a vacillating nature, and could not determine to ally himself with either party; moreover, the Fitzgerald exchequer was nearly exhausted by the late war, so Munster and the west were quiet. Not so the east. The plantation of King's County and Queen's County had not succeeded. Some of the O'Connors and O'Mores had escaped extermination, and their decendants, led by the famous outlaw, Rory Oge O'More, perpetually harassed the new settlers till, after eighteen years of petty warfare, he was slain in 1577. O'More being dead, a convention of the heads of the neighboring Irish families was called together in the queen's name. Four hundred obeyed the summons, and assembled on the hill of Mullaghmast. As soon as they were gathered together they were surrounded by a triple line of English soldiers and butchered in cold blood. A baser, more cruel, or more treacherous deed it is impossible to conceive. The lowest savage might well be ashamed of such a transaction, and it now seemed clear that no reliance could be placed on English promises, and that the queen's name was no protection to her Irish subjects. The island was filled with horror at the hateful deed, and with disgust when it was known that Sir Henry Sidney, who organized it, was to keep the office of lord-deputy, and Crosbie, who had commanded the butchery, to retain his position in the army.

In the meantime James Fitzmaurice Fitzgerald was trying to raise forces on the Continent, and to help him in this he tried to give to his rebellion the color of religious warfare. In vain he applied for help to the kings of France and Spain, but he persuaded Pope Gregory XIII. to issue a bull encouraging the Irish to fight for their religion, and also to fit out a small expedition, which was placed under command of an English adventurer named Stukely. But on his way to Ireland Stukely encountered the Portuguese fleet bound for Morocco, and this affair being more to his mind he joined it, carried off the whole expedition, and was never heard of more.

Fitzmaurice knew nothing of Stukely's desertion till, with about fourscore Spaniards, he landed at Dingle, in July, 1579, when he found that nothing had been heard of the expedition. He now found himself in the unenviable position of a man who commands a foreign invasion of eighty men, but on hearing of his arrival John and James of Desmond, with 3,000 tenants of the Geraldines, joined the rebellion at once, but the earl still wavered; he feared to ally himself with this forlorn hope, while his sympathy with the insurgents was evident enough to make him distrusted by the English. He probably hoped to keep friends with both parties till he could make sure whether or no the expected Spsnish force would arrive. But before the little band of invaders had been a month in the island Fitzmaurice was killed by his kinsmen, Ulick and William Bourke. John of Desmond was now the leader of the rebels, and for some time he held the field successfully against Sir William Drury, but Elizabeth was raising sufficient force to crush a much greater rising, and a proclamation was also issued declaring Desmond a traitor unless he came into the English camp within twenty days. Forced to make up his mind, Desmond remembered his own imprisonment, the fate of the Kildare branch of his family, of Brian O'Neill's six hundred men, and of the O'Mores and O'Connors at Mullaghmast, and so unwilling to draw the sword against his own brothers, he openly declared for the rebels. Malby and the infamous Crosbie were committing atrocities that surpass description; still the advantage was with the rebels, and Elizabeth now sent over the earl of Ormonde, whose loyal zeal was strengthened by private enmity to the Geraldines. He and the new deputy, Sir William Pelham, marched across the island in two columns, wasting the country, destroying the houses, and murdering every living creature, man, woman, and child, that they encountered. To resist such an army was impossible to the half-naked rebels, who were armed only with knives and swords. Wherever the army passed, it left behind it ruin and desolation. Desmond and his followers were soon reduced to the condition of hunted fugitives, nor were the men at arms the only sufferers in those days of savage warfare. Sir Nicholas Malby, the commander of the English army, has left us a graphic account of his proceedings in Connaught during the winter of 1576. "At Christmas," he writes, "I entered their territory, and finding that courteous dealing with them had like to have cut my throat, I thought good to take another course, and so with determination to consume them with fire and sword, sparing neither old nor young, I entered their mountains. I burnt all their corn and houses, and committed to the sword all that could be found. . . . This was Shane Burke's country; then I burnt Ullick Burke's in like manner. I assaulted a castle, where the garrison surrendered. I put them to the misericordia of my soldiers. They were all slain. Then I went on, sparing none that came in my way, which cruelty did so amaze their followers that they could not tell where to bestow themselves. Shane Burke made means to me to pardon him and forbear killing of his people. I would not hearken, but went on my way. The gentlemen of Clanrickarde came to me. I found it was but dallying to win time, so I left Ullick as little corn as I had left his brother, and what people was found had as little favor as the other had. It was all done in rain and frost and storm, journeys in such weather bringing them sooner to submission. They are humble enough now, and will yield to any terms we like to offer them." Ormonde, counting up his services, boasts that he has slain "88 captains, 2 leaders, with 1,547 notorious traitors and malefactors, and above 4,000 others." That many of these others were old men, women, and children does not seem to have detracted from the honor of having been the slayer of nearly six thousand persons. Pelham, with fiendish cruelty, refused pardon to any rebels who did not bring with them the heads of some of their comrades, "for this," he said, "sows dissension among them, as they will not forgive blood."

At last, too late to help the rebels, the Spaniards, commanded by Sebastian San José, arrived, and occupied the Fort del Oro. Lord Grey, who was now deputy, was marching southward, and at the same time Winter and Bingham prepared to attack the place by sea. The garrison were in a desperate case, and San José determined to make his submission. Such of the Irish who were there entreated him to hold the town to the end, but in vain: without striking a single blow, the cowardly Spaniard threw himself on the mercy of Grey. He trusted in what had no existence; and by order of Grey, and under command of Sir Walter Raleigh, the whole garrison was either shot or hanged. The victory of the English being now assured, Grey organized small bands of soldiers to hunt down the rebels in the mountains. So insatiable was this man's thirst for blood that it was said of him that he left Elizabeth nothing but ashes and corpses to rule over in Ireland; and the officers who served under him seem to have been equally devoid from human feeling. Achin, when he seized the castle of Kildimo, slew 150 women and children. Ormonde caught and hanged Lady Fitzgerald, of Imokelly, and executed 134 other persons; Morris massacred 600 women, children, and sick persons at Rathlin; and in Dublin the less important men were hanged in batches, the blue blood being reserved for the more distinguished adjuncts of drawing and quartering. The history at this time has a sickening smell of blood. At length the news came that John of Desmond had been caught and mortally wounded; he died at once, and his body, thrown across his horse, was taken to Cork. His head was sent to Dublin to be spiked in front of the castle, and his body was hanged by the legs in chains on the gates of Cork. Here it remained a loathsome sight for three years, till one stormy night the wind took pity on the ghastly frame that had held so brave a soul and blew it into the sea. The earl, surrounded by a few tried friends, was chased from mountain to mountain, watching by night and hardly venturing to sleep by day. At last, in 1583, he was caught and killed, and his head sent to Elizabeth, to be impaled on London Bridge.

All authorities are agreed that the state of Munster was now truly horrible. The fertile province had become an arid waste; year after year the harvest had been burned, so that plague and famine had completed the destruction began by the sword. Such poor wretches as survived looked, says Spencer, "more like anatomies than human beings. They did eat dead carcasses, yea, one another, soon after, in as much as the very carcasses they spared not to scrape out of the graves." Sir William Pelham, too, says that the people "offer themselves with their wives and children, rather to be slain by the army than to suffer the famine that now beginneth to pinch them."

The province being ripe for plantation, Elizabeth resolved

to re-people this desert with English subjects, so a parliament was called, and the Desmond estates, amounting to more than 574,628 acres of profitable land, were confiscated and offered to English undertakers on the easiest possible terms.

The land was divided into tracts varying from 4,000 to 12,000 acres. No rent was to be paid for the first three years, and after that only half rent for three years. The full rent, therefore, would not be paid for six years after occupation, and this rent itself was so low as to be almost nominal; two-pence per acre in Limerick and Kerry counties and three-pence in Waterford and Cork. For ten years the undertakers were to transport their produce free of duty—no slight advantage in those days. Large tracts were granted to soldiers who had been engaged in the war, and younger sons and brothers were invited to plant. There was, however, a dark side to this dazzling prospect. Elizabeth's object was not merely to enrich her soldiers and adventurers, but also to get rid of the native Irish. None of these were to be taken as tenants, nor were they to be employed as carpenters, builders, wheelwrights, blacksmiths, or indeed in any skilled trade.

Everything except "hewing of wood and drawing of water" was to be done by English colonists. But here arose a difficulty; the English farmers and artisans could hardly be persuaded to go to so barbarous a country, and when they got there the natives made things so unpleasant for them that many returned at once. The hungry, starving Irish desperately resisted this attempt to root them from their soil; they formed secret societies to destroy the settlers, and were known by the name of "Robin Hoods." What the English would not concede them because it was just they gave in to for fear of violence, and gradually the Irish were taken as tenants, and some of the undertakers, sick of the job, gave the land back to its old owners. Thus the scheme failed; the natives were not exterminated, but exasperated by so much cruelty looked out for a chance of revenge.

CHAPTER IX.

ELIZABETH'S WAR WITH HUGH O'NEILL.

ONE of the officers who had led the English cavalry during the Munster rebellion was Aodh or Hugh O'Neill the son of Matthew, baron of Dungannon, who had been killed to make way for his brother Shane. Matthew had left a little son Hugh, who had been brought up partly in Ireland and partly in London at the court of Elizabeth. There was, in appearance and manner, nothing of the wild Ulster chieftain about young Hugh. He was a courtly and well educated personage, wearing English dress, capable of speaking English, and quite willing to bear the title of earl of Tyrone. The attainted and forbidden name of O'Neill he kept in the background as long as he was on English soil.

In Ulster, however, he was the Irish chieftain, and was worshipped by the clansmen, who elected him The O'Neill, and refused to acknowledge the authority of old Tirlough.

The blood-thirsty lord Grey had been recalled, and Sir John Perrot appointed deputy, to the immense pacification of Ireland, for the severity of Perrot fell equally on Saxon and Celt, and despite his hasty temper he gained the respect of the natives. In one instance only did he try to enforce order by gross injustice. He suspected The O'Donnell of treasonable designs, and seeing no fair means of getting hostages for good behavior, he had recourse to treachery, and sent a supposititious Spanish trading vessel, laden with real Spanish wine, round to the coasts of Donegal, bidding the captain invite young Ulster chiefs on board to taste the wines.

O'Donnell's son, Red Hugh, a boy only fifteen years of age, two sons of Shane O'Neill, and some others, accepted the offer; they went on board and drank deeply of the Spanish wine. When they were half tipsy they were disarmed and fastened under the hatches; the anchor was weighed, and the ship set sail for Dublin Bay, and for four years and a half the unhappy boys were kept prisoners in Dublin Castle. This outrage, however, called forth no rebuke from the government of the Pale, or from the queen, and it does not seem to have made Perrot really unpopular with the Irish. Under his rule the country was quieter than it had been for years, but at length Elizabeth heard that the deputy had refused to punish O'Rourke for making an effigy of herself, and dragging it at the cart's tail. For this offence Perrot was recalled and beheaded, and to the misfortune of Ireland Sir William Fitz William was appointed to succeed him. In the meantime, Hugh O'Neill had settled in Ulster and had married a daughter of The O'Donnell. He had sent his son to be fostered by his former enemy, O'Cahen, and at the death of old Tirlough, openly assumed the forbidden title of "The O'Neill."

Elizabeth was uneasy at Hugh's "degeneration." As yet, nothing was known to his discredit, but rumors and vague whispers filled the air. It was reported that he constantly changed the men in his army, so that all the men in Tyrone should by turns get a military education. It was darkly hinted, too, that the lead ostensibly imported for the roof of his house at Dungannon was really intended to take the form of bullets. Probably neither rumor was true; or, if O'Neill did train the clansmen of Tyrone, he had at first no rebellious intention. His Munster experiences had made him too well aware of the power of England for him to wish to plunge Ulster into what must be a state of misery. But he was half unconsciously drifting into rebellion. Under the rule of Sir William Fitz William the Irish saw they need look neither for justice or mercy. The first act of the new deputy was to imprison, on false charges, Sir Owen O'Toole and Sir John Dogherty, both loyal gentlemen. His next, to affirm that Mac-Mahon had, some years ago, levied rents with military force, and for this imaginary offence MacMahon was hanged, and his lands, being forfeited to the crown, were graciously bestowed upon the deputy, Sir Henry Bagnal, and other accomplices in the murder. Bagnal was now created marshal of the British army in Ireland. He became O'Neill's personal and implacable enemy, for, O'Neill's first wife being dead—or, as some say, divorced from him—O'Neill and Miss Bagnal met, and notwithstanding differences of race and religion, they resolved to marry. Bagnal got wind of the affair and sent his sister to Dublin, under the care of friends, with strict injunctions that she was not to see her lover. So when O'Neill called at the house, the lady was not admitted to the room where he was received. Hugh made himself most fascinating to the rest of the family, and quite won their good graces. The poor, solitary woman was for the time forgotten, but at length Tyrone took his leave, and Miss Bagnal's friends rushed to her room to tell her how charming they thought her rebel—but the bird was flown! While O'Neill had engrossed the household, she had, by a previous arrangement, ran off with a confidential friend of her lover, who took her to an appointed place of meeting.

The poor woman must have had many a heartache, for there was no meanness Bagnal would not stoop to, to injure his brother-in-law. He trumped up all manner of false charges against him, and care was taken that O'Neill's letters disproving these calumnies should not reach their destination. O'Neill's continued friendship with the family of his first wife is the best proof of the falseness of some of these slanders.

Tyrone now found himself driven into precisely that course of action he most wished to avoid. The continued barbarity of Fitz William maddened the people of Ulster, and they turned to O'Neill as their leader, urging him to take up arms. Bagnal's enmity goaded him to the same course, for any letters or explanations he wrote to the queen were stopped, and he found himself entrapped in a network of misrepresentations. At this time Hugh of the Fetters—an illegitimate son of Shane—gave information against O'Neill to the government, and for this offence Hugh in a high-handed manner strangled the rebel. This act made no small sensation, and the earl found it necessary to go to London to make his peace with the queen. Free from false dealing and treachery, he had no difficulty in convincing Elizabeth of his loyalty, and entered willingly into articles with her, the more so as he had not the slightest intention of keeping them longer than suited his convenience. About this time Red Hugh O'Donnell and the sons of Shane O'Neill succeeded in escaping from their prison in Dublin. Their flight was in winter time, and so intense was the cold, that Art O'Neill was frozen to death, and Red Hugh's feet were so frostbitten that his toes had to be amputated, and it was many months before he recovered the use of his legs, but at length, after much suffering, he reached his home in Tyrconnel. He was still only nineteen years of age, and his four years of captivity coming at a time when he was young and impressionable had embittered his mind toward the English. He never forgot or forgave the injury he had received, and his life was spent in attempts at vengeance. His youth, his sorrows, his perils, and his sufferings all endeared him to the clansmen, and at his return his father resigned the title in his favor. Reports of Fitz William's cruelty were now becoming too frequent to be disregarded, and Elizabeth recalled him and sent out Sir William Russell, son of the earl of Bedford. Young Tyrconnel had now risen in arms against the English, and O'Neill, sick of the treachery, crooked ways, and barbarity of the administration, threw in his lot with the rebels. O'Donnell was not restrained by any sentimental gentleness toward his late gaolers, and began the war with vigor, defeating the English at Enniskillen with great slaughter, and at Blackwater they received a yet more terrible blow. Half the British army was destroyed, Sir Henry Bagnal being among the slain. All Ireland was now in arms—Ulster, Connaught, and Munster, under O'Neill's earl of Desmond, "the Sugane earl" or earl of Straw, as the new earl was called, he being an earl of Hugh's making, for the true Desmond was a prisoner in London. Even loyal Leinster turned against the English, and for the time it seemed as though Ireland was to regain her independence.

Elizabeth was sick of the Irish difficulty, so she sent over an overwhelming force to stamp out the rebellion, and as far as possible exterminate the rebels. 20,000 foot soldiers and

2,000 horse were landed under the command of the earl of Essex. The Irish harassed this army in skirmishing matches, and greatly reduced them, but were too wily to encounter such a superior force in the open field, and Essex marched his troops through Leinster and back to Dublin without producing any effect. At length, on the banks of the Blackwater, he and O'Neill met; they held a deep and earnest conversation, at which no third person was present. What passed can never be known, but O'Neill stated his grievances to Essex, and having proposed terms, an amnesty for six weeks was agreed to. Essex was afterward accused of a traitorous understanding with Tyrone, and it was rumored that he had agreed to leave O'Neill unmolested on a promise of his assisting Essex to the English crown. The clamor was so great that Essex thought it necessary to return to England, where the fickle queen caused her whilom favorite to be beheaded. Blunt, lord Mountjoy, was now sent to Ireland, and in him O'Neill found a very different sort of adversary—Mountjoy was too wise to allow himself to be entrapped into woods and morasses where he knew the Irish would have the advantage. The terrible weapon he wielded against his enemies was devastation, burning the corn and destroying the dwellings. Thus the Munster and Connaught Irish were reduced and many of the chiefs taken prisoners. All this while Spanish succor was expected, but some of the chiefs, unable to make longer resistance, came in. "But what if the Spaniards should arrive?" inquired the president of one of these. "In that case," answered the Irishman, "let not your lordship rely upon me, nor on any of those lords who seem most attached to your service."

At length a very battered and dilapidated Spanish fleet arrived at Kinsale, under command of Don Juan d'Aquila. Why in Kinsale no one knew. Don Juan had been sent to help the rebels of Ulster, and he seemed to have pitched on the fort furthest from his allies. Most of O'Neill's men were militia, and would not bear arms out of Ulster; but, in spite of difficulties, he collected 5,000 men and marched the length of the island. A second Spanish contingent now arrived, and the O'Sullivans and O'Driscols, who had hitherto remained passive, threw in their lot with the rebels. The besieging army was now besieged—on one hand were the Spaniards in Kinsale, on the other the Irish marching from the north, and the advanced season afflicted the English, who were willing to raise the siege when Don Juan pressed O'Neill to attack them. Tyrone resisted this persuasion. He knew by experience of what stuff an English army is made, and could not believe the Spaniard's account of the distress and demoralization of the British force, but at length he let himself be overruled and the attack was made by night; but Don Juan had revealed the plan of action to the English, and the Irish were completely defeated.

The war was now practically over. O'Donnell went to Spain, where he died of a broken heart. The Sugane earl was betrayed and killed, and O'Neill made his submission to Mountjoy just at the time when Elizabeth was breathing her last.

When Tyrone heard that the queen was dead he bitterly lamented his submission—a few hours more resistance would have enabled him to make peace with the new king on a very different footing, but the die was cast, and Hugh had resigned forever the name of The O'Neill before he knew that his enemy was dead. Elizabeth's death was the cause of much rejoicing in Ireland, for James Stuart was supposed to be sympathetic to the Catholics, and was descended from the Scoto-Milesian kings. His Celtic blood brought little advantage to his Irish subjects, nor did they derive much benefit from his leanings towards Catholicism. He enforced the penal code which under Elizabeth had remained more or less a dead letter, and he assured his Romish subjects they need look for no toleration. To break the power of the O'Neill's the lands were subdivided among the smaller chieftains of the clan, and the ordinary clansmen reduced to the condition of tenants. But it was soon found that though nominally crushed Hugh of Tyrone, backed by Rory O'Donnell, earl of Tyrconnel, was a very powerful adversary, and also there was grave discontent in England that a war which had cost so much blood and such unheard of sums of money should bring no advantage at all to the conquerors. It was, therefore, decided that O'Neill must be got rid of, and his estates which had already been bestowed among his clansmen be made to revert to the English crown, and for this purpose a sham plot was had recourse to. An anonymous letter was dropped in the council chamber of Dublin mentioning a design to murder the lord deputy. This paper named no names in connection with the supposed plot, but the government stated that they had evidence proving Tyrone and Tyrconnel to be implicated and called upon them to appear. They, seeing the impossibility of disproving such charges, fled with their families to Europe, and ultimately died in Rome.

At the time, their flight was held conclusive proof of guilt, they were declared traitors and their estates forfeited. In 1604, when it had so suited James, he had pronounced that Tyrone and Tyrconnel had no right over the lands of petty chieftains, but now, six years later, the law was found to have another meaning; not only the estates which had been left to O'Neill and O'Donnell were confiscated, but also those which had been declared the property of the lesser lords. The counties of Tyrone, Derry, Donegal, Armagh, Fermanagh, and Cavan, in all 2,836,873 Irish acres thus came to the crown, and were parcelled out to undertakers as Munster had been in the time of Elizabeth.

CHAPTER X.

THE PLANTATION OF ULSTER.

JAMES profited by Elizabeth's Munster experience; he made smaller grants of land, and passed stringent laws against absenteeism, and he had the wit to perceive how fit were the industrious and thrifty Scots for the work of colonization. Differences of religion, as well as of race, divided these new-comers from the natives, and there was in consequence less degeneration; indeed, to this day the descendants of these Scotch Presbyterian settlers differ in character from the Irish of the other provinces. Still, the plantation system was never throughly carried out; the Scotch settlers, seduced by offers of exorbitant rent, admitted the Irish as tenants, and thus the natives retained a foothold on the soil they loved so well. After a time many of the Scotch and English planters, tiring of their exile, returned to their own country, first selling their interest in their holdings and the value of the improvements they had made. From this arose the practice of buying and selling the tenant right, a custom still peculiar to Ulster, and familiar to us as the Ulster Tenant-Right. Compared with any of Elizabeth's efforts, the plantation of Ulster was a marked success. The people, starved, poor, plague-stricken, and broken-spirited, crept meekly into the bogs and morasses, and only in Cavan made any stand against the new-comers, or protest against the cruelties of Sir Arthur Chichester, the Ulster deputy.

Perhaps a feeble rebellion would not have been wholly unwelcome to the rapacious Stuart, who could have used it as an excuse for confiscating Leinster and Connaught, but the Ulstermen at that moment were less vindictive than the worm. Wherefore James bethought himself of a new pretext for appropriating Leinster and Connaught. He first turned his attention to Leinster, and discovered that the titles by which the estates were held being many of them defective, a commission of inquiry must be held at once. Courts were assembled and juries empanelled, and as those jurors who did not find for the king were imprisoned, pilloried, and branded half-a-million of the Leinster acres were declared crown property. Connaught was now the only province free from confiscation. James had resolved to turn that also to account, but he thought it well to pause for a season, for the Leinster men had not borne their wholesale eviction with the meekness of their Ulster compatriots. Too broken-spirited to rebel, they had sought to intimidate the planters by agrarian outrage, thus depreciating the value of land without entailing the penalty of treason.

The king next turned his attention toward the construction of the Irish House of Commons. The proportion of Roman Catholics to Anglicans in Ireland being then a hundred to one, there was naturally a large Catholic majority in the House of Commons. The Upper House being mainly filled with bishops of the Established Church and Elizabethan peers, had an Anglican majority, but in the Commons the Papists had it all their own way. The welfare of the native and Catholic Irish was, of course, the interest of this body, who were therefore opposed to the policy of James; and he, to obtain a Protestant majority, created seventeen new counties and forty boroughs, towns as yet unbuilt, but belonging to the new Protestant undertakers of Ulster.

The first business of the reconstructed parliament was the election of a speaker. The Protestant candidate was Sir John Davis, and the recusant Sir John Everard. On a division being taken it was found that the Protestants had a majority of twenty votes, but in the meanwhile the recusants seated their candidate in the chair. The Protestants thrust Davis into his lap, and then dragged Everard from under his successful rival amid a disgraceful uproar, and after this undignified scene the Catholic party left the house in a body, thus giving the Protestants a clear field for making any laws they pleased against recusancy or non-attendance at an Anglican place of worship. Relieved from all fear of opposition, the parliament now passed laws prohibiting Catholic worship, and imposing a fine of one shilling, payable each Sunday for recusance; ordering all Romish priests to quit the kingdom within forty days, and subjecting any priests found after that date to the penalties of treason, and making any person harboring a priest liable to a fine of forty pounds for the first offence, to imprisonment for the second, and to death for the third. Many other restrictions were put upon Irish Catholics, who were now made subject to the laws which already oppressed their English brethren. But in England Papists were few and far between, whereas in Ireland ninety-nine out of every hundred persons were Catholic; this oppression of the many by the few was of course the greater persecution, but in reality their great number relieved the recusants from the penalties of the law, for it was found impossible to enforce them. From time to time priests and prelates were seized and killed, with every conceivable torture, and recusants were sometimes forced to pay the weekly fine; but the only result of this fitful and ineffectual persecution was to foster a spirit of religious intolerance, and awaken a desire for revenge.

The Leinster titles had been defective through the carelessness of the landowners who, having possessed their estates for centuries, had imagined themselves perfectly secure, but the Connaught titles were found to be equally defective, for though the landowners had surrendered their estates to Elizabeth, and received them back with new titles, either through negligence or by design the patents for these had never been made out, and this omission made the titles invalid. James was, of course, in honor bound to make good the defect. The titles were paid for, and their defectiveness was the fault of the crown, not of the Connaught landowners; but honor was an obligation which never bound a Stuart, and the titles were declared defective. At this juncture the Connaught men, astutely perceiving the king's weak point, offered to buy new titles. The temptation made James swerve in his purpose of confiscation; he could not determine whether he preferred the greater or the more immediate gain. He never made up his mind, for while he still vacillated he died, and was succeeded by his son Charles.

At the time of the accession of Charles, Falkland was deputy of Ireland, but being a man of inconveniently high principle he was recalled, and viscount Wentworth, better known by his later title of lord Strafford, was sent to replace him. Wentworth was sent to wring money out of the Irish nation, and this task he faithfully fulfilled. Under his rule the inspection of the Connaught titles proceeded briskly, and the recusancy fines were strictly enforced. The Irish perceived that both this reforming zeal and the inquiry into the titles sprang from the Stuart love of money, and accordingly offered to pay £120,000 in exchange for 51 privileges or "graces," by which, in addition to the removal of many minor grievances, it was provided that the Connaught landlords should be permitted to make a new enrolment of their estates; that the undisputed possession of land for 60 years should constitute title; that recusants should be allowed to practice in the courts of law on taking an oath of civil allegiance to the king, and that a parliament should be held to confirm these graces. The money was to be paid in three equal annual instalments. The conditions were agreed to, the first £40,000 were cheerfully paid, and then parliament was called. The deputy, faithful to his master, now announced that two sessions would be held—the first for the king, the second for the people. The object of the king's session was, of course, money; and the Commons, elated at the prospect of the confirmation of the graces, readily voted the large sums asked for by the deputy. The people's session was next held, but, to the dismay of the people, Wentworth announced that though some of the requests would be complied with, the king could not agree with others, and among those parts of his promise which Charles found himself unable to keep was that relating to the confiscation of Connaught. This business was at once taken in hand. In Roscommon, Clare, Sligo, Mayo, and Limerick the juries were frightened into finding verdicts for the king, but in Galway they refused to consider his claim legal, and for this offence they were each fined £4,000 and their possessions confiscated till the money was paid. Never had rapacious sovereign a truer servant than Charles found in Wentworth; never was devoted service so ungratefully repaid; in all quarters the deputy was active in raising money for his worthless master. Among other sums he extorted £17,000 from the O'Byrnes of Wicklow, on pretence of a defect of title, and from the Corporation of the City of London, who were the great undertakers of Ulster, he wrung £70,000, but in this last step Wentworth had over-reached himself. The English undertakers would not submit to such oppression, and this act of tyranny contributed largely to his final overthrow.

His cruelty and oppression in Ireland bore forth abundant fruit, but his administration though evil was intelligent. He founded and promoted the linen trade, which, though it never flourished in his day, became at a later period almost the only manufacture permitted to the Irish; but on the other hand he did all in his power to crush the fast increasing wool trade, which he dreaded as a rival to that of England.

CHAPTER XI.

THE CIVIL WAR OF 1641.

FEW events in modern history are enveloped in more mystery than are the rebellion and civil war of 1641. Much has been written on these subjects by Catholics and Protestants—English and Irish—but the writers who lived at or near the time of the rising were so swayed by party feeling, terror, and indignation that their evidence is most contradictory, and of little use in helping us to arrive at a just conclusion.

That both parties were guilty of barbarous cruelty there is but little doubt; historians of every shade of opinion concede as much, only they have not agreed as to which side began the atrocities which make this episode so dark a blot on the history of England and Ireland. To which ever party commenced the indiscriminate murderings, drownings, hangings, strippings, and other horrors, belongs the greater guilt, but we can never know certainly whether the massacre of the Papists by the Scotch and English at Island Magee, or the atrocities of the Ulstermen under Sir Phelim O'Neill, were earlier in date; but indeed the murder of women and children with nameless cruelties, because other men have done the same by other innocent and defenceless creatures, is so barbarous a retaliation that it is surprising that two civilized peoples have been eager to claim this mean excuse.

The causes of the rebellion were many and complicated: the murderings, torturings, burnings, and destroyings of the Elizabethan troops; the confiscation of large tracts of land under that queen and James I.; the fitful and apparently meaningless persecution of the Catholics; the tyranny of Wentworth, and the weak despotism of Charles, all conspired to make the Irish disaffected and disloyal. Within the last forty years Munster, part of Leinster, and Ulster had been planted, and the Connaught landlords were perpetually threatened with the same fate. These and many minor grievances had rendered the country as inflammable as a tar barrel, and all that was needed was the match to set the whole country in a flame.

After the Elizabethan wars, great numbers of Irishmen had fled abroad and served in foreign armies. Thus an army of soldiers, hostile to the English rule, had been trained and these exiles resolved to free their country from the English yoke. Among the foremost of these were young Hugh O'Neill, son of the great earl of Tyrone, and Rory O'More, whom the English call "Roger Moore."

Hugh and Rory served together in the Spanish army; a mutual sense of wrong, a mutual love of Ireland, and still more a mutual hatred of England, made them great friends. Between them they hatched a scheme for rebellion, and having obtained promises of help from their comrades they set off for Ireland to see what could be done with the old Irish families there. Rory went straight to Ireland, but Hugh travelled by way of Brussels, to recruit the Irish there. In Brussels he was assassinated, and his cousin Phelim stepped into his place. Meanwhile, Rory was organizing rebellion in Dublin with quite unexpected success. All the old Irish were willing to rise, and Rory was just the man to make such an enterprise succeed. Handsome, brave, honest, and of winning address, the Irish were all his devoted slaves, and trusted to him so implicitly that it became a saying that the Irish put their faith in "God, the Virgin Mary, and in Roger Moore." O'More undertook to manage the Dublin rising, and Phelim went to arrange an outbreak in Ulster, where his name and lineage carried a weight that his personal character did not warrant. Brought up in England, a member of the Established Church, Phelim O'Neill had lost his fortune by dissipation and extravagance, and he now, by turning Romanist and rebel, sought to better his condition.

The 23d of October was the night fixed for the rising in Dublin and in the provinces. O'More organized his part without much secrecy—the apathy of the government was so great that he believed he had nothing to fear.

Since the recall of Wentworth, the government had been entrusted to two chief justices, Sir William Parsons and Sir John Borlase, who, taking their ease, left the Pale to care for itself, and it is to be feared they rather wished for a provincial rising. "The more rebellions the more confiscation," they were often heard to say, alluding to the custom of bestowing the confiscated lands of rebels on the officers of government who, in many cases, tolerated rebellion for the sake of the goods it brought them—and in more than one instance trumped up false charges of treason to secure the property of their victims for themselves.

On the 22d of October a member of the conspiracy informed the justices of what was about to take place, and several persons were arrested, though O'More and the other leaders escaped. So far as Dublin was concerned the plot was now a failure, but all the Ulster risings came off, and the Irish took most of the towns, expelling the new settlers from them and from the country houses. Barbarous acts of cruelty are related against Phelim and his men —a rabble of about 30,000 untrained laborers—those "hewers of wood and drawers of water" who had been permitted to remain in Ulster at the time of the confiscation. This was the hour of revenge, and egged on by Phelim they committed hideous cruelties. The season was exceptionally severe; the ground was hard and white with frost and snow. The pitiless Phelim turned the settlers from their homes, stripping even the women and children of their clothes, and driving them naked into the woods, to perish there or find their way as best they might to Dublin. Many died of cold and hunger on the grim journey. Many, too, were hanged, ripped up, or driven into the river by Phelim's barbarous rabble, whom he was pleased to call "The Catholic Army of Ireland." Here and there the Romish priests or some kind-hearted Catholic sheltered and cared for the wretched fugitives, but in the main the English of Tyrone had a bitter time of it. In other parts, and under better leaders, matters were different. In Cavan, under Philip O'Reilly, the revolution was bloodless, and the settlers were safely escorted to Dublin by the rebel soldiers.

The state of that city can well be imagined. Men, women, and children were pouring in naked, starving, wounded, and ruined; all they possessed had been taken from them, and their relatives had died or been murdered on the road. Many a ghastly tale of horror was told. Some of these tales were true, many were exaggerated by fear, horror, and the natural instinct that prevents tales from losing in the telling, others were false. So great was the exaggeration of horrors, that though the total English population of Ulster was not more than 20,000, it was stated that 145,000 had perished. Yet, with these tales of agony coming daily to their ears, with naked, wounded, starving fugitives trooping into Dublin, the infamous lords justices did absolutely nothing to quell the rebellion. Dublin they strongly fortified, and then not only refused to attack the rebels themselves but rejected the numerous offers of help that were made them by the loyal Anglo-Irish families.

Parliament was prorogued, and the sitting of the law courts adjourned, on the ground that for the safety of Dublin all who had no business there must leave the city, those who had left their country seats and fled to Dublin for safety were now turned out and forced to return to their homes, which were by this time mostly in the hands of the rebels. The loyal Catholics were now on the horns of a dilemma; fate was driving them, as it had driven Desmond and Hugh O'Neill, into courses of rebellion, for the government not only did nothing to quell the rising, but had absolutely refused protection to loyalists from the province. The atrocities of Phelim, which had seemed unparalleled in loyal Dublin, sank into insignificance compared with the accounts given by the rebels of the barbarity of Munroe and of Coote, who, in quelling the Ulster rising, ordered that no Papist should be spared, "if it were but the child a hand high, for nits will be lice;" and a bill which was then passed in the English parliament for the extirpation of the Romish religion led the Catholics to believe that this policy of extermination would shortly be applied to the whole Romish population.

Driven undefended into the rebel quarters, and with

England preparing a death-blow for their creed, it is small wonder that the loyalty of the Anglo-Irish lords gave way, and that in December both they and the Munstermen threw in their lot with the rebels. A pardon was now proclaimed, but with limitations which made it worse than useless. Longford, Cavan, Meath, and Westmeath (in two of which counties there had been no rebellion), were the only places to which the amnesty was offered, and even there no freeholders were included, so the O'Reillys and others who had restrained the mob were to be hanged, and their lands confiscated, and any ruffians were to be pardoned, provided they had no property.

The Roman Catholic archbishop of Armagh had convened a provincial synod, at which the war or rebellion of the Catholics was pronounced lawful and pious, and whereat arrangements were made for a national synod to be held at Kilkenny during the following year. In May, 1642, the synod assembled, and formed a provisional government for the control of the country until such time as a parliament could be called. It was arranged that this provisional government should consist of twenty four members, six for each province, to be elected by a general assembly of fourteen Roman Catholic peers, the Roman Catholic bishops and clergy, and 226 Roman Catholic deputies from the counties and towns. Arrangements were made for the settlement of legal and provincial matters, and the following October was fixed for the meeting of the first convention, which was to be held at Kilkenny. The May synod also issued a manifesto explaining their conduct, and denouncing the murders and outrages which had disgraced the Catholic cause. But Phelim did not find this pacific denunciation binding to his conscience, and continued his barbarities till, in August, his cousin, Colonel Owen Roe (Red Owen) O'Neill came over from Flanders in response to an appeal for help from the old Irish rebels, and at about the same time a similar call from the Anglo-Irish was answered by the appearance of Colonel Preston in Wexford harbor, both leaders bringing with them about a hundred officers and a large supply of arms. Owen Roe O'Neill was disgusted at the undisciplined condition of the Catholic army, and he announced that if another outrage were committed he would quit the country or fight for the enemy. Phelim now resigned the command, and eventually both he and O'More retired from the movement. Against the character of Owen Roe O'Neill not even the bitterest antagonist has ever breathed a word: as a general he was perhaps too cautious to succeed in such an enterprise as he was now engaged in, but he was courageous, truthful, high-minded, and merciful—and the very type of chivalry. His influence on the Ulstermen was magical; under his command the barbarous rabble soon became a respectable army. In the meantime Irish exiles were returning in shoals, bringing with them arms and a knowledge of warfare acquired in foreign armies.

In October the convention of Kilkenny assembled, and passed a number of useful measures; it excommunicated all persons guilty of outrage, and placed the command of the army in the hands of four generals. To Owen Roe O'Neill was consigned Ulster; Munster to Gerald Barry; Leinster to Preston; and Sir John Bourke was made deputy commander of Connaught, the supreme command being reserved for the loyal and gallant earl of Clanrickarde, Charles, most faithful subject. By this time the movement had lost its character of rebellion, and had developed into a civil war, to which there were now four distinct parties. First, there were the old Irish who had began the rebellion, and who aimed not only at religious equality but national independence; to this party belonged the Ulstermen, headed by Owen Roe O'Neill. Then there was the Anglo-Irish party, to which Colonel Preston belonged, and who only desired religious liberty, security for their property, the repeal of the Poyning's Law, and a general confirmation of the graces. This party were rebels against the government only—not rebels against the king—their interest was very different to that of the old Irish, but ties of religion, and in many cases of blood, held them together. The third was a small but very important party, and called itself the king's party; it was composed of Catholics and Anglicans, whose attachment to the king was great enough to overcome differences of race and creed.

The leader was the powerful earl of Ormonde, who afterward became lord deputy; other prominent members of it were the earl of Clanrickarde and the infamous lord Inchiquin. "bloody Murrough O'Brien." The fourth party, at first insignificant, but destined to crush the other three, was Parliamentary and Presbyterian. The Confederation of Kilkenny had been so ably conducted and managed with so rare a spirit of justice and toleration, that the conviction was forced upon Charles that his Irish subjects were quite capable of governing themselves. The royal army, too, was in a wretched state, and in every battle the "Confederates," as the Irish anti-government party was called, had been victorious. Charles now began to negotiate for a truce, and in September, 1643, the Confederates agreed to a cessation of hostilities for one year. This cessation was the ruin of the rebels, who, during the years of enforced peace, found time to foster those dissensions which always have been the ruin of national movements in Ireland, and Charles meanwhile was collecting soldiers and making plans of what he would do when the year expired. He now appointed Ormonde lord lieutenant, and applied to him for advice. "Let them alone, and my countrymen will be sure to ruin themselves," replied the earl, with cynical wisdom, and in August the king, already perceiving the wisdom of this policy, proposed a further truce of six months. To this the Confederates agreed; they were by this time hopelessly disunited. The Pope had sent over his nuncio Renuncini, and the Confederates had split into moderates and ultramontanes; they hoped to settle their difficulties in the prolonged truce, and, moreover, neither English nor Irish wished to fight in the winter, but when spring came a further truce was agreed upon, and hostilities did not begin again until June, 1646. Owen Roe then marched against the Scottish general, Munroe, and, after crossing the Blackwater, gained a signal victory at Benburb. In O'Neill lay the only hope of the Confederates, now terribly weakened by internal disunion, and one party was trying to make terms with the Protestant and anti-Irish Ormonde, though he had declared that, rather than make terms with the Papists, he would deliver

Ireland to those Puritans who were in arms against his king.

Charles had long since commanded Ormonde to make peace on any terms, "and," said he "if the Confederates stipulate for liberty of conscience and the repeal of Poyning's Law, I shall not consider it a hard bargain." For long Ormonde disregarded the king's command, but, at the close of 1648, he saw that the royal cause was too weak to make a longer resistance, so he agreed to make terms, and the Confederates, too weary of war to be deterred even by the threat of excommunication, signed a peace on the 17th of January, 1649; but seventeen days later this was invalidated by the execution of Charles. In August of the same year, Cromwell, attended by his son Henry, Ireton, Ludlow, and others, went to Ireland to preach the gospel and quell rebellion. To attain these ends he took with him an admirably organized force of soldiers, a number of scythes and bullets, and a large supply of Bibles. The scythes and bullets hit their mark, but the Bibles were a dead failure. In the first place, few of the natives could read; in the second, English was an unknown tongue; in the third, the conduct of the Cromwellian troops was not calculated to ensure their reception as messengers of the Word or preachers of the gospel of peace. True, "Jesus and no quarter" was their battle-cry, but the association of that name with butchery savored to the Papists rather of blasphemy than holiness.

Cromwell's first act was to lay siege to Drogheda, and after a time the garrison surrendered on promise of quarter, but no sooner had they laid down their arms than Cromwell took back his word and slaughtered every man, woman, and child in the city, so that five days are said to have been spent in this ghastly massacre. At Wexford, the same miserable scenes of treachery and butchery were enacted, and all over the country Sir Phelim's atrocities (which had already been paid off in the earlier part of the war) were revenged on innocent people who had had nothing to do with them.

By the death of Owen Roe, in December, 1649, the Irish had been deprived of the man whose influence and talent were the sole support of their falling cause. The loss of their leader and the ferocity of the Puritans broke the neck of the rebellion, and in the spring of 1650 Cromwell left Ireland, making his son Henry lord-lieutenant, and his son-in-law, Ireton, commander of the army. Ireton's measures were even more rigorous than those of the Protector himself had been, and his death fifteen months later was a relief to his own party as well as to the enemy. Ludlow now took the command, and marched to help Coote who was encamped before Galway.

Sore pressed and famine-stricken, and moreover terrified at the bloodthirsty reputation of Coote, in whom love of slaughter amounted to madness, Galway surrendered in May, 1652. The ten years' war was at an end. How to make the wasted, depopulated, famine-stricken country pay the debt incurred by the war was Cromwell's next consideration.

CHAPTER XII

THE PLANTATION OF CROMWELL.

DESOLATE though Munster had been after the Desmond rebellion, the whole island was now in a worse condition. During the ten years' war, the country had been neglected, and the practice of burning the harvest had so greatly discouraged the few who were able to till the land that agriculture had been abandoned. All the live stock had been eaten up by the armies, and though after Cromwell had taken the command the soldiers had paid for all they had, the country was in so miserable a condition that many of the wretched natives were driven not only to eat the flesh of the many wolves that attacked them, but even the corpses of their neighbors.

Cromwell felt that a people so reduced, so starved and plague-stricken, must of necessity submit to any measures he proposed, and his first idea was to utterly exterminate the Irish race; but this scheme he abandoned as being at once too difficult and too brutal, and he devoted himself to measures which, if more humane, were infinitely less efficacious.

An Act of Settlement was passed by the English parliament in August, 1652, decreeing that a full pardon should be extended to all whose possessions were worth less than £10. It was perhaps less mercy than self-interest that led to this step; for, had the laborers been removed, the new settlers would have had even to do the very roughest work for themselves, whereas these natives could now become hewers of wood and drawers of water for their new masters; but the clergy, as well as the landed proprietors, were exempted from this Act of Grace, both as to life and estates. If caught they would be hanged and their goods confiscated; but several other classes profited by it in a greater or less degree. Officers of the royal army were to be banished, but were to retain the value of one-third of their property, which was to be assigned for the support of their wives and children. Those also who had taken so small a share in the rebellion as to be considered entitled to mercy were, after forfeiting their estates, to receive land in Connaught to the value of one-third, but the most fortunate were naturally those who were held perfectly innocent—a very small class, as the payment of even a forced subscription to the rebel army was proof of guilt. These few innocent persons were also obliged to give up their lands, but they received territory in Connaught to the value of two-thirds; but to obtain these benefits from the Act of Grace, all landed proprietors had to give up their title deeds and resign all claim to their old possessions. Some defied Cromwell and kept their titles, but their lands were taken from them and they had to fly for their lives into the bogs and forests. Destitute and deprived of all they ever had, they took to a wild life of robbery, and were called Tories, from an Irish word meaning a plunderer.

Of the Irish soldiers 45,000 were transported and took service in foreign armies, but of these the greater number were unable to take their families with them. These families should have been provided for out of that third of their property which was to be returned to them, but justice is a patroness of the powerful, and between six and seven thousand women and children were kidnapped and sent to the West Indies, where the boys were sold for slaves to the sugar planters, and the girls and women reserved for a more dishonorable fate.

All this time military tribunals were sitting to try such rebels as were, for various reasons, excluded from the Act of Grace, and from their blood-thirsty verdicts these courts were called "Cromwell's shambles." In the meantime, the government survey of the three provinces, Ulster, Leinster and Munster, was proceeded with; the acreage was noted and the land valued—the best at four shillings an acre and some as low as one penny: bog and unprofitable land was thrown in and not counted. And now in the harvest time of 1653 the drums were beaten and the trumpets blown throughout the land to assemble the people to hear the news, that by the first of May next they must cross over the Shannon and go into exile in the rainy waste lands of Connaught. Connaught was from henceforth the Ireland of the Irish; fertile Ulster, green Leinster, and lovely Munster were for the Cromwellian settlers, who, by an Act of Grace, gave Connaught to the native Irish. This province was chosen for the Irish not only because it was the least fertile, but also, because, encircled by the ocean and the Shannon, it was most easily converted into a natural prison.

The flight was to be in the winter, for after the first of May, 1654, any Irishman found within the three provinces, in England, or on the high seas, was liable to be put to death.

Not only the old Irish families, but the Anglo-Norman settlers came under this proscription. The Fitzgeralds, Butlers, Bourkes, Plunkets, Dillons, Barnewells, Cheevers, Cusacks, who 500 years earlier had driven the Scoto-Milesians from their inheritance, were now to share the misfortune of their old enemies, and by a common misery to be united with those from whom they had held aloof. The men were to go first, to wrest the land allotted to them from its rightful owners, and to build shelters for the women, who were speedily to follow. Without servants, without money, without cattle, these Irish gentlemen—

many of them with no knowledge of farming—went to earn their living in Connaught. Death was the penalty if they returned; death if they entered the gates of Galway, the one city of this penal settlement; death if they ventured within four miles of the sea or two miles of the Shannon; and to enforce this regulation soldiers were planted round the river-side and the sea-coast. It seems as though a choice of deaths were offered to these unhappy creatures—the swift sword of the soldier or the slow starvation of hunger and cold in Connaught; and, to make matters worse, Cromwell's officers refused to stir in the matter of the allotment till they had been bribed by money or promises of a share of the land. Then arose a new difficulty, for the lands were found to be too small for the exiles; but many of them solved the question by quietly dying of cold and exposure. And now the women began to follow. The winter was wet, and the roads (neglected during the late war) nearly impassable. The country was famine-stricken, and the women, weakened by want and burdened with the sick, the aged, and the children, could not get away by the dreaded 1st of May. Very slowly the squalid procession dragged along the heavy, slushy roads, and many were still east of the Shannon when their time was up. So indifferent, so listless were they, that it was found necessary to hang some and imprison others to stimulate the flagging energy of the remainder. The walled towns which had been peopled with English settlers were cleared like the country, but the merchants, not being entitled to the benefits of the graces, carried their enterprise to foreign cities. Thus the three provinces were cleared, and the lands so acquired were devoted to the payment of the adventurers who had advanced money to Cromwell, and the soldiers whose wages were hopelessly in arrears. The claims of the adventurers were first satisfied, and then lists were made out of the claims of each regiment. The regiments next drew lots for the various localities, and in the same way each man received by lot his own plot of ground. Company after company they were marched to their new homes, disbanded, and put in possession, but all this took time, and it was not till the end of '55—three years before

Cromwell's death—that the last regiments were disbanded. Many of the soldiers sold their plots at once to their comrades and officers, but others settled into farmers, and numbers, sick of bloodshed, turned Quaker. But in their agriculture they were balked by the Tories, in their pastoral enterprises by the wolves, and their souls were distressed by the ubiquitous priests, who, by no fear of death, could be induced to leave the country. "We have now three burdensome beasts to destroy," said Morgan, then member for Wexford. "The first is a wolf, the second a priest, and the third a Tory." A price was put on the head of each of these objectionable animals—a wolf and a priest had the same market value, £5 per head, and the wolves were gradually exterminated, but the priests seemed rather to increase than diminish. The price for a Tory's head was, for a public Tory, £20, but only 40s. for a private Tory. They, like the priests, were very difficult to catch, for the peasants who had been allowed to stay on the lands to work for the new settlers respected them as their old chieftains, and sympathized with their robberies.

But in spite of extermination, exile, and kidnapping the old tale of degeneration was to be enacted. Many of Cromwell's soldiers married the daughters of their Irish laborers, and forty years later numbers of the children of these Puritan settlers were unable to speak a word of English. But long ere that time Cromwell had ceased to be troubled by questions of policy, for on September 3d, 1658, he died, and in 1660 the prince of Wales was proclaimed Charles II.

CHAPTER XIII.

THE RESTORATION.

WHEN the king came to his own again, the Irish royalists supposed that they also would be restored to those possessions they had lost through their devotion to his cause, and a few of them, acting with more zeal than discretion, proceeded at once to turn out the settlers by force. But though the number of these fanatics was small, they were enough to revive the old cry that the Irish Papists were rebelling again, and to serve the government with an illustration of the dangers of Catholic landlordism in Ireland.

The Papists, in truth, had no idea of rebelling. They knew that if Charles had not been actually received into the Church of Rome all his sympathies were Catholic, and they expected to have their lands returned and their religion respected. They petitioned for an immediate restoration of property, and proposed to pay a third of their income for two years to the Cromwellian soldiers and adventurers, and for five years to those who had bought lands during the protectorate. The soldiers and adventurers were naturally furious at this proposal. The estates had been granted them in place of money advanced or owed as wage. The fortune of war, which had seemed just enough when they were the victors, now appeared barbarous and uncivilized. By the sword they had won the fertile lands of Ireland, and by the sword, if need be, they would retain them.

Charles was now in a difficult position, for Coote, Broghill, and others of his father's enemies, seeing the turn of the tide, had been foremost of those who had helped him to the throne. Friends such as these needed buying, for their principles went with their interest. Their estates were therefore extended, and their titles confirmed. "Make much of your enemies, for your friends will do you no harm," was Clarendon's cynical advice, and in it Charles saw the only solution of the Irish land question.

By every tie of honor the king was bound to reinstate those who had suffered for his father and himself, and at first he did not mean to desert them. He was told that there would be land enough to meet all claims, and he tried to believe the flattering tale. But the settlers resented being evicted, with the doubtful prospect of fresh lands somewhere, to be given some time; and Charles, remembering that these Cromwellians were powerful enough and resolute enough to raise a rebellion, acted on Clarendon's advice, and resolved to confirm their tenure. His hold on the English throne was of the weakest; he feared to estrange any class, and he simply dared not favor the Catholics; whereas, no wrong, however great, inflicted on Irish Papists was likely to call forth resentment in England. Things being thus, and Charles being a Stuart, there could be no doubt which cause he would espouse.

In May, 1661, the Irish parliament, after a lapse of nearly twenty years, was once more assembled. The business they were to discuss was a bill of settlement confirming the claims of the "new interest." In the Lower House, consisting almost entirely of Cromwellians, the bill was easily passed, but in the Lords there was a hard fight; though by the influence of Ormonde it was pushed through. But lest this bill might provoke too much indignation among the Catholics, a Court of Claims was instituted, wherein certain of the Irish might have their case tried, and, if proved innocent, get their lands restored. None who had joined the rebels before '48, or who, in the final split of the Confederates, had adhered to the nuncio's party, or had accepted lands in Connaught, were allowed to plead; and with a view of cutting down the number of claimants, it was held proof of rebellion to have lived peaceably in the rebels' quarters even without taking any part in the war; therefore not only all Catholics who had taken arms when the English parliament had passed a bill for the extirpation of their religion were excluded, but also those who had dwelt quietly with the defenders of their faith. The gates of Dublin had been closed against all who had no business in the city, and as nearly the whole of the rest of Ireland had been in the hands of the rebels, it must have been difficult to find a home out of their quarters. The Protestant ascendancy thought it had little to fear from a Court of Claims bound by such restrictions; still, to make assurance doubly sure, no pains were spared to secure "friendly commissioners." Yet with all these precautions the court was crammed with applicants, and at the end of three months, out of about two hundred cases tried, only nineteen applicants were declared *nocent*, the vast majority being judged *innocent*, and in consequence, entitled to the restoration of their estates. The Cromwellians, wild with anger and dismay, talked loudly of an appeal to arms, and Charles, seeing he must now definitely sacrifice one party, decided that the weakest must go to the wall. Houses, lands, wealth, children, liberty, and life these men had given up for him, and for the faith both he and they professed, yet when he had to choose between them and his father's executioners he did not hesitate which should be honored and which despised. The action of the Court of Claims was accordingly restricted to one year—four thousand claims had been entered, but only seven hundred heard when the court rose, and the hopes of more than three thousand unheard claimants were at an end forever.

An "Explanatory Bill" was next passed, which provided that the soldiers and adventurers should give up one-third of their grant to increase the fund for reprisals, but in spite of this surrender hardly a sixth of the profitable land of Ireland remained to the Catholics, for in all cases of competition between Papist and Protestant all ambiguity was to be decided in favor of the Protestant. By special favor twenty persons were restored, but all other claims which had not been heard for want of time were held disqualified by the "Black Act," as the bill for closing the Court of Claims was called in Ireland.

The land question was now settled, and after twenty-one years of fighting, confiscating, and restoring, the Irish Catholics held just half as much land as they had done when they sought to reinstate themselves by the rebellion of 1641.

The tenure by which the new landlords held their estates had been so insecure, the fear of war and harvest burning so great, and the chance of eviction so considerable, that few cared to sow corn which their enemies might reap or destroy, and as a consequence the greater part of the country had been laid down in grass.

The profits of agriculture were greater than of pasturage but the return was slower, and the mischief done by an invading army far greater. Moreover, larger capital is needed to work an agricultural than a grazing farm, for with ploughing, harrowing, sowing, weeding, cleaning, reaping, and threshing much more labor is required than on pasture land. It is just for this reason that an agricultural country is more thickly and more intelligently populated than a pastoral one. Already, in Elizabeth's time, Spencer deplored the pastoral tendency of the Irish, bewailing the few and idle hinds needed on a pastoral farm compared to the many intelligent, industrious laborers on an agricultural one. Indeed, modern economists tell us that other conditions being equal, there is twenty times more pauperism in grazing districts. But the Cromwellian settlers could hardly be expected to enter into these considerations, and the population had been so thinned by war, plague, exile, and transportation, that the pastoral tendency of Ireland was not then so disastrous as it became at a later period. The sole wealth of the country at this time was cattle; rent, taxes, and subsidies were paid in this inconvenient coin, and the only trade of the country was the exportation of beasts to England and Scotland. The civil wars and confiscations that had ruined Ireland had also lowered the rents of England; but the politicians of the day, failing to realize that the unsettled state of the country was the cause of its poverty, assigned various reasons for the disaster, and at last the duke of Buckingham declared he believed the importation of Irish cattle the root of the evil. The idea was eagerly received. The Irish, good for nothing else, were a most convenient scapegoat. The importation was declared a "nuisance," and prohibited, and for the time Ireland was ruined. Subsidies and taxes could no longer be paid; the country was in the direst distress; but happily all classes and both nationalities were affected by this calamity, and Ormonde and other nobles set to work to help themselves and their country. They could not get the embargo taken off the exportation of cattle, but they persuaded Charles to allow Ireland free trade with foreign countries, "whether at peace or war with his majesty"—a truly astonishing measure for that time, and one of hitherto unheard-of liberality. Ormonde also introduced skilled weavers both of woolen and linen to come over from Flanders and teach their art to the Irish, who, in retaliation for the Scotch embargo on cattle, refused to admit Scottish woolen goods. All classes combined to encourage Irish manufacture, and Ireland now seemed in a fair way to prosperity. The iniquitous sham Popish Plot caused some misery to the Catholics, but a reaction soon set in, and they enjoyed more liberty than they had done since the reign of Mary, when, in 1685, Charles died, and his brother James, duke of York, ascended the throne. James was an avowed Roman Catholic, and was moreover the most unpopular man in England. He would probably never have been crowned, but that he was already fifty-two years of age, and had no legitimate son. His daughter Mary, wife of William of Orange, was next heir to the throne, and the English people preferred waiting till James's death for her accession to a violent and unnatural usurpation.

The accession of a Catholic king was naturally a great joy to Catholic Ireland, though James personally was disliked by, and disliked, his Irish subjects. On the other hand Protestant Ireland was much distressed at the ascendancy of a Papist, and the new interest quaked for their rights, but their fears were somewhat calmed by the appointment of the Protestant lord Clarendon to the office of lord lieutenant, though at the same time, Sir Richard Talbot, a most bigoted Papist, was created earl of Tyrconnel and given the command of the army.

But James had the audacity to announce that he intended to establish religious equality, a joyful proclamation to Papist and Presbyterian, but greatly distrusted by the Episcopalians who saw in it the first step towards Catholic ascendancy.

Probably they were right: James was not wise enough, or liberal enough, to care about religious equality for its own sake, nor were the Catholics sufficiently ahead of the age to be content with simple justice. An illustrious Irishman of our own day has summed up the relations between England and Ireland as "a course of brutal repression on the one side met by savage retaliation on the other," and the Episcopalians of James's time were well aware that their oppression had been brutal enough to call down a fearful retribution, should the Catholics ever be capable of revenge. Encouraged by James's favor the Irish royalists again petitioned for a reversal of the Act of Settlement, and a restoration of their estates, and it seemed likely that their request would be granted; for Clarendon was merely a tool in the hands of Talbot, who pushed forward the Roman Catholic interest. The army was first opened to Catholics, then Episcopalians were excluded, and the Monmouth rebellion was made the excuse for disarming the Protestants. After this injustice the Tories, emboldened by the defenceless condition of the settlers and shielded by the peasantry, made raids on the Cromwellian farms and carried off the cattle, and thousands of beasts were slaughtered out of pure mischief and hatred for their owners. The old proprietors now urged the tenants to refuse rents to the new interest on the plea that they had no right to the land; and as the disarmed Protestants dared not evict them, the laborers defied their masters openly. Murders and outrages were committed and a foundless rumor got abroad that the Papists intended to massacre the whole Protestant population, who fled to the towns or barricaded themselves in their houses in abject terror. At this juncture (Feb., 1689) Clarendon resigned, and Talbot was appointed lord lieutenant.

This step confirmed the fears of the settlers; they were now convinced that the savage retaliation was to begin. Five hundred families left Dublin with Clarendon, and all the sea-ports were thronged with refugees. Still the expected massacre did not come off, though the cattle-lifting and theft by the Tories continued. Talbot's administration was really alarming; every Protestant was turned out of office, all the privy councillors, judges, and mayors were Irishmen and Romanists. The English ascendancy was for the moment overthrown, and the lives and fortunes of the settlers were at the mercy of the natives, but in June, 1688, the birth of a prince of Wales brought matters to a crisis. By the birth of a Catholic heir to the throne the Papists felt secure; but the same event drove the English to action and brought about the revolution, for a number of English nobles invited the prince of Orange to come over and take possession of the country. These gentlemen were patriots, but most undoubtedly they were also traitors and rebels. They risked their life, their honor, and their possessions for their country and their faith, and their cause succeeded. The Irish, who remained staunch to James, risked as much in the same holy cause, and they lost; still, though both were patriots, it was the Williamites, not the Jacobites, who were the traitors. Ireland took no part in the invitation to William. War, massacre, and confiscation were associated in the Irish mind with Protestant ascendancy, and the majority knew nothing of the invitation to William till the news reached them that, on the fifth of November, "The Deliverer" had landed in Torbay, and that James had absconded to France. For a moment the Catholics were paralyzed by the blow, and the flight of James by no means added to the dignity of the situation. But Talbot immediately resolved to fight, and quickly raised 30,000 irregular troops of volunteers, or "rapparees," as they were called from the Irish name of the short pike or spear which in most cases was their only weapon. The news of the muster of these troops increased the terror of the Ulster Protestants. The youthhood of Derry and Enniskillen determined to protect themselves against the bloodthirsty Papists, and thus, from a courage born of desperation, began those famous feats of long-sustained valor, the sieges of Derry and Enniskillen. Meanwhile, in the early months of '89, the conventions of England and Scotland declared that James had abdicated, and offered the crown to William and Mary.

James, either from cowardice or policy, resolved to make his stand on Irish ground. Neither the English nor the Scotch were unanimous in their wish for William of Orange, and James hoped his adherents in Great Britain would keep the Williamites busy till he could convert the Irish irregulars into an army serviceable for the invasion of the larger island. Personally he disliked the Irish; he cared nothing for their land difficulties, and certainly had he succeeded in regaining his throne he would not have granted them an independent parliament. The Irish leaders, on the other hand, had no taste for a policy which, even should it succeed, would reduce their country once more to a state of dependence—their aim was to regain their country for their own people. Thus the king, and the men who were to fight for him, had entirely different aims, and when, on the 12th of March, 1689, James landed at Kinsale he found that the old war of races had begun, and that half of Talbot's army was engaged before the walls of Derry, whose weak defences were bravely held by a force of seven thousand English settlers.

CHAPTER XIV.
THE REVOLUTION.

ON the twelfth of March, 1689, James landed at Kinsale, attended by his natural sons, the duke of Berwick and the grand prior Fitz James, and a few Irish and French officers, among them Generals d'Avaux and de Rosen, and about 1,200 troops. James's misfortunes had wiped out from the memory of the Irish people the remembrance of his unpopularity and his cowardly flight from England. Blinded by their sympathies, they saw in James the noble upholder of their faith, persecuted for righteousness sake, deserted by his English subjects, and dethroned by his own daughter because of his steadfastness to his religion. The obstinate, weak-minded old coward was for them a saint. They forgot that they, like every one else, disliked and despised him, and they refused to see how intensely indifferent he was to their national aims and ambition. Irish hospitality and sympathy had prepared a warm welcome for their king, who enjoyed an ovation from Kinsale to Dublin, and a perfect triumph in the capital, where ten days and nights were spent in festivities, levees, and receptions. But there was more serious business to attend to, and parliament was called. James and the Irish entirely differed as to the uses of parliament—to James it was a machine for wringing money out of his subjects; to them it was a means for wringing a constitution out of James. A long experience of the Stuart character made them well aware that when once James had got their money his interest in the Irish parliament would vanish, so they refused to make any arrangement with regard to subsidies, till certain acts were passed.

Their first care was for the repeal of Poyning's Act, by which, since the time of Richard II., no act passed by the Irish parliament could become law, till it had been approved by the English privy council, by whom it might be altered and amended to any extent, but on its return to Ireland it might receive no further alteration, but must either be rejected altogether or passed just as it was returned. Having disposed of this hated law, acts were passed to secure religious equality. Since the reformation, Papist and Protestant alike had had to pay tithe to the clergy of the Established Church. The Irish Catholics now practically disestablished the Irish Church by decreeing that all persons should pay tithe to the clergy of their own denomination. Measures for the security of trade were also passed; but the great business of the session, from the Irish point of view, was the reversal of the Bill of Settlement, and it was decreed that all Catholics who had held land before October, 1641, were to be reinstated. By the subsequent defeat of James, these acts were rendered waste paper, but they are important historically as showing the views of Irishmen of that day with regard to the needs of their country. Parliament now voted to the king the subsidies of £20,000 a month, but, James being dissatisfied with this sum, they consented to double the amount. It had been well for the reputation of the Irish parliament had it now risen, for their next measure was one of simple retaliation—they attainted 2,000 persons of treason, and declared them subject to the penalties of that crime. The lists were drawn up with extreme carelessness—some names were inserted twice or even three times, many were put in from private spite, and a few of the most prominent Williamites were forgotten. All this time the war was going on, and the gallant Derry 'prentice boys—the descendants of the planters sent over by the city of London in the time of Charles I.—were valiantly holding the town. James marched from Dublin to the devoted city, and the Derry governor prepared to capitulate, but the mob followed up his negotiations with a storm of bullets, and elected a clergyman named Walter for their leader; and, despite the most terrible sufferings from starvation and disease, held the town till the end of July, when they were relieved by the English fleet. Long before then, James, discomforted by their warm reception, had returned to Dublin, leaving Hamilton in command. The Irish troops—raw, untried levies—were discouraged at the absence of their king, and they did not get on well with the French generals. Moreover, they were extremely badly armed, having only a thousand really serviceable arms among thirty times as many men. They were, also, in want of money, and in every way the war went against them throughout the summer, so that when in August William's general, Schomberg, arrived with 4,000 men he hoped soon to close the campaign. But through the winter it was Schomberg's troops that suffered, and though the timorous James refused to allow his soldiers to attack the enemy in their damp encampment, fever and disease fought for the Irish, and swept off half of Schomberg's forces before they could retire to winter quarters.

William was becoming seriously alarmed about the Irish war, and his ill success there told against him in England. By losing Ireland he would lose England also; indeed, discontent was so openly expressed that he thought of resigning the crown and returning to Holland. He had also another reason for wishing to settle the Irish question, for his troops were wanted for his war with France, the issue of which was terribly imperilled by the enormous force he was obliged to pour into Ireland. On the other hand, it was to the interest of Louis to prolong the Irish war. He could easily have spared men enough to place victory within reach of James, but, delighted at having the Williamites so plentifully occupied, he sent over only just enough arms and money to keep the Irish from the necessity of surrender, and employed his own troops in pushing his own victories in France. In the spring of 1690, the French generals, d'Avaux and de Rosen, obtained their recall, but not before de Rosen had so far forgotten himself as to tell James that "if he had ten kingdoms he would lose them all." But Louis, who contemplated the annexation of

Ireland to France, felt that by this recall he had left the Irish too much their own masters, so he sent over General de Lauzan, with 5,000 men; but this was rather a loss than a gain to the Jacobites as the same number of Irish, with Colonel Justin M'Carthy, Lord Montcashel at their head, were, in exchange, sent over to France. The French did little good in Ireland. They did not know the country and they suffered much from hardship and the damp climate, to which the Irish were quite indifferent. Throughout the spring Schomberg's troops were engaged in reducing Charlemont, which was gallantly held by O'Regan and a very small garrison. But though neither party made much progress in the war, the "English," as the medley of Dutch, Danes, English, and French Huguenots were called, were becoming so discouraged and demoralized, that William, hoping his presence would have some effect on them, landed at Carrickfergus on June 14, and found himself at the head of 40,000 men.

The arrival of William in Ireland reduced James to the same helpless condition that his appearance in Torbay had done eighteen months earlier, but he made a desperate effort not to run away, and insisted on a battle being fought on the banks of the Boyne. Still he felt a depressing presentiment of defeat, sent his heavy luggage on to Dublin, and chartered a ship to wait for him in Waterford harbor in anticipation of disaster. But notwithstanding these overwise precautions James was bent on proving his valor before William, and on the 20th of June the armies met. The Jacobites had the best position, the Williamites the larger force, and the inestimable advantage of being headed by a prince who knew no fear. Brave to recklessness, William, though wounded and in pain, was always in the front of the battle, leading his men and encouraging them at the post of danger. James watched his army from a safe distance, anxiously regarding the ever-changing tide of fortune, as now the Irish, now the English, got the best of the desperate encounter. At last, when the Jacobites, after seven hours' fighting, began to retreat in good order, James, wild with terror, spurred his horse, and never stopped till, with a scanty retinue of contemptuous gentlemen, he arrived, blown and breathless, in Dublin city—the bearer of the news of his own defeat. The king thus flying, his horse spent and heated, turned the defeat into a rout in the mind of the country. "Change kings with us," cried the sorrowful troops, "and we will fight you again;" but James was determined there should be no changing kings—he had had enough of this terrible warfare. Next morning he fled, though no man pursued him, and never rested till the ship his foresight had provided bore him in safety to France.

Glad though he was to leave Ireland, his troops were still better pleased to be rid of him. But he had ruined his cause. Drogheda surrendered on hearing of the defeat at the Boyne, and William marched into Dublin. The Irish now retreated to the south and west, and congregated at Athlone and Limerick, and round the latter city about 10,000 foot had gathered as if by instinct. De Lauzan looked with contempt on the antiquated fortifications, and refused to try to hold the place. "Are those your ramparts?" he sneered to Sarsfield "Then the English will need no cannon; they can take them with roasted apples." Sarsfield had a higher opinion of the stronghold. But he allowed De Lauzan and his troops to go to France by way of Galway and held Limerick alone. On the 9th of August, William appeared before the despised fortifications, but could not begin operations, as his siege train had not arrived from Dublin; nor did it ever reach the camp, for Patrick Sarsfield, by a daring and skillful maneuver, intercepted it, dispersed the escort, burst the guns, and burned the carriages and ammunition. More guns were sent from Waterford, and by the end of the month the damage was in a measure repaired; but the success of the adventure had restored the Irish confidence, and when, after a long bombardment, the English effected a breach and stormed the town, they met with a resistance so desperate and determined that they were forced to retire, and eventually the autumn floods compelled them to abandon the siege for that year.

William's presence was urgently needed in discontented England, and having restored the courage and striven to correct the morals of his troops, he now left Ireland, sending Edward Churchill, Captain Marlborough, with 8,000 fresh troops, against Cork and Kinsale. Fortune favored the young commander, for both towns capitulated to him, and after a six week's campaign, he went back loaded with honor. Throughout the winter hostilities were continued, in which both armies suffered, though neither gained. The French help, so often looked for, was slow in coming. Old Talbot had gone in the summer to collect arms and money, but he still tarried, and the Irish were becoming a ragged, hungry, and penniless set of troops, when in February Talbot returned, bringing with him 14,000 louis d'or, and the news that he had left almost as much in Brest to be expended in oatmeal.

The old tale of dissension was once more ruining the Irish cause. The French and Irish officers disagreed on every subject, and entertained for each other a most profound contempt, and matters were only made worse when in May Saint Ruth was sent over, and made first in command.

William, pressed for money and soldiers, and "touched by the fate of the gallant nation that had made itself the victim of French promises," was anxious to close the war, and offered very fair terms to the Jacobites, but they, still hopeful of a complete victory, made no response. Through the early summer the war dragged on, the last engagement being on July 12, at Aughrim. Saint Ruth was in command, and, jealous of his brother officers, had confided to none his plan of battle. Under him the Jacobites were gaining the day, and Saint Ruth cried out that they would drive the English back on Dublin; but as he spoke an English ball took off his head, and the Irish, deprived of a commander, were utterly defeated. Only Galway and Limerick now remained, and Galway, having no ammunition, was forced to surrender. The garrison asked and received good terms. They were to march out with all the parade of war and join the rest of the army at Limerick. That ancient city was now the only hope of the Jacobites, but it seemed to both parties that it would hold for ever, for the western side being uninvested by the enemy, food and ammunition could be brought in from Connaught. The French fleet were expected daily, and the Irish knew that when winter set in floods and fever would compel the enemy once more to raise the siege. Still the prospect was a dreary one, and both sides were weary of the struggle. The Irish and French hated each other more cordially every day, and the former began to suspect that France intended to annex their country instead of helping them to win their independence. Next the Williamites gained the island part of the town, and though this was so separated from the rest of the city as in no way to affect its safety, it nevertheless depressed the troops, so that the commanders thought it would be better to close the war while their position was strong enough to ensure favorable terms. Accordingly, a truce of four days was proposed on the 24th September, and three days later the Jacobites offered to conclude a peace on condition of a general pardon for all past offences, religious, civil, and military; of municipal liberty being granted to the Catholics; and soldiers, if they wished, being received into their majesties' armies. The Williamites, delighted at the prospect of peace, assented to these terms, which were amended, drawn up into thirty-two articles, thirteen civil and nineteen military, and on the 3d of October, 1691, the generals of both armies signed the famous Treaty of Limerick.

CHAPTER XV.
THE TREATY OF LIMERICK.

THE signing of the Treaty of Limerick was an event of enormous importance in Ireland, and its ruthless and dishonorable violation perhaps did more than all the cruel confiscations to ruin the country and foster that race-hatred which plays so prominent a part in the relations of England and Ireland. The treaty was a compromise, and, as such, not quite satisfactory to either party, for the Catholics had been fighting for land and liberty of conscience, and the Protestants for land and Protestant ascendancy, and the treaty, while it insured religious equality, conferred the land on the Cromwellian settlers. The civil articles were of the greatest general importance, as they affected the welfare of the entire country and should have secured it from religious persecution for ever.

The first article provided that "the Roman Catholics of this kingdom shall enjoy such privileges in the exercise of religion as are consistent with the laws of Ireland, or as they did enjoy in the reign of Charles II., and their majesties, as soon as their affairs will permit them to summon a parliament in this kingdom, will endeavor to procure the Roman Catholics such further security in that particular as may preserve them from any disturbance upon the account of their said religion."

This was the whole of the first and most important article: we shall see later how it was kept.

The second granted pardon and protection to all who had served King James, on their taking the following oath of allegiance:—"I, —— ——, do solemnly promise and swear that I will be faithful and bear true allegiance to their majesties King William and Queen Mary: so help me, God." The old oath of supremacy, which declared the English sovereign to be the supreme head of the church, had been the cause of much oppression to the Papists, for they, being unable to take any such oath, had, by its means, been excluded from honorable and valuable appointments. To prevent a renewal of this tryanny, the ninth article provided that "the oath to be administered to such Roman Catholics as submit to their majesties' government shall be the oath aforesaid (of allegiance), *and no other;*" and this article was kept as faithfully as the rest of the treaty. Articles III., IV., V., and VI. extend the privileges of the first two articles to merchants and other classes of men; the seventh permits Roman Catholic noblemen and gentlemen to carry arms and keep a gun in their house, and the eighth gives the right of removing goods and chattels without search.

The tenth article guarantees that no person who hereafter breaks any of these articles shall cause any other person to lose the benefit of them; the two next stipulate for the ratification of the articles within eight months. The thirteenth and last provides for the debts of Colonel John Brown, commissary of the Irish army.

The nineteen military articles provided for the honorable exile of all who wish to leave the country and to serve in foreign armies, for the reception into William's army of any who wished to remain, and for the cessation of hostilities. The stone on which the famous treaty was signed in Ginkle's camp is still to be seen at the north end of Thomond bridge—a silent testimony to Irish misery and English perfidy.

After the treaty had been signed, it was discovered that, in the fair draft, two lines had, either by accident or design, been omitted, and the Irish refused to evacuate the town till they had been inserted; but, scarcely was the ink of this second writing dry when the long-promised help from France sailed up the Shannon, with men, money, and ten thousand stand of arms—too late! Great was the grief in Limerick, and some of the officers were now for breaking the treaty and going on with the war, but Sarsfield indignantly refused to soil his country's name with so foul a stain of treachery.

Sad and silently the Irish troops marched from the beloved city, most of them to take ship for France, and never again to see their native land. Some few took service under William, and many, warned that if once they enlisted in foreign service they must never more return, went quietly to their homes. Still the greater part—in all some twenty thousand men—enlisted in foreign armies, chiefly in that of France, where, under Montcashel, Clare, and Dillon, they laid the foundation of that Irish brigade to whose valor England owed many a defeat. For many years the supply of Irish soldiers in the French army was kept up by constant recruiting, and the number thus taken from the country must have been very great, since in the succeeding fifty-four years four hundred and fifty thousand Irishmen *died* in the service of France alone.

Besides the tremendous loss of life, the war had cost England ten millions of money, and as an effort to recoup some portion of this, 4,000 Irish were outlawed, and 1,060,792 Irish acres, equal to 1,918,307 English acres, were confiscated—so heavy was the penalty for having been worsted in a fair stand-up fight.

Since the accession of James I. the extent of the whole island, with an excess of 276,147 acres, had been confiscated, for though some very few Anglo-Irish noblemen still retained their property, a good part of the country had been declared forfeit twice within eighty years.

I have been able to find no account of the amount of land which changed hands during the confiscations of Henry VIII. and Elizabeth, nor of the lands taken from the Connaught landlords by order of Cromwell for the Irish of the other three provinces, but lord Clare's table of the confiscations of James I., of Cromwell, and of William, makes a fitting close to the unhappy history of the Stuart dynasty in Ireland.

The acreage is given in Irish acres, which are to English acres about the proportion of eight to thirteen.

Ireland is estimated at 11,420,682 acres, and the confiscations of the eighty years ending 1691 amounted to 11,697,629 acres, or an excess of 276,147 of the entire acreage of Ireland.

After the flight of Hugh O'Neill, James I. had confiscated the whole of Ulster, amounting to --- 2,836,839 acres.
At the Restoration there were set out by
the Court of Claims --- --- --- 7,800,000 ,,
And William's confiscations amounted
to --- --- --- --- --- 1,060,000 ,,

Total, --- --- --- 11,697,629 ,,

CHAPTER XVI.

THE PENAL CODE.

THE ink of the Treaty of Limerick was hardly dry before the ninth article was broken, for at the meeting of parliament Roman Catholic peers and commons were required to take an oath which denied the doctrine of transubstantiation, and pronounced the sacrifice of the mass "damnable and idolatrous." No sincere Catholic would take such an oath, and by it Papists were for ever excluded from the Irish parliament.

The remaining civil articles of the treaty were soon disregarded as ruthlessly as the ninth had been, and the Irish parliament began to build up a penal code against Roman Catholicism. Laws were made forbidding any Papist to send his child to be educated abroad, and at the same time Catholics were prohibited from keeping schools in Ireland. Statutes were passed authorizing a search for arms in the houses of Papists, either by night or by day, and forbidding makers of arms and weapons from receiving Catholic apprentices. The regular Romish clergy were commanded to leave the kingdom before the 1st of May, 1698, and bishops and priests of that creed were forbidden to enter the country on pain of imprisonment and banishment for the first offence, and death for the second.

The Irish parliament of those days was elected for an unlimited number of years, and was usually dissolved only by the death of the sovereign, and the parliament elected after the death of William, in 1702, sat throughout the fourteen years of the reign of Anne.

At the time of Anne's accession the Protestants in Ireland were only about a sixth part of the population. They were a small dominant class, holding nearly all the land, and alone eligible as members of either house of parliament. Planted amid a very naturally discontented population, they lived in a perpetual state of terror, and, with a ferocity born of fear, passed a crushing penal code against Catholicism. That the Papists would once more get the upper hand was the nightmare of the "Protestant garrison," for the Stuart cause was still far from hopeless—Presbyterian Scotland and Papist Ireland alike favored the pretender, whose claim was also supported by the powerful king of France—and until the suppression of the rebellion of 1745 there was always the possibility, and the greater or less probability of the return of the Stuarts, with all its attendant evils.

Ireland was felt to be the weak point of the Orange party,

the stronghold of rebellion, and this ill-conditioned state of mind was deemed to be due to the influence of the Catholic religion. It was easy for a staunch Protestant to persuade himself that by oppressing Papists and degrading their social standing, he was furthering the cause of the true religion, and when his zeal enlarged his property, he felt that a blessing was upon him and that he had come in for the promised inheritance of the meek. So in Ireland the Protestants, and in Switzerland the Catholics, persecuted their neighbors in the interests of true religion.

The oppressions of William faded into insignificance before the sterner penal code which was framed during the reign of Anne.

To pervert a Protestant to the Roman religion was declared premunire, and punishable with imprisonment for life. Education was further prohibited to Catholics, for it now became criminal for a Catholic to employ or to act as a private tutor. Papists were forbidden to buy land, and were forced to leave their estates in gavelkind (that is in equal portions to all their sons) unless the eldest son conformed, in which case he inherited the whole property, and could force his father to allow him a third of his income during his lifetime. No Papist could take a lease of more than thirty-one years, nor could he raise money on his estates. The civil services, municipal offices, the army, the navy, the learned professions, save medicine, and all positions of public trust were now closed against the Catholics, who in addition to the oath of allegiance were required to take an oath of abjuration, declaring that "no foreign prince, person, *prelate*, state, or potentate, hath *or ought to have* any power, jurisdiction, superiority, pre-eminence, or authority, *ecclesiastical or spiritual* within this realm." The bill which thus aimed a blow at the Catholics and all supporters of the house of Stuart, was sent over to England in this form, where a clause was added, providing that "any person entering the courts, the civil service, or any place of trust, shall, in addition to this oath, receive the sacrament according to the rites of the Church of England." The insertion of this clause raised a clamor among the dissenters, for by Poyning's Law the bill could receive no further alteration on its return from England, but must be received or rejected entirely; but rather than lose so glorious an opportunity of spiting the Catholics, the Irish parliament accepted it, and thus all Protestant dissenters were excluded from every public office, from that of lord lieutenant to that of common postman.

Papists were next forbidden to employ more than two apprentices in any business except the linen trade, and were nominally excluded from the cities of Limerick and Galway. Catholic gentlemen were prohibited from carrying and from keeping arms in their houses, nor might they go more than five miles from home without a passport. Under these circumstances a horse, except for farm purposes, was a superfluity to a Papist, and he was not allowed to keep one over the value of £5. If a farm held by a Catholic yielded one third more than the yearly rent, any Protestant might, by simply swearing to the fact, evict the tenant and take possession; and any Protestant suspecting another of holding an estate in trust for a Catholic, might file a bill against him and take the estate from him. No Papist might, under a penalty of £500, become guardian to any child, and any child who conformed could demand of his Catholic father an allowance of one-third of his income. Any Protestant marrying a Catholic became subject to all the disabilities, and any woman who conformed was freed from her Papist husband's control, and could demand an independent allowance. These regulations with regard to private life caused much heart-burning and misery. The unloving wife, the dissolute and undutiful son, had but to add the hypocrisy of a pretended conversion to their sins to reap a rich reward, and the last hours of the dying Catholic were darkened by the thought that his children must be brought up in a creed which was to him heretical.

But it was against the priests that the law was most severe. There were to be 3,000 priests registered for the whole country, and any unregistered priest was liable to be put to death. No bishops were allowed in Ireland, and when the priests died the irregisters died with them, so that had the Irish been a law-abiding people, Catholicism must soon have become extinct. Under this law a race of priest-hunters grew up, who were rewarded for their discoveries according to the standing of their victims. £50 was the reward for a bishop, £20 for an unregistered priest or begging friar, and £10 for a schoolmaster. But, besides these professional "discoverers," any Catholic over 16 years of age could be seized and, on pain of imprisonment, be made to swear when and where he had heard mass, and who was the officiating clergyman, and he, if he were not registered, was liable to lose his life. Still, though the registered priests died, Catholicism did not: bishops, priests, and schoolmasters continued to fulfill their duties though by so doing they became members of the criminal classes. They lived hidden in the mountains or in the wretched cabins of the peasantry. Sometimes they were caught, imprisoned, and banished, but the people were generally very faithful to them; and the chief result of the code respecting the clergy was to create a hatred of law and foster a sympathy with crime; nor could the clergy preach obedience to law, when by their very existence they themselves broke the law every day of their lives. It was impossible for a Catholic to obey the laws of his church and his country, and as his conscience forced him to break some part of the law of the land, it soon permitted him to disregard others, and if he were unlucky enough to be found out and sent to gaol, there was no moral stigma attached to the name of criminal, since his religion was itself a crime.

But the cup of Catholic degradation was not yet full; ignorant, poor, and criminal as were the Papists in the days of Anne, they still might, when otherwise qualified, vote at the election of members of parliament, and of civil corporations. But at the accession of George II. these last remnants of civil liberty were taken from them, and thenceforward they had no vote in the elections of members either of parliament or of civil corporations. Indeed so numerous were the restrictions on Papists that a judge declared that "the law did not suppose the existence of any such person as an Irish Roman Catholic, nor could they even breathe without the connivance of the government."

CHAPTER XVII.

THE COMMERCIAL RESTRAINTS.

The penal code affected only five-sixths of the people of Ireland, but there were restrictions which fell on Catholic, Anglican, and Dissenter alike. England looked on Ireland, not as a sister country but as a dangerous rival, whose prosperity must be checked for fear it should endanger her own. In the time of Charles II. cattle, meat, pork, ham, cheese, and butter had been excluded from the English market. In consequence of this embargo the Irish farmers converted their pasture into sheep walks, and soon produced the best wool in Europe. Quantities of it were exported raw both to France and Spain, but there was also a large and growing industry in the north, where woolen goods were manufactured both for home consumption and for exportation. But this industry excited the fear and envy of England, and early in the eighteenth century the exportation of wool, either manufactured or in a natural state, to any foreign country or to any colony, was forbidden under penalty of £500, together with the loss of the ship and cargo.

England thus secured to herself the monopoly of the best wool in Europe at her own price; the Irish, deprived of all other bidders, had to accept anything that she chose to offer, till at the time that French fleece wool was fetching 2s. 6d. per pound, Irish was selling at fivepence. The farmers suffered greatly, but they repaired their loss as much as possible by smuggling wool to France, and a huge illicit trade sprang up between the two countries, till there was not a cave on the Kerry coast that was not stocked with wool. Every one—magistrates, landlords, priests, farmers, and peasantry—knew of and connived at the illicit trade. The coastguard was powerless to cope with the numbers of smuggling cutters which brought

French wines and brandy, priests and prelates, to Ireland, and carried away wool, or a still more valuable commodity, entered on the ships' books and spoken of as "wild geese," but in reality soldiers recruited for the service of France.

There was, however, a class that suffered much more deeply than the farmers—the weavers. These were chiefly Protestants, the descendants of English and Scotch settlers. From a condition of comfort, earned by honest industry, forty thousand of these poor creatures were in a day reduced to poverty and enforced idleness. There was no other trade for them to take up, so they had no alternative but emigration. By the restrictions on the Catholics, England and the Protestant ascendancy between them had driven hundreds of thousands of men into the armies of France and Spain and Austria, to fight against, to kill, and be killed by Englishmen; and now, by a like short-sighted policy, the friendly northern Protestants were changed into enemies, who paid off old scores in the war of American Independence.

The only great industries now left to Ireland were the linen and shipbuilding trades. In early times, Ireland had been a densely wooded country. Since then, much wood had been consumed in the working of mines, and successive generations of colonists, holding their land on insecure tenure, had hastened to realize what money they could by felling whole forests of timbers. Still in the early part of the eighteenth century there was plenty of good oak, much esteemed for shipbuilding. But England, too, was a shipbuilding country, and the fiat went forth that henceforward Ireland was to use none but English-built trading vessels, and was to trade directly with no country save England. By this law the sea-port towns were ruined, and their inhabitants, along with the shipbuilders and merchant sailors, were forced to emigrate, or try to live by agriculture.

Her position and magnificent natural harbors seems to have destined Ireland to be a great shipping center, where English and American exports could be exchanged, but the shipping trade was to be henceforward an English monopoly, and Ireland was prohibited from sending or receiving any article to or from any colony or foreign state. Calicoes and other cotton goods were already beginning to have a baneful influence on the linen industry, which was now further crippled by heavy duties on sail-cloth, and checked, striped, and colored linens. The mischief done to Ireland by these restrictions which deprived her of *all* export trade, were of a deeper and more lasting nature than appears at first sight. For a country to succeed in manufacture, capital, skilled labor and industrial habits are needed—habits of diligence, order, and thrift, which it takes generations to acquire. The principal industries of England were founded in the time of the Tudors, and have an almost unbroken history since those days. The Irish of the seventeenth century had made a heroic effort to create a national trade, but so soon as any branch succeeded it was stifled by the selfish and shortsighted policy of England.

The Irish did what little they could for their ruined trade; they resolved "to burn everything that came from England but her people and her coals;" and Swift, in his famous letters to the Irish people, wrote that, "even a stay-lace of English manufacture should be considered scandalous." But trade cannot flourish under such conditions; the home consumption was not great enough, especially as the whole nation was miserably poor; home manufactures made under so many disadvantages were dearer and less good than foreign ones; and goods were often sold as Irish, at Irish prices, that were made abroad. So trade, though bolstered up for a time, dwindled and sank. The people who had once been employed in the factories were driven back on the country, and the competition for land was something unheard of. The little farms were let by auction, and fetched more than they produced, so that the nominal rent could never, by any possibility, be paid. Evictions for nonpayment of rent became very frequent, and, as the century rolled on, great tracts of country were laid down in grass. The Irish parliament now stepped in and passed a bill providing that at least five out of every hundred acres must be tilled, but England, having been in the habit of exporting wheat to Ireland, threw the measure out.

There was now no work to be got in the towns or in the

country, and emigration was too expensive a luxury for the really destitute. Thousands who were willing to work were forced to beg, and, from a necessity, idleness grew into a habit. Fellow feeling made the poor wonderfully charitable to one another, and none who had a crust or potato grudged his neighbor half. One fatal consolation was left to this poor, starving nation; hunger could be stifled, cold be driven out, misery, want, and nakedness forgotten at a very small expenditure, for, with all the commercial restraints that bound down Ireland, rum might be imported duty free.

CHAPTER XVIII.
THE LAND DIFFICULTIES.

PARALYZED by the penal code and the heavy commercial restraints, Ireland, at the beginning of the eighteenth century, was in truth a "most distressful country." The towns afforded little occupation for any one; but the army, navy, law, all civil offices, and wholesale trade being Protestant monopolies, the Catholics had to content themselves with such small businesses as could be carried on with the help of two apprentices, or take to the overstocked business of farming. The class of Catholic landlords was rapidly dying out. Many eldest sons secured their inheritance by conforming to the English Church, and those who did not change their faith sank in a few generations to the class of farmers, for few Catholics had held estates large enough to bear even the first sub-division, and when the process had been gone through two or three times the owners sank to the condition of cottiers, or sold their little properties. Papists might neither buy land nor hold it on a long lease, so all that came into the market was of necessity bought by Protestants. In many cases land was acquired simply as a speculation; it was cheap because as five-sixths of the population were forbidden to purchase, the market was restricted; it could be let at a high rent because five-sixths of the people being by law prohibited from almost every occupation but farming, there was immense competition, and people were willing to offer exorbitant rents. But many a man who had bought large tracts of land disliked the thought of living on his new possession, the trouble of collecting rents from small tenants, so estates were often let on long leases to middlemen at a very moderate rental. These middlemen sub-let the land to tenants or to other middlemen at a higher rental, till on many properties there were five or even six middlemen between the landlord and the actual tiller of the soil, who, to enable all these deputies of deputies of deputies to make a living, was charged an extortionate rent, often a rack rent—that is, a rent higher than the value of the total production of the land. Such a rent could not be paid in full, even in a good season. The middleman got as much as he could out of the tenant, and the tenant paid as little as he could induce the middleman to accept. Even with a good will the wretched middleman could not afford to be merciful, as his living depended on the difference of the rental paid him by the tenants and that which he paid the middleman over him. In good seasons the tenants managed to rub along somehow, but in bad years they were reduced to a fearful state of misery, often culminating in eviction and starvation, and there were several actual famines. The most terrible was that of 1746, when mothers devoured their children, and children their dead mothers. Docks, nettles, and shamrocks were the staple food of many thousands, and when at length fever, dysentery, and exhaustion put an end to the sufferings of these poor creatures, the thin corpses were as green as the unwholsome food on which they had prolonged their miserable existence.

Extortionate rent, whose payment was enforced by threats of eviction, was not by any means the only trouble of the Irsih farmer and cottier; short leases, or still worse, yearly tenancy hampered him, and there was the great grievance of the tithe which every one was forced to pay to the Anglican vicar or rector of his parish. Many of these clergy held several livings, and, having no congregations, lived entirely in England; it was therefore inconvenient for them to collect the tithes themselves, and they usually employed a "tithe proctor" who paid a certain sum to the clergyman, and whose profit depended on the degree of rigor with which he collected his tithe.

That this tithe was a fruitful source of ill-feeling can well be imagined; the small farmer barely able to find his children bread, and bound to maintain his own priest, bitterly resented this tax to the absentee heretic whose face he never saw. Moreover, the tithe was levied with great inequality and injustice. Munster, as a whole, paid one-third more tithe than any other province, and some parts of Munster were more severely rated than others. The great tithes of wheat and corn which were general throughout the country were usually paid with a fairly good grace. It was the potato tithe, a tax almost peculiar to Munster, that was so desperately resisted, as being a weight which fell most heavily on the poorest. Pasturage was most unjustly exempted by a law made in 1785, so from that time the grazier had a clear advantage of ten per cent, over the agriculturalist. This naturally prompted men to lay down their land in grass, and another inducement to Catholic farmers was the law which prohibited them from making a profit of more than one-third of the rent. The gains of pasturage are less easy to ascertain than those of agriculture, so the Papist farmer, who by luck, skill, or the leniency of his landlord, cleared a large profit, laid down his land in grass that he might run less chance of being discovered and evicted—a fate from which, in this case, his landlord was powerless to save him.

The tithes and the penal code were slowly turning Ireland into a grazing country, but when, in the middle of the century, the restriction on the importation of cattle, meat, butter, and cheese into England was removed, in consequence of murrain which had destroyed English beasts, a perfect grazing fever set in. While the land was being turfed and prepared, the effect of this change was not apparent, but the process once completed tenant after tenant was evicted, homestead after homestead destroyed, common and waste lands, whereon hitherto many a poor man had kept his goat or cow, were enclosed, and thousands of families, through no fault of their own, were turned out on the roadside, without even such funds and shelter as have, of late years, been provided for their successors by a disloyal and illegal organization.

Estates that had supported twenty or thirty laborers could now be tended by two or three herdsmen, so nine out of every ten men on the transformed estates were discharged, and, with their families, turned out of their homes.

Emigration was then far more costly than now, and therefore impossible to the greater part of the tenantry, who flocked into the towns, hoping for work. But trade was so shackled and bound down that there was no work even for skilled artisans, and for these evicted tenants no hope or chance of work. Starvation was very near, and fever soon laid her burning hand upon the little children. The Irish cottiers of the eighteenth century were well used to hardship; the poorest food, the scantiest dress, the roughest shelter, were all they had known; but the wail of the dying children, lying shelterless and starving in the ditch, was more than they could bear. The old cabin had been pulled down to prevent the return of its tenants, and on its site stood the new cow-house and the sheep-pen. These men were very ignorant—in that, at least, they obeyed the law which forbade education to Papists. They knew nothing of economic principles, or of the law of demand and supply; they had never even heard that the the object of farming was to produce the most with the least possible amount of labor. As Catholics, they were forbidden the right of public meeting or of framing petitions, but in any case they would all have been dead long before any petition could reach that tender mother of the poor— the State.

They had no hope but in themselves, no friend but the priest, a man as poor, as hungry, often nearly as ignorant as themselves. As for the enemy, the cause of all their misery, did not the new cow-house and the sheep-pen tell them who he was? The landlord, the middleman, the tithe proctor, the parson, and the priest, all these they had managed somehow to pay, and had still kept a roof above their heads; but this gentle, silent, innocent supplanter had deprived them of all they ever had. Moreover, this enemy was food himself, food in abundance was comfortably housed around them, while they, their wives, and little ones, were dying in agonies of hunger and of cold. Silently, by the cold light of the winter moon, the men arose and killed the cattle in hundreds and in thousands. The Munster hillsides rang with the cries of the dying beasts, whose owners, paralyzed with fear, lay quaking in their beds. So began the famous Whiteboy outrages; and then arose that spirit of desperation and revenge, which led not only to a wholesale slaughter of cattle but to crimes of a far worse nature. Murders, maiming, and mutilations were dealt out with horrible barbarity, as punishment to men who laid down their land in the grass, to tithe proctors, and to several extortionate clergymen and priests. The law at first was powerless, for most of the peasantry sympathized with the Whiteboys, and such as had the will had not the courage to give them up, for Whiteboy revenge was far more certain and more terrible than legal penalty. Stringent laws were passed against Whiteboyism, and many offenders were hanged or shot; still it was years before the organization was suppressed.

At the time that the Whiteboy outrages were terrifying the Munster graziers, two organizations were made by the Protestant tenantry of Ulster. The roads were in those days repaired by public unpaid labor, every man being forced to give six days' work yearly. At sowing time, at hay time, or at harvest he might be required to give his week's labor. The rich were, by custom, not by law, exempted, and the cottiers naturally contended that the rich, who used the roads, should be forced to pay a substitute to do their share of the work for them, and not leave the burden entirely on the poor. To right this grievance a great number of tenants pledged themselves to resist the law till all classes were made subject to it. Members of this organization wore an oak branch in their hats, and thus obtained the name of "Oakboys."

The "Steelboys" were more like the Whiteboys of the south. They were tenants of Lord Donegal who, when his leases expired, instead of raising the rent, demanded a very high premium for their renewal. This the tenants could not pay, though they would willingly have acceded to an increase of rent. They were evicted, and their farms taken by capitalists and laid down in grass. The wretched tenants resisted as desperately and as vainly as the Whiteboys of the south, and, like them, gained nothing by their lawlessness but the gallows and the gaol.

CHAPTER XIX.

WOOD'S HALFPENCE.

THE Whiteboy movement brings us down almost to the time of the declaration of Irish independence, but we must now see what was passing in Dublin and the great cities in the early part of the century.

The ever-increasing disabilities of the Catholics, their consequent poverty, ignorance, and social stigma, drove them more and more from the towns into the country and into the armies of foreign powers. In the country, the better class of Catholics often contracted friendships for, and even intermarried with their Protestant neighbors, till in many places the greater part of the penal code was a dead letter. But in the towns the "Protestant garrison" had society enough among themselves without admitting the "common enemy," and the contempt in which Catholics and Jacobites were held was such that "no Papist may presume to shew himself even in the galleries of the houses of parliament."

The political history of Ireland in the eighteenth century is therefore entirely the history of the Protestant ascendancy and of Englishmen who were sent over to fill the best offices, for to be born—even of English parents—in Ireland was to begin life heavily handicapped. Throughout the century the lord lieutenant and the primate were always English, and the only Irishmen who held office as chief secretary and lord chancellor were Clare and Castlereagh: the bishop, justices, and other high officials were also mostly English, to the great and natural discontent of the conforming Irish.

At the end of the seventeenth and the beginning of the eighteenth century, the hatred and fear of Popery was so strong among the Anglicans that all other distinctions were forgotten; but as years rolled on common nationality, common though unequal oppression, and common poverty softened party feeling, and the unbroken loyalty of the Catholic killed the fear and hatred of the Protestant. Common interest also grew up between the two creeds. There was the vast smuggling trade to which all classes were party, and in 1722 the nation laid aside its animosities, to wage a common war against "Wood's Halfpence."

For many years no copper had been coined in Ireland, and one William Wood, an English hardwareman alleging the scarcity of copper coin, procured a patent for coining £108,000 sterling of halfpence and farthings to pass as current money. The whole patent was an infamous job, and Wood must have hoped to make an extortionate profit since he thought it worth while to pay £30,000 for the patent, a profit which, if it was to be made off the coinage of poor penniless Ireland, ought certainly to have gone to her revenue and not to the pocket of Mr. William Wood of London. Moreover Ireland did not need a tenth part of the copper which Wood was to supply. In England, the whole of the copper never exceeded a hundredth part of the currency, and exclusive of the brass already in use, £108,000 was more than the quarter of the currency of Ireland. Jonathan Swift, then dean of St. Patrick's, had already taken a lively interest in Irish politics, and had exhorted the people to use and wear only goods of Irish manufacture. He threw the whole of his energies into a war against Wood's halfpence, which he argued would ruin the already poverty-stricken country. Writing in the character of a draper, Swift drew a lively, but not a very scrupulous, picture of the ruin the copper would bring with it, and exhorted every one to refuse to take the money, for by the provisions of the patent no one was *bound* to receive it. The whole nation responded loyally to Swift's appeal; and for a time political animosities and distinctions of race and creed were alike forgotten in the bond of common nationality. Wood's copper was entirely "boycotted," and had to be withdrawn; and, though Wood was compensated out of the Irish revenue, Ireland felt that she had achieved a national victory. But the matter did not end here, for it created a class of men and founded a new party in politics.

The "English garrison" had realized that Ireland was, after all, their country, and that her interest was theirs, and from the copper war arose the "Patriot Party," which from that time has never ceased to be a power and influence in Ireland. The success of the agitation had also led men to believe that in agitation and passive resistance lay the redress for Irish grievances. A long string of confiscations and disabilities was all Ireland had got by armed resistance, but by agitation Irishmen had at last gained a victory; a new way had been discovered, a new era in Irish history began.

The English and Protestant dean Swift had created a new class of politicians—the Irish agitators.

CHAPTER XX.

THE PATRIOT PARTY.

The national spirit created by the agitation against Wood's halfpence never again forsook the "Protestant garrison." Their hatred of the Papist softened into contemptuous indifference among the worldly, and among the religious into a desire to "compel them to come in" to the pale of the Establishment. The gentler spirits among the Anglicans, the good, high-minded bishop Berkeley, primate Boulter, and others, felt that it was not by penal codes or persecutions that real conversions would be made, and in the hope of moulding the young in the ways of the establishment, charter schools were founded about seven years after the close of the copper war.

These charter schools were originally free day schools, where children of every creed could be taught and instructed in the orthodox Anglican faith, but in this form they did not answer. Many of the Catholic poor preferred ignorance to even a risk of heresy, and among such children as frequented the schools, home influence was far stronger than any that could be gained at a day school. Accordingly the institutions were changed to boarding schools, where only Papists were received, and that they might be utterly cut off from the pernicious influence of home, the children were sent to distant parts of the country. The effect of this may easily be imagined: the charter schools became more dreaded than the gaol. Only in time of famine could the parents be induced to send their children to the institutions, and when once the hour of starvation was passed they rescued their little ones from the wiles of the heretic. Perhaps had the schools been well managed, and the wan little children returned home fat and rosy, a different feeling would have grown up; but the sad old tale of funds misappropriated, officials growing fat and children thin, haunted the charter schools, and Howard, who visited them toward the end of the century, describes a scandalous state of dirt, hunger, misery, and squalor.

A more successful, because less bigoted, effort of patriotism was the Dublin Society, which was founded about the same time as the schools, and which had for its object the increase of industrial knowledge and the encouragemnt of agriculture and manufacture in Ireland. Each member on his admission chose some branch of natural history, husbandry, manufacture, agriculture, or gardening, about which he learned all he could, and then drew up a report which was read to the society, and published in the public prints. For many years hardly a newspaper appeared that had not some hint for the struggling manufacturer, some recipe for the farmer, some bit of knowledge about manure, or the rotation of crops. Farming lectures were delivered throughout the country, and though want of capital prevented many of the farmers applying what they learned, much useful knowledge was diffused. Prizes were given for Irish lace, homespun, and silks, and thus a little zest was thrown into the languishing manufactures, and it is probably largely owing to the efforts of the Dublin Society that Irish industry did not utterly collapse.

The patriotism of this was much purer and wider than that which inspired many politicians of the patriot party, for not a few of these used their patriotism merely as a stepping stone to office, for the corrupt government was willing to buy at a high price the silence of malcontents who exposed the abuses of the pension lists and kindred waste of public money.

The patriotism of Swift himself, though sincere, was not of an exalted nature. For the Anglicans only he reserved his sympathy; and though all the severe laws against the Catholics were passed during his lifetime, he never wrote a word for the defence of his oppressed countrymen.

After his death, his place as leader was filled by a man as honest, more bigoted, and infinitely less able than the old dean—Charles Lucas, a Dublin apothecary, now chiefly remembered as the founder of the *Freeman's Journal*. Lucas entered the Irish parliament in 1745, four years before the death of Swift. His career was stormy, and at one time he had to leave the country for some years. On his return he was the idol of the people, and again headed his party in parliament; still, the patriots were a small minority, never throughout the thirty-two years of George II.'s reign able to count on more than eight-and-twenty votes in a parliament composed of three hundred members. The powers of the Irish parliament, already stunted by Poyning's Law, were further curtailed by an English bill, passed in the time of George I., by which the English parliament was enabled to make laws to bind the Irish people, and the Irish House of Lords was at the same time deprived of its right to judge, or affirm, or reverse any judgment, so that the Irish parliament became nothing more than a provincial assembly, whose decision was always liable to be overruled by the superior powers of the English legislature. Its construction was also extremely corrupt; not even the Protestant minority was fairly represented. Of the three hundred members, two hundred were elected by a hundred individuals, and nearly fifty by ten. Two hundred and sixteen members were returned for closed boroughs and manors, mostly owned by members of the House of Lords. The earl of Shannon commanded sixteen seats, lord Hillsborough nine, the Ponsonbys fourteen, and so forth. The House of Commons, instead of representing the nation, represented a few favored peers, who made large sums of money by the sale of their seats.

Both houses were intensely anti-Catholic, and many of the most oppressive clauses of the penal code originated in the Irish, not the English parliament; and the policy of grinding down and degrading the Papists was usually advocated and supported by the viceroy, the court, and the primate. But in seasons of political crises conciliation was had recourse to, and this was notably so during the rebellion of 1745. Encouraged by the news of the defeat of the English at Fontenoy, the Scotch and English Jacobites took up arms, and a rising was daily expected in Ireland. Chesterfield was accordingly sent over as viceroy, with orders to conciliate the Catholics. No rising took place in Ireland; by a little kindness and humanity the danger was staved off; but while England was torn by rebellion, Catholic chapels were opened in Ireland, mass was said publicly, and priests and friars walked about in their habits. But Prestonpans sealed the fate of the loyal Irish, as well as of the Scotch rebels; Chesterfield was recalled, and the old penal system set up on its feet again.

Meanwhile the little band of patroits continued what seemed a hopeless agitation for the control of the national revenue and the reform of the pension list.

But hopeless though the struggle seemed, the party was gaining ground and was joined by several of the powerful nobles, among them the earl of Kildare, eldest son of the duke of Leinster, who was head of the historic house of Fitzgerald. England now felt how dangerous was the almost unlimited power of the aristocracy to return members of the House of Commons. A combination of some half-dozen peers might entirely change the character of the lower house, and to meet this possible difficulty a legislative union was proposed, but the idea was received in Ireland with such evident hatred that it was abandoned, and in the following year (1760) the death of George II. dissolved the parliament, which had sat every alternate year throughout the 32 years of his reign. In the parliament elected at the accession of George III., the patriots, for the first time, became a formidable minority. Most members of that party who had sat in the last parliament were returned again, and several able men were now elected for the first time; among these new politicians were Denis Daly, Hussy Burgh, and Henry Flood, a young man of seven-and-twenty. It was very clear to the patriots that little reform could be hoped for so long as parliaments were elected for the lifetime of the king. Members after a time became lukewarm, their zeal not being renewed by the prospect of a general election; constituents had no chance of freeing themselves from an unsatisfactory representative, and the opposition, once the opposition, was always the opposition. Lucas brought in a bill for limiting the duration of the Irish, like the English, parliament to seven years. Each session the measure passed through the Irish houses, but was three times thrown out by the English privy council. The fourth time it was sent up it passed, merely altered from a septennial to an octennial bill, and parliament, having now been elected eight years, was dissolved and the first limited parliament elected. The patriots were returned in greater force than before. The septennial bill had been a popular measure, but the great cause of the popularity of the party was their agitation for the reduction of the Irish pension list. By a curious irony of fate, Ireland was forced to provide for the poor relations, cast-off mistresses, and natural children of the monarchs of that dynasty whose accession she had so desperately resisted, and the Irish nation was made year by year to increase the pension list, which now stood at £72,000 per annum, whereas the king's private revenue for Ireland—whereon alone it could be charged with decency—amounted only to £7,000, so that £65,000 of the public revenue was yearly devoted to this purpose—exclusive of French and military pensions. The reduction of this list, and the reform of the army which, by mismanagement, cost nearly double what it ought to have done, were benefits easily understood, and the agitation of the patriots, though utterly ineffectual, made the party very popular throughout the country. After the elections, they continued the pension list agitation, and this new parliament began a repeal of the penal laws. The first concession to the Catholics was a small one; it only allowed them to take long leases of bog, provided the bog were at least four feet deep and a mile outside a town, but it paved the way for other boons, and accustomed people to the idea of the gradual repeal of the code.

In 1775 a new and very important figure made his first appearance in politics. In that year Henry Grattan was nominated by lord Charlemont to represent the borough of Charlemont. The young politician, though only twenty-five years of age, at once took a prominent place in the patriot party, and among the orators of his day. He soon succeeded Flood as the idol of the people, for Flood had lost much of his popularity by taking office under government.

When Grattan entered parliament, England was already in serious difficulties with the American colonies, and in the following year the war of American Independence broke out. Ireland had now to decide whether she, struggling for her own independence, should raise her hand against a colony where precisely the same struggle was going on, or whether she should look on in silent sympathy. The government proposed sending four thousand Irish troops against the insurgents, and on this question Flood and Grattan disagreed with a violence that rendered impossible the continuance of the friendly relations that had hitherto subsisted between them.

Flood and the government triumphed; the troops went, and Ireland, being now involved in the war, was prohibited from exporting salt meat to the colonies.

Trade had been bad enough before the war, but it was now at a deadlock—there was no money, public or private, and the Irish government was forced to borrow both of England and of a private Dublin bank to carry on at all. In the autumn of '77 came the news of the loss of Saratoga, and also that despotic France had joined the insurgents in their war for liberty. The news caused a still deeper depression both in England and Ireland. In Dublin alone twenty thousand persons were thrown out of work, and the government had to raise money by increasing the national debt, but throughout all this time of distress, the pension list was not reduced by a halfpenny. With France and America allied against her, England was in extremity; her palmy days of power seemed over, and victory favored the insurgent cause. Thousands of Irishmen strengthened the armies of the enemy, and England, fearful of an alliance between Ireland and France, sought to conciliate the Catholics by a gradual repeal of the penal code.

While England was dreading an alliance, Ireland was in terror of a French invasion, and also feared the attacks of the noted pirate, Paul Jones. French ships were seen off Belfast, and the mayor sent to Dublin for a force to defend the town. Sixty able-bodied troopers were all that could be spared to hold Belfast against the armies of France, for of fifteen thousand soldiers that Ireland was supporting, not one quarter were in the country. This being so, the island must fall a prey to the first enemy who became aware of her unprotected condition, or else she must undertake her own defence.

CHAPTER XXI.

THE VOLUNTEERS.

The French are off Belfast, and 60 troopers nold the city! More men cannot be spared—the army is abroad fighting England's battle, and England cannot spare a man to save the sister island! What will the Ulstermen of Belfast do? Why, like their forefathers at Derry, rise and defend themselves. But this is no civil war, no strife of creeds and races; it is a struggle of all Irishmen, whether of Celtic, Norman, or English blood, to keep their country from a foreign foe. The grandson of the Derry 'prentice boy, and the grandson of the Jacobite of Limerick stand side by side in the great army of the Irish volunteers.

In every town, in almost every village, sprang up a corps

of volunteer defenders, clothed and equipped at their own expense. The French ships did not land in Belfast; but the danger was not over—for any day a fleet might sail in to any port of Ireland—and the volunteer army grew quickly in strength and discipline. Soon it became an ample defence for the country. The highest in the land were its officers. The duke of Leinster, the earl of Claremont, Henry Flood, and Henry Grattan were among its leaders, and few were the half-hearted Protestants who were not members of their local corps. Each regiment elected its own officers and chose its own color—blue, white, scarlet, orange, or more often the beloved green, and all the uniforms were made by Irish tailors, of cloth woven in Irish looms, of wool sheared by Irish peasants from the backs of Irish sheep, and thus an impetus was given to Irish trade.

The Papists had little share in all this patriotism; the drillings and the marchings, the brilliant uniforms and the reviews were still a Protestant monopoly. The Catholics begged to be allowed to join the ranks, but, mainly owing to the prejudice of Flood and Claremont, were refused, and had at first to content themselves with helping on the cause with money.

Still, they had powerful friends among the leaders. Hervey, earl of Bristol and Anglican bishop of Derry, and Henry Grattan were their staunch supporters, and at a later period many Catholics were enlisted. The government looked with no cordial eye on this growing army, which soon amounted to 100,000 armed men and over 200 cannon. Still, while discouraging the volunteers, the government was bound to sanction them, and give them a cold support, for nothing but the fame of these unpaid soldiers kept the French war-ships outside the Irish ports. Government was alive to the danger of such a corps—the wishes of a nation are more potent when supported by 100,000 men at arms—and the Irish felt that this truly was their hour and this the moment to demand free trade, so Grattan and Hussy Burgh, brought forward a motion for colonial free trade in the Irish House of Commons, and, in obedience to the threats of the volunteers, Ireland was at length permitted to trade freely with the colonies.

The next move was a bolder and an infinitely more important one. Grattan brought in a bill declaring that the king, the lords, and the commons are the only powers competent to enact the laws of Ireland. The bill was first brought forward in the session of 1780, which was already illustrious as having carried the free trade measure, but it was withdrawn till the next session, and in the interval the whole force of the volunteers was brought to bear upon the question, so that government was made clearly to understand that it was a national demand. In April, 1782, Grattan again brought in the bill, which passed without a division, and England, in repealing the statute of George I., resigned her claim for making laws for the Irish people. Ireland was now, in some measure, a free country, but this boasted freedom left five-sixths of her people without political rights, and even the Protestant minority could hardly be said to elect its own representatives to a house of which considerably more than half the members were nominees of peers and government officials. The volunteers having so far succeeded in forcing legislation at the point of the bayonet, resolved by the same means to carry parliamentary reforms, and had it not been for the difficulties of the Catholic question, and the divisions of the Irish leaders, they could have gained their end.

But Flood and Grattan were now in open enmity, and differed on every subject. The final rupture had come directly after the declaration of independence. The first act of the free parliament had been to break her own chains by repealing Poyning's Law, and then Grattan had moved an address of gratitude to England for sanctioning her liberty, and repealing the law of George I. The generosity of England did not appeal to Flood's less gentle nature. He argued that England had freed Ireland merely because she was too weak to hold her, and that should she ever recover her power she would once more reduce Ireland to the condition of a province. He therefore considered that the repeal of the law of George I. was an insufficient guarantee for Ireland's liberty, and that England must be made to declare that she would never again meddle in Irish affairs. Grattan held that such a course would be ungenerous in the extreme; that England was not a foe, but a trusted friend in whom confidence could be placed, and who must not even be asked to make so humiliating a confession of past error and injustice. Grattan's view appealed to the chivalry of the house, and his address was carried with only two dissentient voices, but during the debate he and Flood had heaped on each other much abuse, and established an enmity, embittered on the part of Flood by jealousy of his rival and the humiliation of defeat.

On every point these two great men differed. Flood was at once more radical and less liberal than the conservative Grattan, who considered that the mission of the volunteers was now fulfilled, that the legislature of armed politicians was defensible only in extreme necessity, and that Ireland being now free to make her own laws, should legislate only in a constitutional manner. Flood was the upholder of the volunteers, and advised them to agitate for complete parliamentary reform, for he believed the interest of the borough owners would prevent it being effected except by intimidation or force.

Charlemont, the president of the volunteers, was inclined to agree with Grattan, but held with Flood that Catholic emancipation must be resisted, as it would inevitably lead to the disestablishment of the Irish church. The bishop of Derry, whose influence in the volunteers almost equalled that of Charlemont, agreed with Flood on the necessity of volunteer intervention to secure parliamentary reform, but held with Grattan that this must be accompanied by Catholic emancipation. Thus there were four parties among the patriots, and Grattan's popularity waned daily, while Flood was fast recovering lost ground. The volunteers resolved that, as 1782 had been the year of independence, '83 should be the reform year. A hundred and sixty delegates of the volunteers met in the Rotunda, on the 10th of November, to draw up the resolutions for reform, and to decide whether the Catholics should or should not be included. Flood and Charlemont prevailed, and the former presented the bill to the commons in its mutilated form. A long and fierce debate ensued on the motion for leave to bring in the bill, but at length this was refused—not on the merits of the bill, but as an attempt to intimidate the house. With some who voted against the measure the alleged was the real reason for casting out the bill, but the placeholders, borough owners, and pensioners grasped eagerly at so good an excuse for maintaining their power. Grattan, to his honor, voted for his rival's bill.

All night the wordy battle raged, while the delegates, cold, depressed, and tired, sat in the Rotunda waiting the result of the debate. In the morning came the news of their defeat, and the warlike bishop exhorted them to an appeal to arms. But the power of the volunteers was already on the wane; by excluding the Catholics from the Reform Bill they had ruined their own cause, and in the gray light of the November morning the delegates, realizing that their hour was past, wisely followed Charlemont's prudent advice and dispersed, never again to regain their old power and might.

The defeat of the Reform Bill was followed by riots both in Dublin and the provinces, and though the volunteers were in no way responsible for the disorder, it detracted from the dignity of the organization. The moderate and anti-Catholic parties resigned and formed the Whig club, while the democratic party, taking up the cause of reform and Catholic emancipation formed for these ends, and these ends only, a perfectly open and loyal society, called "The United Irishmen."

CHAPTER XXII.

GRATTAN'S PARLIAMENT.

THE concession of free trade with the colonies, and the declaration of parliamentary independence, had an almost magical effect on the prosperity of the capital and the larger provincial towns. Once more the warehouses were filled, the looms at work, the harbors gay with ships, and the streets noisy with traffic. During the fifteen years that followed, many fine houses were built and decorated in Dublin, and the quays, the bridges, the law courts, and the custom house all date from this short time of Irish prosperity.

But the well-being of the towns did not extend to the country, where feud and faction still raged between the peasantry of the two creeds. In the north, the "Orangemen," or "Protestant boys," turned thousands of their Catholic neighbors out of house and home, and these organized for self-defence the society of "Defenders." In Munster, Whiteboyism had revived, and the peasantry once more tried to obtain redress for their grievances by outrage and intimidation. The condition of the peasantry was most pitiable; the little plots of potato ground were let at a rental of £6 per acre; but this was not paid in coin, being worked out in labor at the rate of sixpence a day, so that for one acre of potato ground a man gave the work of 240 days. He had, therefore, only his one acre of ground and the toil of 70 working days for the support of himself and his family. Beyond this, he had to pay tithe to the Anglican clergyman and contribute to the support of his priest.

The unhappy creatures, starving and desperate, ruined their cause by barbarous outrages, and to meet the needs of the case government brought in a stringent Coercion Bill. This was opposed by Grattan, on the plea that the outrages were the result of mad despair, and would best be checked by a mitigation of the miseries of the people. Accordingly, he brought in a measure for the consideration of the tithe question, but Fitzgibbon (lord Clare); while admitting that the condition of the Munster peasantry was more wretched than human beings could be expected to endure, maintained that coercion must go before conciliation. The majority were of his opinion. The Coercion Act became law, and the Tithe Bill was thrown out.

The new nation was only three years old when she had her first difficulty with England. Although colonial free trade had been granted, the commercial relations of England and Ireland still remained unaltered, but in 1785 the Irish House passed a bill for removing some of the trade restrictions between the two countries. Such a bill was, of course, useless unless approved by both countries, and was therefore sent to England, where a number of restraints on Irish colonial trade were suggested as the price of free trade with England. These not only deprived the measure of its usefulness, but were resisted by the Irish as an attempt upon their newly-acquired liberty, and accordingly the bill was thrown out, to the great annoyance of Pitt, who probably intended it as a step towards a union. Three years later another difficulty arose. The king's mind gave way, and it became necessary to appoint a regent. With regard to the person of the regent there was no dispute, both countries appointed the prince of Wales, but the question was, whether the regent should have limited or unlimited powers. Pitt and the English Tory majority voted for limited powers; Fox and the Whig minority for unlimited powers. Ireland, unfortunately, went with the Whigs, and, anxious to prove her independence, hastily offered the prince unlimited regal powers in Ireland. The Whig party was just then in the ascendant. Many of the Tory placemen deserted and swelled the majority. Suddenly there was an unexpected *denouement*. The king got well; the Whigs were out, and all placemen and officials who had voted with that party were turned out of office, and the pension list was augmented by £13,040 per annum for the reward of the faithful placemen. Seven commoners were ennobled for their good offices, and nine peers were raised a step in the peerage.

The regency difficulty had resolved Pitt to carry a union, and to further this scheme he stooped to a course of bribery and corruption unparalleled in history. An eighth part of the revenue of Ireland was now divided among members of her parliament, and besides the nominees of the House of Lords, the English government held 110 commoners in her pay. Whatever the merits of the union, there can be no doubt as to the baseness of the means by which that important measure was carried.

In 1792 both branches of the legal profession were opened to Catholics in Ireland, and in the following year a bill was passed granting them the right to vote at elections, but they were still prohibited from sitting in either house of parliament. In this year, too, the pension list, which then amounted to over £110,000 yearly, was revised, and it was enacted that in future no pension of more than £1,200 a year should be granted except to persons of royal blood. The concession of the elective franchise had raised the hopes of the Catholics, who thought that the right to sit in parliament could not be withheld from them much longer, and the national demand for Catholic emancipation and parliamentary reform grew stronger every day. Pitt, who had always supported a repressive policy and was the arch corrupter of the parliament, suddenly turned round and at the close of '94 announced himself a convert to the cause of conciliation and emancipation. The reason of this change of front we can never know; it may have been sincere or it may have been merely an attempt to induce Ireland to vote large sums of money toward the expenses of the French war, but its immediate result was that Fitzgibbon, lord Clare, was deposed from the viceroyalty, and lord Fitzwilliam, an ardent advocate of emancipation, sent to replace him, with power to act as he thought fit. The new lord lieutenant at once dismissed the ministers and replaced them by patriots, and emancipation and reform were a foregone conclusion. The delighted nation, in an excess of prospective gratitude, voted £1,800,000 for the French war, and raised 20,000 men for the navy. Early in the February of '95, Grattan brought in a bill for Catholic emancipation, but the king now unexpectedly stepped in: his mind had taken four months to grasp the situation, but he now told Pitt that he would *never* consent to such a measure. Pitt was accordingly forced to make his choice between resignation and the reversal of his new policy. He decided to sacrifice his policy rather than his office; so Fitzwilliam was hastily recalled and all his appointments reversed. Clare was made lord chancellor, and lord Camden appointed viceroy. The rejection of the Emancipation Bill was now beyond doubt, the 110 members paid by the government and most of the 123 nominees of the House of Lords turned round, and Grattan's bill was supported only by a minority of 48.

That was the death-blow of the Irish parliament; the

nation, cheated and angry, could not fail to grasp the situation. The independent parliament was but the tool of an English statesman; not one quarter of its members were chosen of the people, the remainder were a venal crew of placemen paid to pass measures dictated to them by the English government. Reform was hopeless, and independence but a name. Heart-sick and weary were the patriots, and many of them failed to attend the parliament of '96. In '97, Grattan made one last hopeless effort to bring in a Reform Bill. The division was merely a farce; and, with a feeling that for the time at least further parliamentary effort was lost labor, most of the patriots resigned—Grattan, Curran, and the milder spirits to watch from a distance the struggle of their country. Fitzgerald and O'Connor to attempt by an appeal to arms to right those wrongs which peaceful agitation proved powerless to redress.

CHAPTER XXIII.

THE UNITED IRISHMEN.

NOTHING could be less sinister than the original aims and methods of the Society of United Irishmen, which was conceived in the idea of uniting Catholics and Protestants "in pursuit of the same object—a repeal of the penal laws, and a (parliamentary) reform including in itself an extension of the right of suffrage." This union was founded at Belfast, in 1791, by Theobald Wolfe Tone, a young barrister of English descent, and, like the majority of the United Irishmen, a Protestant. Some months later a Dublin branch was founded, the chairman being the Hon. Simon Butler, a Protestant gentleman of high character, and the secretary a tradesman named James Napper Tandy. The society grew rapidly, and branches were formed throughout Ulster and Leinster. The religious strife of the Orange boys and Defenders was a great trouble to the United men, who felt that these creed animosities among Irishmen were more ruinous to the national cause than any corruption of parliament or coercion of government could possibly be. Ireland, united, would be quite capable of fighting her own battles, but these party factions rendered her contemptible and weak. The society accordingly set itself the impossible task of drawing together the Defenders and the Orangemen. Catholic emancipation—one of the great objects of the union—naturally appealed very differently to the rival parties: it was the great wish of the Defenders, the chief dread of the Orangemen. Both factions were composed of the poorest and most ignorant peasantry in Ireland, men whose political views did not soar above the idea that "something should be done for old Ireland." The United Irishmen devoted themselves to the regeneration of both parties, but the Orangemen would have none of them, and the Protestant United men found themselves drifting into partnership with the Catholic Defenders. To gain influence with this party, Tandy took the Defenders' oath. He was informed against; and, as to take an illegal oath was then a capital offence in Ireland, he had to fly for his life to America. This adventure made Tandy the hero of the Defenders, who now joined the union in great numbers; but the whole business brought the society into disrepute, and connected it with the Defenders, who, like the Orange boys, were merely a party of outrage. That a prominent United man had been a sworn member of the Defenders, and that many Defenders had joined the union was considered proof that it also was an organization for crime, and, accordingly, one night in the May of '94 a government raid was made upon the premises of the union. The officers of the society were arrested, their papers seized, the type of their newspaper destroyed, and the United Irish Society was proclaimed as an illegal organization. Toward the close of this year all need for a reform society seemed to have passed. Fitzwilliam was made viceroy, and emancipation and reform seemed assured. His sudden recall, the reversal of his appointments, the rejection of Grattan's Reform Bill, and the renewal of the old coercive system convinced the United men of the powerlessness of peaceful agitation to check the growth of the system of government by corruption.

They accordingly reorganized the union, but as a secret society, and with the avowed aim of separating Ireland from the British empire. The Fitzwilliam affair had greatly strengthened the union, which was joined by many men of high birth and position, among them lord Edward Fitzgerald, brother of the duke of Leinster, and Arthur O'Connor, nephew to lord Longueville, both of whom had been members of the House of Commons. Fitzgerald had held a commission in the English army, and had served against the Americans in the war of Independence: his military knowledge caused him to be chosen military leader of the United Irishmen, but the ablest man of the party was Thomas Addis Emmet, a barrister, and the elder brother of Robert Emmet. The society gradually swelled to the number of five thousand members, but throughout its existence it was perfectly riddled with spies and informers, by whom government was supplied with a thorough knowledge of its doings. It became known to Pitt that the French government had sent an English clergyman, named Jackson, as an emissary to Ireland. Jackson was convicted of treason, and hanged, and Wolfe Tone was sufficiently implicated in his guilt as to find it prudent to fly to America. But before leaving Ireland he arranged with the directors of the union to go from America to France, and to try to persuade the French government to assist Ireland in a struggle for separation.

While Tone was taking his circuitous route to Paris, government, to meet the military development of the society, placed Ulster and Leinster under a stringent Insurrection Act: torture was employed to wring confession from suspected persons, and the Protestant militia and yeomanry were drafted at free quarters on the wretched Catholic peasantry. The barbarity of the soldiers lashed the people of the northern provinces into a state of fury: the torture did indeed extort some confessions, but for every man whose scalp was torn off by a pitch cap, or whose ribs were laid bare by flogging, there were a hundred recruits to the union, and these new recruits were animated.

not by love of country, but by hatred of their persecutors and thirst for revenge.

In the meantime the indomitable Tone—unknown, without credentials, without influence, and ignorant of the French language—had persuaded the French government to lend him a fleet, ten thousand men, and forty thousand stand of arms, which armament left Brest for Bantry Bay on the 16th December, 1796.

Ireland was now in the same position as England had been when William of Orange had appeared outside Torbay. Injustice, corruption, and oppression had in both cases goaded the people into rebellion. A calm sea and a fierce gale made the difference between the English patriot of 1688 and the Irish traitor of 1796. Had the sea been calm in the Christmas week of '96, nothing could have stopped the French from marching on to Dublin, but just as the ships put in to Bantry Bay, so wild a wind sprang up that they were driven out to sea, and blown and buffetted about. For a month they tossed about within sight of land, but the storm did not subside, and all chance of landing seeming as far off as ever, they put back into the French port.

This was a fearful blow to the United Irshmen, but Tone was undaunted, and persuaded the Dutch Republic to give him an expedition. This expedition sailed in the following July, but fortune still favored England, and the second fleet met with a worse fate than the first. The government now had recourse to strong measures. The Insurrection Act had failed to pacify the country, for the people, instead of being cowed by the barbarities of the soldiers, were half mad with desperation, and to quiet them martial law was proclaimed in Ulster, where the army, consisting of half-trained Irish, Welsh, and English yeomanry and militia, was in a scandalous state of insubordination. Sir Ralph Abercrombie was now appointed to the command. The gallant and humane old Scotchman was aghast at the condition of the army, which, he said, "rendered it formidable to every one but the enemy," and he refused to sanction the use of torture, or to countenance the free quarter system. But finding himself powerless to control these abuses he threw up his command, in which he was succeeded by General Lake, to whom these practices were not repugnant.

Meanwhile though spies and informers kept the government supplied with the details of every movement of the society, no arrests were made in Dublin till the March of '98. Nineteen of the leaders were then taken on one day, and their places in the society were filled by men of more extreme views, who, with Fitzgerald, preferred to risk an immediate rising to the more prudent policy of awaiting help from France, and it was resolved that Dublin and five counties should rise simultaneously on the 24th of May. On the 19th, Fitzgerald was arrested after a severe struggle, and two days later Byrne and the brothers Sheares, who were members of the new directory, were also taken and eventually hanged. On the 23d, martial law was proclaimed in Dublin.

CHAPTER XXIV.

"NINETY-EIGHT."

NOTWITHSTANDING the imprisonment of Fitzgerald and the Sheares, five counties rose on the 24th of May, and twelve days later the Kildare and Wexford rebels held nearly the whole of their respective counties, but the leaders were all in gaol, and their places filled by men destitute of military knowledge, with no united plan of action, no commissariat, and who were unable to follow up a victory, or to maintain discipline among their followers. Victory was followed by drunkenness, insubordination, and brutal acts of ferocity; and the army, well officered and well provisioned, soon overcame the disorganized mob. Then a very reign of terror set in. Matters were worst in Wexford, where there had been no branch of the United Irish Society, and where the struggle assumed the aspect of a war of creeds. But even there the abortive rising was utterly crushed in less than two months, while in Ulster the rebellion was quelled in a week.

This swift suppression was not effected without much bloodshed; there was no law but martial law, and in very many cases men were shot and hanged without even the scanty justice of a military trial. The streets of Wexford ran down in blood, and the bridge was a stage whereon many ghastly tragedies were enacted, the rebels first, and then the soldiers choosing it as the scene of their most horrible atrocities.

Dublin, dispirited by the imprisonment of the leaders, had not risked a rising. The rebels of the capital were well aware that such an attempt, without the support of French help or military guidance, could only result in disgraceful rioting and bloodshed; moreover, they were overawed by the crushing power of the government. Day and night the cries of the tortured resounding from the Riding House, in Marlborough Street, from the barracks, from the Royal Exchange, from the very entrance to the castleyard, for floggings, which tore the flesh and laid the bones bare, were believed to be the only means of extorting confession. As a further warning to traitors, the scaffolding of the new Carlisle (now O'Connell) Bridge was decorated with the suspended bodies of suspected rebels.

In June Edward Fitzgerald died in gaol, from the effects of the wounds he received in the struggle at his capture; but the Dublin gaols still held between eighty and ninety prisoners awaiting their trail for high treason. At this time Camden, the indolent viceroy, and Lake, the barbarous commander of the forces, were recalled, and lord Cornwallis was sent out to fill both offices.

Cornwallis accepted the viceroyalty with great reluctance; indeed he had only been induced to do so by the desire of having his name associated with the measure of legislative union which Pitt was resolved to carry, and which Cornwallis believed essential to the maintenance of the British Empire.

Fitzgibbon, lord Clare, retained the office of lord chancellor, and Robert Stewart, lord Castlereagh, was appointed chief secretary.

Clare was a stern, fanatical supporter of coercion, and had the effrontery openly to defend the use of torture in the English House of Peers. He was an ardent Unionist, and probably one of the few whose opinion was based on conviction more than self-interest.

Castlereagh was a man of a very different stamp; suave, corrupt, and wily, he proved his utter absence of moral sense by his boast that the government to which he belonged had taken measures to secure a premature explosion of the rebellion, and by his open and unblushing advocacy of a policy of bribery and corruption. He entered parliament as a patriot, but soon abandoned his party, and by his talents and self-seeking rose to be marquis of Londonderry and prime minister of England.

The viceroy was superior to either of his colleagues. Naturally humane and just, if he stooped to dishonorable actions he hated himself for the moral degradation. He would have nothing to do with torture, and saw the immense evils arising from martial law. His first act was to promise protection to all insurgents guilty of rebellion only who should surrender their arms, and soon afterward an Amnesty Bill was passed, but the leaders were excluded from its benefits. Both in Dublin and the provinces numbers of the less prominent men had been hanged by order of martial law while the State trials of the leaders were proceeding. But while Byrne and Oliver Bond were convicted and lay under sentence of death, the remaining eighty-four State prisoners volunteered to give general information as to the designs of the society, on condition of being allowed to go into banishment, and of Byrne and Bond being spared. The negotiations with the government occupied some days, and while they were in progress Byrne was hanged; still the negotiations were concluded. Emmet, O'Connor, M'Nevin, and Neilson, were now examined before a secret committee of the House of Lords, but as they gave only general information, and refused to implicate any of their associates, they disclosed nothing of which the government was not already made aware through the information of spies. Either the government thought the conditions of the treaty had not been fully carried out by the four leaders, or believed that, notwithstanding their word, the rebels would seek the aid of hostile France, for

the State prisoners, and fourteen others, were sent to Fort
George in Scotland, and kept in custody until the peace of
1802. It had been believed that when the State prisoners
volunteered information the rebellion was over, but Tone
was still busy in France. He could not induce the French
government to give him an efficient force, but on the 22d
of August a small fleet entered Killala Bay, and marched
triumphantly to Ballinamuck, in Longford. There they
were overpowered by the troops under Cornwallis, and
forced to surrender at discretion. Tone was good general
enough to disapprove of these small expeditions, but was
forced to accept what he could get, and in October another
small French fleet sailed under command of General Hardi.
The frigate *Hoche*, with Tone on board, arrived outside
Loch Swilly, and for some hours gallantly defended herself
against four English ships as large as herself, but at last
she struck, and was brought into port. For a while Tone
passed for a French officer, but he was recognized by an
old friend, betrayed, and taken in irons to Dublin. Here
he was convicted and sentenced to be hanged; but having
resolved never to endure the ignominy of a public execution
he cut his throat in gaol, and died after a week of agony.
With him perished the last hope of the United Irishmen.
All that now remained was to try the prisoners, and during the three months following Tone's death one hundred
and thirty-four were sentenced to death, and ninety executed, but in the beginning of the year '99 civil law came
in force, and the remaining prisoners were handed over to
its juster administration. The country now being quiet,
the government took in hand the great measure of the Legislative Union.

CHAPTER XXV.

THE PROSPECT OF UNION.

ALTHOUGH Ireland had obtained a nominal independence
in 1782, her position since that time had been one that
could not have contented any nation. A Catholic country

ruled by a Protestant minority; an independent kingdom governed by alien officials, in whose selection she had no voice; a national parliament filled with nominees of those officials and of the House of Lords; an equal of England with no voice in the management of imperial affairs. A position so anomalous could be maintained in no country under heaven; a constitution so rotten and corrupt must inevitably be changed by reform or revolution or be entirely swept away.

For long years the patriots had labored for reform, but with the recall of Fitzwilliam that hope had died. The bolder spirits had then tried the desperate remedy of revolution, and the crushing failure of the premature rising of '98 sealed the doom of Irish independence. This was the moment for which Pitt had striven so long and so unswervingly, for which he had corrupted and bought up both houses of the Irish legislature; but even now, though the parliament was well nigh filled with placemen, though honest Irishmen of all parties were heartsick of the struggle, though resistance seemed hopeless, and any show of national feeling considered proof of sympathy with outrage and with crime, this poor, battered, weary island had to be bought by means of a system of unparalleled bribery. The project of union was fearfully unpopular in Ireland. Apart from the very natural dislike Irishmen felt to having their country reduced from a nation to a province, union was against the interest of almost every class. The peers disliked it, because they were to be degraded from hereditary to representative legislators, only 28 being elected by their body to represent the Irish peers in the Imperial House; the borough-owners, because, as two-thirds of the Irish seats were to be annihilated, they would be deprived of the considerable income they had made by the sale of seats. To the professional men and traders of Dublin the project of removing the parliament to London meant little short of ruin. London, not Dublin, would thenceforward be the capital of Ireland; thither the Irish political world must repair, and, consequently, thither would be drawn all the rank and wealth and talent of the country. To the owners of houses and land in Dublin the prospect was no more cheerful; so the capital was unanimous in its hatred of the scheme. Still, from the English point of view, there were great and weighty arguments in favor of the measure. First and foremost there was the French scare; for had Napoleon taken his fleet to Ireland instead of Egypt the power of England had been annihilated. In after years Napoleon saw how fatal had been his error; but Pitt and the other English statesmen saw the danger at the time, and, knowing the wide-spread disaffection in Ireland, they perceived, as Napoleon did not, that, invaded by an efficient French force, Ireland of '98 might have become a province of France, to the inevitable ruin of the British empire.

This was the main reason for a union. The other arguments were comparatively trivial, and were mainly advanced to convince those who did not think the measure would lessen the chance of a French invasion.

There was the suggestion that one country might wish to go to war and the other refuse to share the expense. The regency difficulty also was revived, and England suddenly became awake to Ireland's wrongs in having no voice in imperial legislation. Catholic emancipation, too, Pitt argued, could never be conceded while Ireland had a separate parliament; whereas, the introduction of a few Papist members into the imperial assembly could place the State in no peril, and, consequently, emancipation would probably be granted directly the union was passed.

Then there was a class of argument whose validity could only be proved after the experiment had been tried. The union would cause an increase of Irish commerce; English capital would flow into Irish trade, English skill improve Irish agriculture. The two races, joined in a brotherly bond of union, could learn to love each other and outdo each other in a generous struggle to legislate for the benefit of the sister country. Rebellion and oppression would alike be past—the healing qualities of union would cause differences of race, creed, custom, interest, climate, and sentiment to be forgotten, and in a few years all that would remain to distinguish West from Great Britain would be the passage from Dunleary to Holyhead.

The anti-unionists argued that union, so far from being a security against foreign invasion, would increase that danger; for the measure, thrust on an unwilling nation, would cause such disaffection and discontent as might bring about this very disaster, and even eventually prove fatal to the British connection, for Irishmen would in future regard rebellion, not as treason, but as a patriotic effort to regain an independence stolen from them without their consent. The anti-unionists considered that the war difficulty was practically non-existent. No such dispute had as yet arisen, and was not more to be dreaded than a disagreement between the House of Commons and the House of Peers; moreover, as the king had power to declare war without consent of parliament, he could overrule any parliamentary differences should they arise.

As for the regency question, the anti-unionists pointed out that there was at that moment a Regency Bill under discussion which would settle that dispute for ever.

Then they asked of what use would the promised emancipation be to the Catholics in an assembly in which they would be an utterly insignificant minority? Indeed, the whole question of parliamentary representation was just then a very sore subject in Ireland. The 100 Irish members might all vote for some local Irish bill and still find themselves in a minority of one to five, so that, practically, Ireland would be, for home legislation, disfranchised; and England had never behaved with sufficient liberality to Ireland to be justified in entrusting her with the management of her affairs; moreover, England was unfitted by ignorance and dissimilarity of temper and situation to legislate successfully for the sister country.

Then, too, they urged there would be great difficulty in finding suitable representatives for so distant a parliament; professional men could not leave their practice for five or six months of each year, and, in point of time, London was then nearly as far from Dublin as New York is now. Ruin must inevitably fall on the capital if the parliament were removed, and as numbers of men of position, having their interests removed to London, would become permanent absentees, the condition of the country must become more deplorable than ever.

At least, urged the anti-unionists, let us wait a while; from delay no danger can arise; before we pass this irrevocable measure, let Ireland have time to recover the effects of the late rebellion, and let the sense of the country be arrived at by a general election, for, even if the measure be a good one, it will be unwise to press it against the public will, and to carry it by such odious means as wholesale bribery and corruption. But if it be a bad one, the consequences will be dreadful. It required no general election to prove that the union was repugnant to the vast majority of Irishmen; both parties sought to test the sense of the country by means of petitions, and, for every signature obtained by the unionists, the oppositiosn party got a hundred; but in this matter the will of the Irish people was to count for nothing. Pitt was convinced of the necessity of union, and resolved to carry it at all hazards.

The measure was first proposed in the viceregal speech at the opening of the parliament of 1799, but, after a very long and stormy debate, the paragraph hinting at union was rejected by a majority of five, and the subject dropped for that session. But the government did not accept their defect as final, and the autumn recess was devoted to a diligent canvas for votes. Cornwallis, believing union to be absolutely necessary for the maintenance of the British empire, stooped to a course of bribery which rendered his life unbearable to him. "How I long to kick those whom my public duties oblige me to court," he writes of the bought supporters of the union; and again, "I hate and despise myself hourly for engaging in such dirty work, and am supported only by the reflection that, without the union, the British empire must be dissolved." A hundred such passages from the viceroy's letters might be quoted, showing what he thought of the means by which the union was passed. But, degraded as Cornwallis felt himself by acting as the instrument of corruption, his hands were clean compared with those of Castlereagh. The chief secretary was without political conscience, and cared little for the purity of the means by which he gained his end. At his suggestion, the objections of the borough owners were removed by the exorbitant "compensation" of £15,000 for each seat. In this way a million and a-quarter of money was expended and charged into the Irish national debt, and the discontent of members who had paid for their seats was annulled by the promise that the money so expended should be returned to them.

Those who were above the reach of direct bribery were seduced by promises of titles and honors, and after the passing of the union, 22 Irish peers were created; five received English peerages, and 20 were raised a step in the peerage; places, pensions, judgeships, posts of profit and of honor, were showered so lavishly that there were not a dozen unbribed supporters of the union. Nor were the anti-unionists free from the charge of corruption; both parties seem to have used equally unscrupulous means to get signatures for their petitions, and tried to outbid each other for such seats in the House of Commons as came into the market.

Grattan had for long been seriously ill, and when, on the 13th of January, parliament assembled, he was still too weak to leave his bed. But the patriots felt that the father of Irish independence would be her best champion, and by an expenditure of £5,000 they secured the seat for Wicklow, which happened to become vacant. The writ was issued on the 15th of January, and by great exertion, and an over-straining of the law, the election was held on the same day, and by midnight Grattan was returned. That night was passed in the Commons in hot union debate, and the thickest of the fight was over when, at seven in the morning, Grattan entered the house. Pale as death, and as thin, worn by sickness to a very shadow of himself, the father of the Irish parliament tottered into the house supported by two friends. Instinctively the whole assembly rose, and after the oath had been administered there was a silence. Grattan rose feebly from his seat, but finding himself unable to stand, asked leave to address the house sitting. As he spoke his weakness disappeared; for two hours his eloquence held the house, but it was powerless to move men whose minds were already made up, and when, after a debate of eighteen hours, the house divided, the unionists obtained a majority of forty-two. It was now a mere question of time, but through every stage the bill was debated on both sides with magnificent eloquence; on June 7th the final passage of the bill was effected in Ireland, and on the 2d of August, 1800, the Act of Union received the royal assent.

CHAPTER XXVI.
THE ACT OF UNION.

THE acquiescence of the Catholics to the measure of union had been gained by promises of emancipation, and the assurances that on this subject the ministers were unanimous; but the more powerful adherence of the Protestants was bought with something more substantial than words, and the passing of the union added an enormous sum to the national debt of Ireland.

The borough owners received £15,000 compensation for each borough, and this alone cost £1,275,000, of which lord Shannon and the marquess of Ely received each £45,000, and lord Clanmorres £23,000 and a peerage. The price of a union vote was £8,000 down, or in instances where ready money would not be accepted, an honorable or profitable office. Indeed, the list of the supporters of the union shows us that, of the 140 members who voted for the measure, only 11 were neither place-holders nor received rewards for their votes, and of these 11, one was General Lake, the commander of the forces through the rebellion of '98. The rebellion and the union had cost Ireland dear, for her national debt, which in '97 had amounted only to £4,000,000, had during four years increased more than seven fold, and at the beginning of 1801 stood at £28,545,134, or nearly one-sixteenth that of England, which then amounted to £450,504,984. Ireland sought to protect herself from the charges of the English pre-union debt by the seventh article of the union, which prescribes that the sinking fund for the reduction of the principal of the debt incurred in either kingdom shall be defrayed by separate taxation; but this article has not been complied with, and the two kingdoms now bear conjointly the charges of the pre-union expenses. It was arranged that for the ensuing 20 years the expenditure of the United Kingdom should be defrayed in the proportions of fifteen parts to Great Britain to two of Ireland, and that after that time a fresh arrangement should be made, and the proportions from time to time revised until such time as the national debt of Ireland should bear the proportions of two to fifteen parts of the debt of Great Britain. This consummation was arrived at in 1817, for whereas during the 16 years of union the British debt had not doubled, the Irish had increased fourfold, and already exceeded the proportion of two to fifteen. Nor was this all that Ireland had to complain of, for in defiance of the seventh article of the union, which provided that the surplus revenue should be expended for the benefit of each country in the proportion of their contributions, the surplus due to Ireland, and amounting in some years to three or four millions, was not so expended.

The sixth article places the two kingdoms on equal commercial footing, and prescribes that neither shall impose a duty on the imports or exports of the other; but this commercial equality was no benefit to Ireland; the English industries were in possession of the market, the commercial current flowed in her direction, and want of capital and the complicated system of rings, exclusive and reciprocal trading, placed insuperable barriers in the way of Irish commerce. That the union did not improve Irish trade is easily seen by a glance at the returns of her imports and exports, which, though they increased with her increasing population, rose much less rapidly than they had done in the years before the union, and became of a less satisfactory character—for the imports consisted yearly more of manufactured goods, the exports of raw material.

The other important articles of the union were the fourth, regulating the parliamentary representation of Ireland, and the fifth, providing for the eternal duration of the Established Church.

By the fourth article it was provided that four lords

spiritual of Ireland, by rotation of sessions, and twenty-eight lords temporal, elected for life by the peers of Ireland, shall sit and vote in the House of Lords; that the non-representative peers shall be eligible to sit for any constituency of the United Kingdom in the House of Commons; and that not more than one Irish peerage shall be created for every three that become extinct. This article also fixes the representation of Ireland in the House of Commons at one hundred members, at which figure it has practically remained throughout the eighty-five years of union, though the principles of proportional representation would have allowed Ireland over two hundred representatives in 1845, and now entitle her to not more than ninety-one. The fifth article enjoins "that the churches of England and Ireland, as by law established, be united into one Protestant Episcopal Church, to be called *The United Church of England and Ireland*, and that the doctrine, worship, discipline, and government of the United Church shall remain in full force for ever, as the same are now by law established for the Church of England, and that the continuance and preservation of the United Church as the Established Church of England and Ireland shall be deemed, and taken to be an essential and fundamental part of the union." This clause formed the great, and, indeed, the sole argument in favor of retaining the Establishment in Ireland.

The remaining articles provide for the succession of the sovereign and the maintenance of the laws. On New-Year's-day, 1801, the union practically commenced, and at the assembling of the first united parliament on January 22d the Catholics looked for speedy measures of relief. But the Catholic claims were not so much as mentioned in the king's speech, and his majesty having declared that he would abdicate rather than consent to Catholic emancipation, Pitt resigned into the hands of the anti-Catholic Abingdon. The hopes of the Catholics were dashed; five of the ministers reported to be in favor of the measure proved to be against it, and Pitt, though he professedly resigned on this question, resigned into the hands of a man whom he knew to be against emancipation, and resigned at a moment when the failure of his continental policy rendered his position as prime minister a painful one. He was probably glad to leave to others the task of making and breaking the Treaty of Amiens, and at least his resignation cannot be put down to devotion to the Catholics, for, when he resumed office in 1804, he gave a pledge to the king never again to trouble him with the subject.

In 1801 things were going ill with England; the allied armies had been victorious everywhere, and the French scare, which had led to the union, induced the ministers to pass, as the first measure of the united parliament for Ireland, an act for the suspension of the habeas corpus, and empowering the viceroy to proclaim martial law. Yet there was at that time no rebellion in Ireland; bad trade, bad harvest, and the abandonment of the Catholic claims rendered the union even more unpopular in reality than it had been in anticipation; there was some little agitation for repeal, but there was no shadow of rebellion.

When the claims of the Catholics were thrown over, Cornwallis gladly resigned the viceroyalty, and betook himself to the more congenial task of negotiating the Peace of Amiens. At its conclusion in June, 1802, the State prisoners were released from Fort George, and a new council of United Irishmen was established in Brussels. Unable themselves to return to Ireland, the United Irishmen sent over as an emissary young Robert Emmet, who was then in his three-and-twentieth year. The young man arrived in Dublin in the October of 1802, and spent the winter in organizing and preparing for rebellion. The moment was almost as unfavorable as any that could have been chosen; the memory of '98 was still green, and England on the alert; the best of the Separatists were all out of the country, and the revolutionary party were without funds. But for these errors of judgment, not Emmet, but those who sent him are to blame, and if we concede that any man has the right to involve his country in the terrible misery and risks of rebellion and civil war, we must admit that the nobility of Emmet's character, and the purity of his aims, entitle him to the hero-worship that Ireland has so lavishly showered on his memory.

His rebellion was worse than a failure, it was a collapse; but his plan of securing the capital and holding it as a rebel fortress is the only one which could have even the remotest chance of success in a country whose center is one vast plain. But after eight months' diligent organization Emmet was followed into the streets by an army of only eighty persons, and his attempt ended in nothing nobler than the brutal murder of lord Kilwarden, one of the best judges that ever sat upon the Irish bench, and his nephew, a clergyman. An hour later the streets of Dublin had returned to their usual quiet, and Emmet, heart-sick, disillusionized, and convinced of the utter hopelessness of the struggle, hurried to the Wicklow hills to prevent a country rising. He might even yet have escaped, but he had resolved to see one person before leaving the country. He could not go without a word to Sarah Curran, the youngest daughter of the advocate, who, at all risks to his life and professional reputation, had undertaken the defence of the rebels of '98. But the meeting between Miss Curran and Emmet never took place; while he was still waiting, he was seized and taken to Dublin.

The story of the clandestine engagement then came to Curran's ears, and he, unable to forgive the secrecy and the injury that this connection was to his reputation as a loyal man, refused to defend his daughter's lover. Emmet lost nothing by this refusal; the result of the trial was a foregone conclusion; hundreds of blunderbusses and thousands of pikes had been discovered in Emmet's arsenal, and with them were some thousand printed placards to be issued by the republican government to the people of Ireland. The evidence against Emmet was complete, and if anything could have saved him, his youth, the manly gentleness of his countenance, and his own marvellous eloquence, would have been his best advocates. On the nineteenth of September he was led in irons to the dock; by midnight the verdict was obtained, and in the afternoon of the next day he was hanged in Thomas Street, within view of his arsenal. "All that I crave of the world," said dying Emmet, "is the charity of its silence; let no man write my epitaph," but by friend and foe alike that request has been denied, and the nameless stone in St. Michan's churchyard alone is faithful to the wish of the dead rebel.

CHAPTER XXVII.
THE PEACE OF 1815.

THE utter collapse of a rebellion organized by a leader of such exceptional enthusiasm and personal charm was proof that in 1803 there was wonderful little tendency to rebellion in Ireland, but the renewal of the continental war increased the dread of a French invasion, and the miserable rising of eighty persons was punished by the imprisonment of three hundred, and the death of nineteen. Martial law was proclaimed, the Habeas Corpus Act suspended, and the whole yeomanry of Ireland put on permanent duty, at a cost of one hundred thousand pounds monthly.

The rising, abortive as it had been, threw back the anti-union party; in the horror and terror of the time Home Rule and Separation were deemed equally disloyal, and any demand for repeal raised a cry of disintegration of the empire. "Do not unite with us, sir," said Samuel Johnson to an Irish friend; "we would unite with you only to rob you;" and in the early years of the century there was a very general impression in Ireland that the union had indeed been, as Byron called it, "The union of the shark with its prey." The continental war gave artificial stimulus to agriculture both in England and Ireland, but by the end of 1804 the Irish national debt had risen to fifty three millions—a rise of twenty-six millions in four years, while in the same time the net produce of the revenue had actually decreased, despite the increasing population. The prosperity of the towns began to flag at once. The removal of the parliament ruined Dublin, which, from a metropolis, sank in a few years to the condition of a second-rate provincial city.

The common dislike to the union drew all parties together; Protestant, Catholic, Whig, and Tory united in the wish for repeal, but while the French scare continued agitation seemed hopeless, and the Catholics set themselves to gain first the lesser, but more attainable, boon of emancipation. They could not tell that the tendency of the century would be towards religious equality and centralization of government; that emancipation must come, even without any effort on the part of the Catholics, while every year would render English statesmen more attached to the union, and would raise fresh difficulties in the way of repeal.

In 1804 Pitt resumed office, and the Catholics, ignorant of his pledge to the king, asked him to present their petition for emancipation. He was, of course, unable to do this, and on March 25th of the following year the petition was presented by Fox in the Commons and Grenville in the Lords. During the debate that ensued, it was proposed to place the Roman Church on the same footing as the Gallican, by allowing the sovereign a right of *veto* on the prelates appointed by the Pope, and thus arose the famous question of *veto*, which was destined to be so bitterly debated before the emancipation question was settled. It was during this debate that Grattan made his first speech in the united parliament, and to this cause he devoted the remainder of his life. The bill was thrown out by a majority of nearly three to one, and when, after the death of Pitt in the following January, the Grenville-Fox ministry was formed, Fox advised the Catholics to let their claims stand over till the next session. So far as Fox was concerned, that next session was never held, for on the 13th of September he died. At his accession to office the hopes of the Catholics and anti-unionists had been high; the act for the suspension of the habeas corpus was allowed to expire, and for a time Ireland was governed by ordinary legislation. The death of the minister dashed these high hopes; and in the next session it was not even proposed to bring forward an Emancipation Bill, though, as a soothing measure, an act to enable Catholics to hold commissions in the army and navy was introduced; but so invincible was the king's opposition to this concession that the ministers were forced to resign, and the "No Popery" cabinet was formed. The duke of Bedford was now recalled, and the duke of Richmond succeeded him as viceroy, with Sir Arthur Wellesley, afterward duke of Wellington, as chief secretary. In this year, for the first time since the union, there was a renewal of Whiteboyism, the objects of the Whiteboys being the usual ones of reduction of rents, security of tenure, increase of laborers' wages, and resistance to tithe. The organization was confined to a small part of the country, and was quickly suppressed by ordinary law, but so great was the dread of a French party that the whole country was placed under an Insurrection Act and an Arms Act.

Notwithstanding the known views of the cabinet, the Catholics continued to urge their claims, and in 1808 Grattan presented a petition for emancipation accompanied by *veto*. The measure was thrown out, to the content of most parties, for the Catholic prelates unanimously declared that they preferred the existing state of affairs to emancipation with *veto*. Two years later the measure was again brought foward, and, as a set-off to the *veto*, the state payment of the Catholic clergy was proposed, but despite the temptation that this must have offered to so poor a body of men, the clergy declared against the measure, and the body of the Irish Catholic laity went with them. The English Catholics, some few of the Irish Catholic nobility and upper class, and the Irish Protestant advocates of emancipation favored the scheme, but the vast majority were against it. In this year Daniel O'Connell was elected chairman of the Catholic committee, and from this time he became the acknowledged leader of the Catholics. O'Connell was now thirty-five years of age, and had already attained considerable reputation at the Irish bar. He had joined the Catholic committee in 1806, and at an earlier date had made speeches in favor of repeal. In 1810 a Repeal Asssociation was formed, and had O'Connell thrown his energies into that channel it might possibly have fallen to the lot of the Irish, not the united, parliament to emancipate the Catholics. But O'Connell believed that in the House of Commons the Irish Catholics would best plead the cause of repeal; and, being himself a Catholic, he felt the political degredation of the mass of his countrymen very keenly. The veto agitation broke up the Catholics into two parties, and the movement seemed doomed to collapse till 1823, when O'Connell, taking advantage of some revival of interest, founded the Catholic Association.

The history of Ireland in the years between 1810 and 1823 is mainly agrarian; the Catholic agitation was continued, and various Emancipation Bills were brought in and rejected—Grattan making his last effort in 1813, six years before his death; but until 1823 the cry for emancipation did not amount to a national demand.

After holding the chief secretaryship for a few months only, Arthur Wellesley resigned it to his brother, Sir Wellesley Pole, who was succeeded by Sir Robert Peel on the formation of the Liverpool-Castlereagh ministry in 1812. Peel's Irish politics are briefly summed up in his nickname, "Orange Peel;" he was intensely unpopular, being too temporizing for his own party and too exacting for the emancipationists. During his tenure of office the long continental war came to an end, and with the peace came a rapid fall in the price of agricultural produce. In England there were two interests—what the land interest lost the trade interest gained by the cheap prices; but in Ireland, where there was no trade, the fall in prices was an unmixed evil. To bolster up the agricultural interest in both countries, Corn Laws were passed prohibiting the importation of wheat till home-grown grain should have reached the price of 80s per quarter. This act remained in force till 1828, when "the sliding scale" was introduced, allowing the importation of wheat on payment of a sliding scale of duty, which varied from £1 5s. 8d. per quarter when the average English price was under 62s., to 1s. per quarter when home-grown grain was above 73s. But notwithstanding this protective duty the peace brought great distress to Ireland, and distress was followed by agrarian outrage. An Insurrection Act was immediately passed and martial law proclaimed, but this measure had no effect on the starving peasantry, and the southern provinces remained practically in revolt against the landlords and tithe proctors. The reduction of prices had been followed by no reduction of rent, and in 1819 the failure of the potatoe crop changed pinching distress to absolute famine. The Coercion Act was renewed, but was ineffectual, and the operation of an act which had been passed two years earlier lessening the cost of evictions had no better result.

In 1822 the potato crop again failed, and to a more disastrous extent. There was grain in abundance, but the peasantry could not afford to buy it. Thousands of quarters of grain were exported weekly to England; while so great was the scarcity in Connomara that half-starved wretches walked fifty miles into Galway in the wild hope of food, but when they arrived in the city they were often so exhausted that they fainted, and the means taken to restore them failed in effect. In the month of June there were 99,639 souls in the County Clare alone living on daily charity, and in Cork there were 122,000; while in some of the remoter villages the whole population died of sheer starvation. Through all this distress the middleman or landlord and the tithe proctor had to be paid, and to the unreasonableness of their claims and their severity in extorting them, those living on the spot, and best competent to judge, attributed the agrarian outrages. Writing in this very year of 1822, Mr. Wiggins, agent to the marquess of Hertford, says in his "Hints to Landlords" that, "goaded by the distreses of laws; irritated also by rents too high even for war prices, by the fallen prices of produce without corresponding reduction of rents and tithes, and by severities which have increased with the difficulties of their collection, the peasantry of Munster yielded to the influence of these, and probably of other less apparent causes, and in the winter of 1822 insurrection and outrage became so extended as to require a large army to check its progress; but," he adds, "it is not by the terrors of the bayonet or the law that a brave and hardy people like the Irish can or ought to be permanently controlled; it is not only entirely in your power, but also greatly to your interests, nay, your bounden duty as lords of the soil, to alleviate these miseries, and to remove this poverty."

CHAPTER XXVIII.

EMANCIPATION.

THE year 1823 marks an era in the history of Catholic emancipation, for in it O'Connell, aided by Shiel, formed the Catholic Association for the furtherance of the cause of emancipation by means of petitions, public discussions, meetings, and the return of members of parliament, who were pledged to support the cause. The association, like its numerous successors, consisted of members paying an annual subscription of £1 1s., and associates who paid one shilling. A standing committee formed the government; meetings were held weekly, and the business consisted of organization, discussion, correspondence, and petitions. At first it was difficult to keep the infant association alive, and at one of the early meetings O'Connell had to entreat two Maynooth students, who were passing the committee rooms, to come in and form a quorum. It was a fortunate accident; from that hour the clergy gave the association their support. The association, once rooted, spread like a fire, and in the next year the "Catholic rent," consisting of one penny monthly, averaged £500 a week, representing nearly half a million associates. The cry for emancipation had become a national demand, and there was a strong feeling in England that it ought not to be resisted, though George IV. regarded the project almost as unfavorably as his father had done. In March, 1825, the association was dissolved by act of parliament, but O'Connell, who boasted that he "could drive a coach and six through any act of parliament," circumvented the act, and reorganized the association under the name of the *New* Catholic Association, and the government took no further means to suppress the society, for at that moment they were constructing a Catholic Relief Bill granting emancipation, but weighting the measure by the disfranchisement of the forty-shilling freeholders, and the State payment of the Catholic clergy. In this form the bill was unpopular in Ireland, and the news that it had been thrown out by the lords was received with pleasure rather than disappointment. The proposal for the State payment of the clergy was held both by priesthood and laity to be nothing better than a bribe, and the forty-shilling freeholders, who were the great bulk of the rural voters, hotly resented the prospect of disfranchisement. During the next three years the vigorous and ever-increasing efforts of the Catholics were unavailing; in 1827 Canning died, and early in the ensuing year the duke of Wellington became premier, and Peel home secretary. Yet this anti-Catholic administration was destined to carry the Catholic Relief Bill, not from any conversion to the principles of religious equality, but, as the premier himself stated, "to prevent civil war." While the Emancipation Bill was being framed, Mr. Vesey Fitzgerald, member for Clare, accepted the office of president of the board of trade, and had to present himself for re-election. To the surprise of every one O'Connell announced his intention of contesting the seat, for though the nature of the oath of allegiance was such that no Catholic could swear it, there was no law to prevent the election of a Papist. The contest was a hot one, and O'Connell was successful, but as the Emancipation Bill was in progress he did not attempt to take his seat till it had been through the house. In the next session it passed, but at the same time the county franchise in Ireland was raised from forty shillings to ten pounds—five times that of England, where the franchise remained unchanged. As the disfranchisement of the forty-shilling freeholders was for many years a standing grievance, it will be well to briefly state the facts of the case.

In 1795 a bill had been passed giving the elective franchise to all lease holders of property to the annual value of 40s. This bill had made Irish landlords very willing to grant small leases, and a whole race of peasant farmers had sprung up. The population had increased rapidly, and in 1821 amounted to nearly 7,000,000. At the fall in prices at the peace of 1815, the cry of over-population of Ireland had first been raised, and the famine of '17 and '22 had confirmed English statesmen in their theory; and it was professedly as a check to the too rapid increase of population that the franchise was raised from two to ten pounds. But, whether for good or evil, the deed was done; the population was there, and the disfranchisement brought an infinity of misery. Such landlords as cared for political power, and looked on their tenants only as voters, refused to renew small leases, and at their expiration ejected the small tenants to bring the value of the leaseholds of such as remained up to the county qualification. The cheap Ejectment Acts that had been passed after the peace of 1815 greatly simplified the process of eviction, and in Ireland a tenant could be evicted in two months and at a cost of £2, while in England the process took at least 12 months and cost £18. The Irish landlord, too, could distrain the young crops of the tenant, keep them till they were ripe, gather and sell them, charging the tenant with the accumulation of the expense.

After the disfranchisement these acts were largely used, and many landlords who did not evict refused to renew small leases, and so the system of annual tenancy increased. It is difficult to conceive what can be said in favor of this system of tenure so ruinous to the cultivator and the soil. The tenant, dreading eviction, fearing that his rent may be raised on the value of the improvements he has made, and unwilling to risk his capital, stints his manure and contents himself with scratching over the surface of the soil, growing potatoes and oats, oats and potatoes, till the impoverished land refuses to yield enough to support life, much less pay the rent; then follows the familiar, miserable story of eviction, starvation, and crime.

By the raising of the franchise, the electors of Ireland were reduced from 200,000 to 26,000, that is to say, nearly seven out of every eight electors were disqualified. Twenty-one years later a Reform Act was passed establishing a £5 freehold and £12 rating occupation franchise for the counties, and an £8 rating occupation franchise for the boroughs, and in 1868 the borough franchise was lowered to £4 and a lodger £10 franchise introduced; but the Fenian movement being then at its height, it was not deemed expedient to lower the county franchise in Ireland. In this same year a lowered franchise added 400,000 voters to the English county constituencies, and household suffrage was granted to the Scotch and English boroughs. This act was superseded in 1885 by a Reform Bill, which practically granted household suffrage to both Great Britain and Ireland.

The parliament which disfranchised the 40s. freeholders and granted Catholic emancipation, was dissolved in 1830 by the death of George IV., and at the ensuing election O'Connell and many other Roman Catholics were returned. From this time "the Liberator" devoted himself to the cause of repeal; this had been his first political aspiration, and now he returned to the old path. But the old allies were gone; the Protestant repealers were no more; religious bigotry had conquered self-interest and national sentiment: dread of O'Connell and the Pope had converted the Irish Protestants into unionists. They could not realize that the days of religious disability were passed for Papist and Protestant, that a renewed Irish parliament could never pay off old scores, no matter how great a majority of its members might be Catholics. They dreaded papal supremacy even more than they hated English ascendancy, and they preferred the ill they knew to the ill they knew not. Moreover, repeal had become a much more complicated question; laws had been made, taxes levied, debts contracted that placed practical difficulties in the way of simple repeal; it was impossible after a lapse of 30 years to go back to the old order of things, and O'Connell had no project of an Irish parliament for Irish affairs, and an Imperial parliament for the settlement of the affairs of the empire. Home Rule, too, was easily confounded with Separation, or was mistrusted as a step towards the severance of the connection of the two countries.

Throughout the reign of William IV. the Irish masses remained indifferent to the repeal question; emancipation had brought them nothing but disfranchisement, and they were mainly occupied with the struggle for existence, with the emigration question, and above all with the tithe war. In vain the rector claimed every tenth sheep; in vain an army as large as that which dragooned India tried to collect the tithe. A purely spontaneous resistance had arisen among the peasantry who, of their own accord, and without leaders or agitators, carried on war by means of outrage and what is now known as "boycotting." It was useless to try to sell the cattle that had been seized for tithe, for though thousands of persons attended the auctions not one bid would be made for cattle seized under the tithe decree. The state of the country was fearful. War, prosecuted on both sides with barbarous cruelty, raged between the peasantry and the tithe proctors, and a stringent Coercion Act did nothing for the pacification of the country.

In the meantime Mr. Stanley, afterward lord Derby, who was then chief secretary, brought in a bill for primary education in Ireland. No religious instruction was to be given in the schools founded under this act; yet, notwithstanding the national objection to mixed education and the denunciations of priests and parsons, the schools prospered. Twenty years later Ireland contained 5,000 national schools, attended by 511,020 pupils, and in 1880 there were 7,590 schools with 1,083,020 pupils. Another much needed reform was accomplished in this reign by the passing of the Church Temporalities Act, whereby ten bishoprics were abolished and the Establishment was made to bear some proportion to the people for whose benefit it was maintained at the cost of so much bloodshed and injustice. The reign was but a short one; for in June 1837 the king died, and was succeeded by his niece, Victoria.

It was impossible that so young a woman as the new queen could have more than a nominal voice in the government of a vast empire, and thus with the reign of Victoria began the era of constitutional government in England. One of the first acts of the queen's ministers was to pass the much-debated measure of poor law for Ireland, and soon afterward the Tithe Commutation Act abolished for ever the scandalous method of collecting tithe. No more were corn and cattle to be seized by force of arms, for in the future the landlord—not the tenant—was to pay a sum of money as tithe. By raising the rents the landlords generally transferred the obligation to the tenant, and by consenting thus to play the part of tithe collector, they attracted toward themselves all the ill-will that had been hitherto bestowed on the tithe proctor.

This same year (1838) made memorable by the Poor Law and Tithe Reform Acts, also witnessed the establishment of two great national movements in Ireland—the repeal agitation and the teetotal movement.

It was an era of conciliation, and O'Connell had agreed to accept "Justice to Ireland" as an alternative to repeal, and for the promotion of this somewhat indefinite cause he founded the Precursor Society, which soon numbered two million members, and which on the formation of the Tory ministry in 1841 merged into a full-grown and avowed repeal association.

The teetotal movement had been founded some years earlier by the Quakers of Cork, but it took no hold on the people till Theobald Mathew, a young Capuchin friar, joined it in 1838. His unfailing kindness and devotion to the poor had already endeared Father Mathew to the lowest classes of the community, and, through his influence, 156,000 persons took the pledge in the first nine months of his mission, and by 1842 he had made a successful crusade in every part of his native land. Without any special gifts or influence beyond that of goodness, this simple friar wrought a moral reformation almost beyond belief. The curse of drink seemed banished from Ireland, and millions took the pledge. With a rapidly-increasing population, crime rapidly decreased; in '39, when the movement was beginning, there were twelve thousand committals and sixty-four capital sentences, while six years later, when the movement was at its height, there were but seven thousand committals and fourteen death sentences. But these statistics give only a very faint picture of the extent of the reform. In five years, public opinion changed utterly, no man was any longer ashamed to be temperate, and many who felt no need to bind themselves by a pledge abstained from strong drink. The friar wisely, and in true Christian spirit, refused to make his mission a question of politics or creed, and administered the pledge with equal kindliness to Leinster Repealer and Ulster Orangeman, and thus a common bond of interest was established between creeds and parties.

CHAPTER XXIX.

THE REPEAL YEAR.

THE formation of the Peel ministry, in 1841, shattered O'Connell's hopes of justice to Ireland, and the Precursor Society, by a change of name, became the Repeal Association. The movement gained ground rapidly; there was abundant oppression and distress, and all the Catholic or "lower" nation cried loudly for a change. In the early days of the Association the Repealers were almost exclusively Catholics of the middle or lower class: indeed, the peasantry of the three southern provinces became Repealers almost to a man. The Anglicans were held back from the movement by the conviction that the first act of an Irish parliament would be the disestablishment of the English Church, and, moreover, O'Connell's attitude towards Protestants was not such as to encourage their national aspirations. The "Saxon" in any form was abhorrent to O'Connell, and for purely political purposes he revived the race-hatred which had become almost extinct. But the masses were blind to the faults of the Liberator, and his eloquence, his ready sympathy, his wit, his pathos, his rich and tender voice, gave him complete mastery over his audience. But looking back to a distance of forty years, we can see that O'Connell had the faults common to his temperament; like most persons of quick sympathies and many moods, he was only tolerably truthful and moderately sincere, and, like many public orators, he allowed himself to win the support and gain the confidence of his public by a species of moral bribery, by flattery of his supporters, and wholesale abuse of his antagonists. The personal abuse which he showered upon his opponents can be condoned on the score that it was but retaliation in kind for the coarse invectives and insults they heaped upon himself, but nothing can justify or even palliate his deliberate revival of the memory of long-forgotten wrongs. For the purpose of arousing latent passion, he drew moving pictures of the treachery of Elizabeth at Mullaghmast, the barbarity of Cromwell's troops at Wexford and Drogheda, and he even asserted that, given the power, England would reproduce those acts of treachery and blood. These speeches had a twofold result; they made the Irish hate the English, and they made the English despise and detest the Irish, for had an English orator striven to arouse race-hatred by a description of the atrocities of Phelim O'Neill, the only sentiment he would have evoked would have been one of disgust against himself, and a reaction in favor of the Irish, against whom no more modern offences could be brought up. But in Ireland it was different; a chain of injustice and oppression linked the present with the past, and had O'Connell contented himself with anything less dramatic than wholesale massacre under a flag of truce, he might have made out a very good case without going back to the protectorate.

But though O'Connell's method of agitation pleased the peasantry, such young men of the more cultured classes as joined the Repealers disapproved strongly of his practice of appealing to passions of race and creed. To these young men it seemed more to the point that the English government of 1842 was countenancing wholesale eviction than that the government of Elizabeth had connived at treachery. They felt no need to awaken the memory of bygone wrongs; it was enough for them that almost one-fourth of the cultivable land of a country which was held to be overpopulated was lying waste; that in Mayo, alone, there were 500,000 acres of improvable waste land; that Catholic peasants paid tithe for Protestant rectors; that no tenant had security for his tenure or compensation for his improvements; that the rack-rented peasantry had no redress; that juries were packed, and the poor law badly administered. To air these and other grievances, to give the public a fair view of contemporary history, three young Repealers—Thomas Osbourne Davis, John Blake Dillon, and Charles Gavan Duffy—founded the *Nation* newspaper. Such a journal was much needed; O'Connell's organ, *The Pilot*, was conducted on the most bigoted principle conceivable, and it was the ambition of the founders of the *Nation* to establish a journal worthy of the cause of nationality and free from religious bigotry. Like the vast majority of Irish leaders, Thomas Davis was a Protestant; Dillon and Duffy were staunch Catholics, but absolutely free from prejudice or fanaticism, and all were men of exceptional talent and purity of motive. Davis was possessed of poetic gifts akin to genius. Under the guidance of these young men the *Nation* at once took a high position; indeed, even now, after a lapse of more than 40 years, the early numbers are still fresh and interesting, while it is impossible to read without emotion some of the patriotic ballads which appeared in its pages. Many of the historical articles are excellent, but the contemporary articles convey the most useful information, and from them we learn that in the year 1843, 42,000,000 lbs. of grain, almost 1,000,000 head of live stock, besides great quantities of butter, eggs, and bacon, were exported to England alone, while in this same year a surplus population of 100,000 souls were forced to emigrate, so that had Ireland exported neither food nor people those who under existing circumstances were forced to emigrate might each have eaten 10 beasts and 420 lbs. of grain.

O'Connell had declared that 1843 should be the repeal year, and all through the summer the most intense excitement prevailed. Enormous multitudes attended the repeal meetings, and between forty-eight and forty-nine thousand pounds were subscribed for the association. Larger and larger grew the meetings; Tara and Mullaghmast had each been the scene of a peaceful triumph, and a monster meeting was announced to take place at Clontarf on Sunday, the 8th of October. The English government now took alarm, and though O'Connell maintained that "no political reform is worth the spilling of one drop of human blood," the attitude of the country was considered dangerous, and on Saturday, Sept. 7th, the meeting was proclaimed. Many thousands had come up from the country, and it was no easy matter to prevent the gathering; but O'Connell decreed that the proclamation must be obeyed, and by strenuous exertions the meeting was prevented. But that was the real end of O'Connell's influence. The people began to feel that that agitation which repudiates action is powerless, and that an army pledged not to fight is no defence. The proclamation of the Clontarf meeting was followed by the arrest of O'Connell and eight other prominent Repealers for conspiracy and kindred offences, and in November the State trials began. At the conclusion of the trials in May, the traversers were all found guilty. O'Connell was sentenced to a year's imprisonment, and the others to shorter terms. The jury had been shamefully and notoriously packed, and the traversers appealed against the judgment, which was reversed by the House of Lords. The released traversers received a triumph; but the repeal movement never regained its strength, the repeal year had passed, and the union was as firmly established as ever. The faith of the masses in the agitation was shaken, and there were divided councils in Conciliation Hall, where the "Young Ireland Party," as the staff of the *Nation* were called, often found themselves unable to subscribe to the ruling of their leader. Throughout '44 the disunion increased, and in the autumn of '45 Ireland fell a prey to that long agony of famine through which all her energies were absorbed in the struggle for dear life.

CHAPTER XXX.

THE FAMINE.

THE autumn of '45 was cold and wet; chill and persistent rains fell over the north of Europe, bringing scarcity and disease in their train. The bad weather set in too late to affect the wheat crops, but the potatoes were seriously damaged, and by the failure of that crop hundreds of thousands were deprived of their usual food. In Germany,

France, Denmark, and Holland, the poor, suffered; but the Irish, being more dependent on the potatoes suffered more. The whole energy of the people was needed to cope with the emergency; all their savings were expended in keeping body and soul together, and in buying seed for next year's sowing. The winter was one of terrible privation; those who had savings lived off them, but among the really poor there was widespread destitution. The loss of the potato crop was valued at £16,000,000, and to replace this with grain would cost £20,000,000, but compared to the extent of the calamity the efforts to cope with it were lamentably inefficient. The starving peasantry—forced to sell their clothes for food—resisted the payment of their rent, and where the uttermost farthing was extorted, barbarous outrages were committed. To meet the difficulty, a Coercion Bill was passed, but in the early part of winter government fearing to overrate the extent of the calamity, refused to take further steps; in the beginning of '46, however, £50,000 were voted to be expended on public works. The amount shows how utterly the government failed to realize what the loss of the potato crop meant; it was only a two-hundredth part of what was needed to replace the loss, and only one quarter of the sum expended in the same year on Battersea Park. But the great measure of the session was the repeal of the Corn Laws which, it was hoped, would prevent a recurrence of such terrible scarcity of food. The English manufacturing towns had long clamored for their repeal, and in England this had become an absolute necessity. Bread was at starvation price, and was actually scarce; British islands were incapable of raising food for their increasing population; and had it not been for the strength of the landed interest in parliament, the Corn Laws must have gone much earlier.

It was as a measure of relief for Ireland that these laws were now repealed. The protectionist party argued that far from giving food to the people of Ireland, the repeal of the Corn Laws would ruin them by destroying the profits of their only manufacture, and taking away from them the very means of procuring subsistence. Time has proved that the protectionists were right. The population of Ireland was rural, the population of England urban; thus the interests of the two islands were diametrically opposed. Ireland was the producer, England the consumer. For years the producer had enjoyed an artificial and most unjust advantage, but the destruction of this advantage could hardly be considered a measure for his relief. Ireland was unable to produce food enough for both countries, but she was capable of raising abundant food for her own population. The famine of '46-'47 was an artificial famine, for in this very year that hunger deprived Ireland of a quarter of her people, she was the largest export country in the world. "The exports of Ireland," says lord George Bentinck, "are greater than those of any country in the world; not merely more in proportion to its people, or to its area, but absolutely more. Its exports of food are greater than those of the United States, greater than those of Russia;" and throughout the famine year an average of 20 steamships laden with food left Ireland daily. In the *Times*, of March 12th, 1849, we find a list of Irish produce which on one single day entered the port of London— we have, unfortunately, no record of the imports to Liverpool, Bristol, and the smaller ports. "No less than 16 ships arrived in the river, laden almost exclusively with food of various kinds, the produce of Ireland, having collectively 14,960 packages of butter; 224 packages of pork; 1,047 hampers and bales of bacon; several of hams; 140 sacks, 22,926 barrels, and 7,889 quarters of oats: 434 packages of lard; 75 of general provisions; 40 of oatmeal; 44 of porter; 259 boxes of eggs; and a variety of articles of lesser importance." The magnificent wheat harvest, the finest that ever ripened on Irish soil, had been swept away earlier in the season. Let us take a nearer look at this fertile country, the greatest food exporter in the world; this island which feeds 8,000,000 of the English people, and whose agricultural produce is valued at £45,000,000.

All through the spring and summer of '46 the people worked on in hope; the season was fine, and the potatoes looked well, till the magnificent grain crop was whitening for the harvest. Then, in July, a blight swept over the land, and in one fortnight the potatoes were totally, utterly destroyed; nothing remained, not even enough for seed. The people endured their loss with an apathy incomprehensible in England. Their food was gone, their savings were spent, the blackened, blighted potato tops were a sentence of death that the most illiterate could read. Weakened by a year of privation, the people met their fate with the indifference of ill health and the patience of despair. Quietly, without murmur or complaint, they went into their cabins, closing the the doors, because the close air made them feel less hungry, and so, without remonstrance or effort, they watched the departure of the heavy carts of golden grain. Potatoes were the exclusive diet of three million persons, the staple diet of two million more;—five million persons were without money and without food. It was useless to sell food even at a moderate price. Potatoes are the very cheapest form of human food, and "to a people subsisting on them, no retrenchment is possible. They have," said John Stuart Mill, "already reached the lowest point of the descending scale, and there is nothing beyond but beggary and starvation." The problem of how to cope with this famine of the thirteenth century with a population of the nineteenth was no easy one to solve; and many and various were the plans suggested. "Close the exports," cried some; "let us eat our own food." "Open the imports," cried others; "import cheap grain;" and this indeed was done, but with very limited success.

Fifty thousand pounds were again voted for relief works, and, in accordance with the laws of political economy, these were strictly unproductive. Roads were broken up, and works were set on foot, which, the inspector reported, "would answer no other purpose than that of obstructing the public conveyances." Further grants of money were made, and at a cost of seven or eight thousand pounds weekly, good roads were broken up and re-made. The Irish party urged that the money would be better expended in draining some of the five million acres of improvable waste land; and lord George Bentinck proposed a scheme for laying railroads on a large scale, but both projects were held to be inimical to private enterprise, and the unproductive works were continued. As the winter wore on the distress increased. The men, weakened by starvation, were unable to work, and many reached the spot only to faint or die. Some had to walk five or ten miles to their work, and were too exhausted to perform the task exacted of them; indeed, so reduced were they that in some districts attendance was obliged to be considered qualification for wage; and one of the superintendents reports that "as an employer he was ashamed of allotting so little work for a day's wage, while as a man he was ashamed of extorting so much." The people crowded into the works, and in March 734,000 heads of families, representing 3,000,000 persons were thus employed. "A nation," said Disraeli, "equal to the population of Holland, breaking stones on the road."

But government was not left to cope with the difficulty alone. All over the world hearts were touched by the appalling misery of the unhappy nation. So dire was the distress that the Quaker commissioners state it would be impossible to exaggerate it. Whole families existed on a daily ration of a few ounces of oatmeal till death ended their sufferings. Typhus of a most malignant and infectious type raged among them, and the dread of contagion overwhelmed even the boundless charity of the poor toward one another. Save in the case of those stricken with fever, there was no limit to the charity of these starving people. Mr. W. E. Forster, who was among the most zealous of the Quaker commissioners, tells us of more than one instance where destitute strangers were housed and fed by families who could rely only on a few ounces of thin gruel for food. "Never," writes another authority," have I witnessed so much good feeling, patience, and cheerfulness under privation. I hardly remember an instance of their murmuring or begging." On the public works the same good feeling prevailed; those whose claims were rejected in favor of a still more distressed applicant submitting with a cheerful patience for which any praise would be insulting. The suffering from cold was only second to that from hunger. During the scarcity of the preceding year no new clothes had been bought, and many old ones sold, so that the poorer peasantry were almost naked. The children suffered least, for the parents stripped and starved that their little one should have food and covering. Indeed, in all accounts of this fearful misery, the one bright spot is the touching and unparalleled unselfishness of the people. Perhaps the most horrible of all the horrors of this time was the fearful condition of the workhouses. The Irish hatred of the poorhouse gave way before the pangs of hunger, and the unions were filled to overflowing. In these loathsome lazar-houses typhus, starvation, filth, and death reigned supreme. Dead and dying lay in one bed or side by side on the floor, and the poorhouse was known to be the gateway to the tomb.

The condition of the towns was no better than that of the country; the people below the middle class were reduced literally to skeletons, and the whole of the poorer class were starving. An appalling picture of the state of Cork is given by the late Mr. A. M. Sullivan in his sketches of "New Ireland." "Daily in the street and on the footway some poor creature lay down as if to sleep, and presently was still and stark. In our district it was a common occurrence to find, on opening the front door in the early morning, leaning against it the corpse of some victim who in the night had 'rested' in its shelter. We raised a public subscription, and employed two men with horse and cart to go round each day to gather up the dead. One by one they were taken to Ardnabrahair Abbey, and dropped through the hinged bottom of a 'trap coffin' into a common grave below. In the rural districts even this rude sepulcher was impossible In the fields and by the ditches the victims lay as they fell, till some charitable hand was found to cover them with the adjacent soil." In the attempt to assuage this awful misery, devoted men and women were daily laying down their lives. The resident landlords, for the most part, did their duty well—establishing soup coppers and distributing cooked food. Many remitted their rent or half their rents, and if others were exacting and extorted their full legal dues, we must remember that their estates were often so deeply mortgaged that they were only less destitute than the tenantry, and, in some cases, were thankful to accept a daily ration of cooked food. Several of their body fell victims to their devotion, and a large number of doctors and of the clergy died of fever, caught in the performance of their duty.

At last the sowing time came round again, and it was found that sickness, death, the poorhouse, the emigrant ship, and the public works, had absorbed the male population. It was clear that political economy was ruining the country, and government now adopted the cooked food system which they had rejected as pauperizing, but which had been employed by private charity throughout. The cooked food relief proved much more efficacious and less expensive than the public works. The rations, including all expenses, cost only 2d. each, and the total expenditure in meal was only a million and a-half out of the millions which were advanced out of the Imperial exchequer, half as a loan to be repaid, and half as a free grant to meet the expenses of the famine. But public works, free food, poor-law, and charity, were insufficient to cope with this vast distress, and east to England and west to America fled the stricken multitude, carrying everywhere the seeds of deadly disease, till England, to protect herself, subjected ships with steerage passengers to quarantine, and several companies raised the rate of steerage passage. Westward now was the only escape from famine, and the poor wretches flooded the emigrant ships to Canada and the United States.

The ships were terribly overcrowded, carrying double the legal number of passengers, and here, as in the workhouses, filth and mismanagement had it all their own way: the death-rate on the passage rose to twelve times its usual extent, and many were landed in such a diseased condition that the deaths in quarantine increased from one and one third to forty per thousand. In Montreal alone eight hundred emigrants died in nine weeks, and in six months the deaths amounted to three thousand. Of the hundred thousand Irish who fled to Canada in the black '47 one out of every five died on the voyage or on their arrival; one out of every three was received into a hospital, and the remainder dispersed among the population, carrying death everywhere, and shunned and dreaded for the contagion they brought with them. Too weak to work, too poor to live without work, the condition of the Irish emigrant was pitiable. The labor market in the towns was overstocked, and these half-starved people were little fitted for backwoods settlers. Such settlers must have means of support from twelve to fifteen months after their arrival, and this cannot be accomplished for less than sixty pounds per family at the lowest estimate, whereas these emigrants had nothing—not even health. The subject of emigration has been discussed with much heat by its advocates and opponents, and in the case of Ireland the subject has been approached with peculiar bitterness. England argues that the miseries of Ireland are due to over-population, and Ireland maintains that a country capable in a year of famine of producing food for sixteen million persons, and containing five million acres of waste but improvable land cannot be said to be too thickly peopled. The falseness of the over-population theory receives some support from the fact that, when Swift wrote his "modest proposal," Ireland, with two million inhabitants, was worse off than she was in '41 with more than four times that population, and in 1886, now that the population has been reduced to between four and five millions, she is little better off than when she fed double as many at home and was a larger exporter of food. An extract from the able paper on the emigration question by Sir Charles Trevelyan, and published in the *Edinburgh Review* of 1848, makes a fitting close to the sad chapter of the famine of '47.

"There is no subject of which a merely one-sided view is more commonly taken than that of emigration. The evils arising from the crowded state of the population, and the facility with which large numbers of persons may be transferred to other countries, are naturally uppermost in the minds of landlords and ratepayers; but her majesty's government, to which the well-being of the British population in every quarter of the globe is confided, must have an equal regard to the interests of the emigrant and of the colonial community of which he may become a member.

It is a great mistake to suppose that even Canada and the United States have an unlimited capacity of absorbing a new population. The labor market in the settled district is always so nearly full that a small addition to the persons in search of employment makes a sensible difference; while the clearing of land requires the possession of resources and a power of sustained exertion not ordinarily belonging to the newly arrived Irish emigrant. In this, as well as in the other operations by which society is formed and sustained, there is a natural process which cannot be with impunity departed from. A movement is continually going on toward the backwoods on the part of the young and enterprising portion of the settled population, and of such of the former emigrants as have acquired means and experience; and the room thus made is occupied by persons recently arrived from Europe who have only their labor to depend on. The conquest of the wilderness requires more than the ordinary share of energy and perseverance, and every attempt that has yet been made to turn paupers into backwoodsmen has ended in signal failure. As long as they were rationed, they held together in a feeble, helpless state; and when the issue of the rations ceased they generally returned to the settled parts of the country. Our recent experience of the effects of a similar state of dependence in Ireland offers no encouragement to renew the experiment in a distant country where the difficulties are so much greater, and a disastrous result would be so much less capable of being retrieved. . . . Those who have inherited or purchased estates in which a redundant population has been allowed to grow up may with propriety assist some of their people to emigrate, provided they take care to prevent their being left destitute on their arrival in their new country. The expense of assisting emigration under such circumstances properly falls on the proprietor. A surplus population, whether it be owing to the fault or the misfortune of the proprietor or his predecessors, must be regarded as one of the disadvantages contingent on the possession of the estate; and he who enjoys the profit and advantage of the estate must also submit to the less desirable conditions connected with it. So long as emigration is conducted *only* at the expense of the proprietor it is not likely to be carried to a dangerous or an injurious extent, and it will press so heavily on his resources as to leave the motives to exertion of a different kind unimpaired. Emigration is open to objection only when the natural checks and correctives have been neutralized by the interposition of government or other public bodies. It then becomes the interest and policy of the landed proprietor to make no exertion to maintain his peopled home, to produce a general impression that no such exertion could be successfully made, and to increase by every possible means the pressure upon those parties who, having the command of the public funds, are expected to give their assistance; and the responsibility of the consequences, whatever they may be, becomes transferred from the individual proprietors to the government or public body which countenances and promotes their proceedings."

CHAPTER XXXI.

YOUNG IRELAND.

THE action of the government in proclaiming the Clontarf meeting forced O'Connell's hand. To forbid such a gathering at such a short notice was a dangerous measure, and might have ended in riot and bloodshed; but the *coup* was a complete success, and by that one blow the neck of the repeal movement was broken. It was not that the crushing power of the government had asserted itself, but the Repealers had been forced to ask themselves what this peaceful agitation meant, and whither it was leading them? and they found that it meant nothing and was leading them nowhere. The younger men were as opposed as O'Connell himself to the idea of insurrection: they knew that nothing but dire necessity could justify such a course, but they could not subscribe to their leader's motto, that no political reform is worth the shedding of one drop of human blood; still, this being merely a theoretic principle, the young men would willingly have left it in abeyance had O'Connell been content to let it rest an open question. The split between the *Nation* party and the Conciliation Hall arose from a fundamental difference of aim and idea. O'Connell's Ireland was the Ireland of Catholic and Celt; he cared nothing for Protestants or Anglo-Irishmen. The patriotism of the *Nation* party was wider; they wished to make the Ulster Presbyterian feel that he was every whit as much an Irishman as the Connaught Catholic. Thomas Davis, their inspiring spirit, was a Protestant and the son of a Welshman; Smith O'Brien, Mitchel, and Martin were also Protestants; and though two out of the three founders of the *Nation* were Catholics, they refused to constitute their paper a Catholic journal; it was simply political, without any denominational bias. For this O'Connell stigmatized the *Nation* as an infidel print and Davis as an unbeliever; but in 1845 Davis died, and O'Connell ceased his invectives on the Young Irelanders. About this time it began to be rumored that O'Connell was negotiating with the Whigs, and ultimately the negotiations were actually begun. The Young Irelanders protested, and O'Connell took offence at the language they used. Finally he required a formal renunciation of the principles of armed rebellion, and this the Young Irelanders would not give. The celebrated two days' debate ensued, and it resulted in the Young Irelanders, headed by Smith O'Brien, leaving the hall in a body,

The rupture was now complete; the youth, the talent, and the enthusiasm of the country had left the association, but the priesthood and the peasantry remained faithful to the old party. The very name of O'Connell had magic in it; O'Connell was the Catholic, the Celt, the Liberator, the founder of repeal; O'Connell, too, was the champion of the Church; the preacher of the beautiful doctrine that right is might, and peace more invincible than war. The Young Irelanders occupied a far less popular platform, and appealed to only a very restricted public. Their leader, William Smith O'Brien, was indeed descended from Brian Boru, but there was "too much of the Smith and too little of the O'Brien about him" for popularity, and he was a Protestant, a landlord, and the member for Ennis. Davis, too, was a Protestant; the son of a Welsh gentleman who had settled in Mallow and married an Irish wife. He had been educated at Trinity College, and was a member of the Irish bar, but never practiced. His influence on his party had been mainly personal, and was the result of a singularly chivalric and enthusiastic nature, tempered by an intense love of justice. He was a profound Celtic scholar, and one of the finest ballad writers of Ireland; but his life of nine-and-twenty years was an active one, and his literary remains are quite insufficient to account for his great influence. His nearest friend, and fellow-founder of the *Nation*, was John Blake Dillon, a young Catholic barrister, who, though possessed of a singularly sweet and gentle nature, was destined to take the most active part in the rising of '48. The third founder, and the editor of the *Nation*, was Mr. (now Sir) Charles Gavan Duffy. But the most remarkable man of the party was John Mitchel. The son of a non-conformist minister, who had himself been a United Irishman, Mitchel had been raised in an atmosphere of hatred to English rule. He joined the staff of the *Nation* soon after its foundation, but in '47 he resigned, and started the *United Irishmen* "for the purpose of inculcating the holy hatred of English rule." Thus in the same year in which by O'Connell's death repeal lost its great champion, separation for the first time since Emmet's rebellion found a powerful advocate. For Mitchel, reckless and embittered as he was, was a man of mental power and literary talent. The *United Irishman* had been preaching the gospel of hatred for only ten days when the sudden revolutionary outbreak in Paris convinced the Young Irelanders that the moment to strike for liberty was come. The terrible incapacity of the government to cope with the potato famine seemed proof to the gentler spirits among the Irish Nationalists of the ignorance of England, while the wilder natures attributed the mismanagement to ill-will. During the last two years, a quarter of the people of Ireland had been swept away, and the *Nation* party and the Mitchelites were both convinced that by some means the harvest of '48 must be retained in Ireland. Then, in February, the French revolution determined them to fight.

The *Nation* party implored Mitchel to adopt some secrecy, but for three months his extraordinary paper instructed the populace in the arts and mysteries of street warfare, and made the most treasonous confidences to the lord lieutenant. It was a paper no government could tolerate. Mitchel was seized, tried, and convicted of treason-felony, and sentenced to fourteen years transportation. Within two weeks of his conviction, a new revolutionary journal, the *Irish Tribune*, edited by Dr. Kevin Izod O'Doherty and D'Alton Williams, succeeded the *United Irishman*, and a fortnight later the first number of the *Irish Felon* appeared, edited by John Martin, a Protestant country gentleman of County Down. Five weeks later, Martin, Williams, Dr. Kevin Izod O'Doherty, and Sir Charles Gavin Duffy were arrested; the Habeas Corpus Act was suspended, and the warrants issued against Smith O'Brien and Meagher—the most eloquent speaker of the party.

The Young Irelanders were now pledged to insurrection; the government, by forcing a premature explosion of the rebellion, had ruined their already desperate game, but, pledged as they were, they felt that to men of honor the only course was to rise before the warrants were put into execution. Smith O'Brien, Dillon, Meagher and others went down into the country and tried to prevail on the people to take up arms. But the peasantry knew nothing of the Young Irelanders, save that they had been denounced by O'Connell and were disliked by the priests, and the poor creatures were too enervated by starvation and disease, to care to fight. The rebels had neither arms, commissariat, nor plan of action, and the rebellion was a miserable collapse. At Killenaule a barricade was erected, under command of Dillon, and at Ballingarry, Smith O'Brien headed a small skirmish in a cabbage garden, and then the rebellion was over. Smith O'Brien, M'Manus, O'Donohue, and Meagher were tried for high treason, and sentenced to be hanged, beheaded, and quartered; but the sentences were at once remitted to transportation. Dillon and P. J. Smyth escaped to America, Dr. O'Doherty and Martin were sentenced to ten years transportation. Williams was acquitted, and the prosecution of Sir C. G. Duffy was abandoned after two trials, ending in the disagreement of the jury. The life sentences were in no case carried out. Mitchel escaped with the assistance of P. J. Smyth, and the other prisoners and refugees were pardoned by a general amnesty in '54. Smith O'Brien never again took any part in politics, and died in '64. Sir C. G. Duffy left Ireland and became prime minister of Victoria: M'Manus, after his death, was the unconscious apostle of Fenianism in Ireland; Mitchel was elected a member of parliament, but died before taking his seat; John Martin, P. J. Smyth, and John Dillon, all became members of parliament, and Dr. Kevin Izod O'Doherty, after a successful medical career in Australia, has entered parliament as a follower of Mr. Parnell and a colleague of Mr. John Dillon, the son of John Dillon of '48. The rising of '48 quelled the national movement as utterly as Emmet's rebellion had done five-and-forty years before, and for a time there was nothing heard of disaffection in Ireland.

CHAPTER XXXII.

THE LAND.

The nunger and the fever of the black '47 left a legacy of misery and want to those who survived them. The years which had starved the tenant had utterly ruined the poorer landlords. Rents had been paid in only a small proportion of cases, and in '48 many of the tenants, instead of being able to pay, were dependent on the charity of the landlord. During the famine years the majority of resident landlords had done their utmost to relieve the misery which surrounded them. But, when the famine was past, self interest reasserted itself, and the war between landlord and tenant was waged with renewed vigor. Throughout the country the bitter struggle continued—the tenant keeping a grip on the land by means of intimidation, outrage, and murder; the landlord rack-renting and evicting him with the help of the civil and military resources of the law. From time to time select committees had been appointed to inquire into the condition of Ireland, and almost all these committees reported that the disturbed state of the country was due to the unfortunate nature of the relation between landlord and tenant.

The land question has an importance in Ireland infinitely greater than England, for in Ireland farming is practically the *only* business. This being so, the whole population is thrown on to the land, and there is never the slightest difficulty in getting a tenant. To obtain possession, men are willing to promise to pay impossible rents, and to retain it pay rents which keep them on the verge of starvation. Eviction is the one dread of the Irish tenant, for once evicted he has before him only emigration, the workhouse, or the grave. In 1845 the Devon Commission reported:—"(1.) That all improvements in the soil were made by the tenant; (2.) that these improvements were subject to confiscation, and were confiscated by the landlord; (3.) that the outrage system sprang from the ejectment system; and (4.) that it was necessary for parliament to intervene to compel the landlord to recoup the tenant for his outlay on the land."

Until 1870 the tenant had not even a nominal right to the value of the improvements he had made; the custom of the tenant making the improvements had endured from time immemorial, and consequently a great part of the value of the estate was justly theirs. Yet tenants were liable to be rented on the very improvements that they had made and paid for, and on their eviction these improvements became the property of the landlord. In some cases the improvements raised the value of the property enormously, as on the Clomber estate, which at the end of the last century had had a rent roll of £3,000 a year; whereas in 1850 its annual value was £24,000. The barony of Ferney, too, originally worth £3,000 a-year, was, by tenants' improvements, raised by 1854 to an annual value of £50,000. In the first of these cases seven-eighths of the value of the property was the creation of time and the tenant; and in the second, tenants' improvements had raised the value of the property to nearly seventeen times the original worth; but by eviction the landlord could confiscate the whole of the capital which the tenant had sunk in the soil, and the tenant had no security against eviction. The commonest cause of eviction was non-payment of rent, but in a great many cases the middleman, not the tenant, was the defaulter; yet, in turning out the middleman, the landlord also evicted tillers of the soil; an enormous number of evictions were also made for the purpose of consolidating farms, and some from sheer caprice, religious bigotry, or disobedience to the rules of the estate. In the ten years following the famine Ireland was a land of evictions; during 1851, 257,372 persons emigrated, and in the following year the number rose to 368,372. Between '49 and '56 nearly a million and a half persons left Ireland, and "not far from one in every five of the multitudes who have swarmed across the Atlantic had been driven by positive physical violence from their homes." "There is not," said Mr. John Bright, speaking of the evicting landlords of 1850, "I say there is not a human being in existence who ought to be more generally scouted than the individual who could commit atrocities like those which have been brought before the House."

In estimating the bitterness of feeling caused by rack-renting and eviction, we must therefore keep clearly before our minds, that land to the tenant was a matter of life and death; that by eviction the tenant forfeited his capital; that knowing this the landlord knew he would submit to any increase of rent rather than forfeit his tenure, and that in consequence of the absence of trade in Ireland the demand for land was greatly in excess of the supply. There was, therefore, no freedom of contract between landlord and tenant; by losing his holding the tenant lost his all, and a sentence of eviction was equivalent to a sentence of death. The landlord's view was that the land was his own —a commodity to be sold in the best market. Men who have possessed salt, and corn, and water in times of siege and famine have sometimes traded in the same manner on the necessities of their fellows, and have commonly met with the fate that befell many of the Irish landlords.

On the other hand, it must be admitted that the Irish landlords, in 1848, were placed in an extremely difficult position; the estates of many were deeply mortgaged, and they depended on the rents not only for their subsistence, but for the money wherewith to pay the interest of their encumbrances. Under these circumtsances the temptation to wring the most out of the land was almost irresistible; the system of annual tenancy had bred an idle and stingy method of farming; the repeal of the Corn Laws had ruined the agricultural interest, and it was believed that scientific farming and grazing would yield a better profit. Large farming was the hobby of the day, and for the consolidation of farms a perfect eviction fever set in. On some estates as many as 700 persons were forcibly ejected on a single day. The sick, the aged, the little children, and the women big with child were alike thrust forth under summer sun or the cold snows of winter, and to prevent their return their cabins were unroofed and levelled to the ground. The wailing of the women, the cries of the children, the still more piteous despair of the strong men was such that the constabulary, whose sad duty it was to carry out these ejectments, often wept as bitterly as their victims. Shelter there was none; the few remaining tenants were forbidden to receive the outcasts, and on some estates they were even driven from the shelter of the ditches. The majority, left penniless by the preceding years of famine, wandered aimlessly about roads and bogs till they found a refuge in the workhouse or the grave; others swarmed over to England, and by underselling the market, ousted the English laborer from the harvest field; such as had funds took ship for America. The fate of these poor creatures could but be deplorable; they and their forefathers had lived their lives on the same plot of ground, and their affections, like their capital, were centered in that one spot of earth. Many could speak no English, and these friendless, penniless strangers brought with them to America nothing but an undying hatred of the power that had robbed them and deprived them of their homes. The over-population of Ireland was fast being remedied. In 1841 the population of Ireland had been over eight million; twenty years later it was between five and six. "In a few more years," wrote the *Times*, "a Celtic Irishman will be as rare in Connemara as is the Red Indian on the shores of the Manhattan," and the same organ discovered that by a curious freak of nature Irishmen removed to "the banks of the Ganges, or the Indus—to Delhi, Benares, or Trincomalee—would be far more in their element than in a country to which an inexorable fate had confined them."

But besides the Celtic tenancy there was another class which needed removal, and that was the debt-laden landlords; and in the interests of this class, and in the hope of creating a class of landlords who would make all improvements themselves, the Encumbered Estates Act was passed in 1849. The act provided that a court of commissioners should be established in Dublin, with discretionary power to sell any encumbered estate on the petition of the owner or of any creditor of that estate, and to give the buyer an indefeasible title. Such a measure had long been needed by the Irish landlords, but much of its good was done away with by passing it at a moment when Irish land was a drug in the market. The landlord was now forced by his creditors to pay or quit, and many noble estates were sold at prices which failed even to realize the value of the mortgages, and were resold a few years later for nearly double the sum that the old owners had obtained for them. In its second object, of creating a class of English landlords, the bill failed utterly, for of the 7,489 purchasers who, up to August, '57, availed themselves of the act, only 309 were English, Scotch, or foreigners, and of the twenty millions and a half realized by the court, seventeen and a half millions was Irish capital. Thus the bill did absolutely nothing for the tenant; the new landlords were of the same class as the old, and managed the estates on the old system. The relation of landlord and tenant was unchanged; rackrenting, eviction, and confiscation of tenants' improvements on the one hand was met by outrage, murder, and intimidation on the other.

The Encumbered Estates Act having failed to relieve the tenants, a number of Irishmen founded, in 1850, the Irish Tenant League, for the purpose of securing for the tenantry of the other three provinces the advantages of the Ulster Tenant Right, and at the general election of '52 half the Irish members returned were nominally members of the Tenant League. By this party was founded the policy of "Independent opposition," whereby Irish members unite and form a third party, pledged to uncompromising opposition to every ministry that refuses or delays to settle the Irish land question. But the opposition of the Tenant League party was of short duration, for when, in the following December, Lord Aberdeen was called on to form a ministry, several of the Tenant League party accepted office. The tenant claims were, however, still forwarded by Sharman Crawford, Sir C. G. Duffy, Napier, Poulett Scrope, Shee, J. F. Maguire, Isaac Butt, and George Henry Moore, and various bills were introduced in successive years, but without success. In 1855 Lord Aberdeen resigned, and a Whig ministry was formed, with Palmerston, the bold enunciator that "Tenant Right is Landlord Wrong," as premier.

The prospects of the tenants now went from bad to worse; every measure brought in by the Irish party was defeated by an overwhelming majority; and the government Land Bill of 1860 was so unworkable that it remained a dead letter. The desperate tenantry, abandoned by the law, sought to redress their grievances by the power of Whiteboyism, and in 1862 the outrages reached the number of 363. Since '47 Ireland had been governed by an unbroken series of Coercion Acts, and no further repressive legislation was possible, but the storm of '62 was purely agrarian, and was succeeded by a calm. "Repeal was buried; disaffection had disappeared; nationality was unmentioned; not a shout was raised; not even a village tenant club survived." Evictions proceeded briskly; the surplus population was shipped off by the thousand daily to America; still no voice was raised, no agitator roused the passions of the people. Political agitation being dead, agrarian outrages on the decrease, it seemed to England that Ireland had no further wrongs to be righted, that the Celts were gone, and that in depopulation the government had at last solved the problem of how to govern Ireland peacefully.

CHAPTER XXXIII.

FENIANISM.

BUT there is a quiet that is not peace; a still that is not calm, but the listening hush of expectation. When on a breezy day the wind drops suddenly, and the leaves are still, we know that a storm is brewing, and that soon not only the leaves but the branches will rock wildly to and fro; so, too, the leaders of men and students of human nature should know that when men no longer cry out against hunger, nakedness, and oppression, it is not that discontent has ceased, but that a storm is brewing.

In 1854 a general amnesty pardoned the rebels of '48, and allowed such as wished to return to Ireland to do so. They were received with little enthusiasm, and the government concluded that "Irish disaffection was dead and buried, and would never trouble the English people more" But in truth the '48 leaders were received coolly, not because the people found them too extreme, but because they looked upon them as reactionaries. It must be remembered that the disaffected Irish have always been divided into two distinct and often antagonistic parties; the Separatists and the anti-Unionists. From time to time they have acted together, but at heart they are utterly distinct. In the rebellion of 1641 the old Irish, under Rory O'More and Phelim O'Neill, were Separatists, and the Anglo-Irish, who subsequently made common cause with them, were Home Rulers; but the rebellion of 1641 was mainly Separatist, and its failure turned the scale of national opinion in favor of the Home Rule party for many years to come, and the agitation of Grattan and the Irish volunteers, ending in so-called parliamentary independence, was a Home Rule movement. But the independent parliament failed to secure justice for Ireland, five-sixths of the people still labored under grievous disabilities; land laws were unjust; the poor oppressed by unjux tastation; the government corrupt, and the parliament, filled with a venal crew of placemen, was merely a tool in the hands of an English statesman. The Home Rule policy, therefore, was judged a mistake, and public opinion swung over to the side of the Separatists. The crushing failures of '98 and in 1803 stamped out the Separatist theory, and through the years of the repeal agitation the Separatist party seemed utterly extinguished, but after the famine of '47 some of the Home Rulers developed into Separatists, and on the extinction of the repeal agitation men's minds again turned toward separation. Thus each party was in the ascendant turn and turn about, and the failure of each has alternately turned the hopes of the disaffected Irish into the opposite channel.

The Fenian movement originated among some of the expatriated '48 men and the victims of the famine clearances; it was first called the Phœnix Society, and was introduced into Ireland by Mr. James Stephens in '58, when the army of England was engaged in quelling the Indian mutiny. Stephens was himself a rebel of '48 who had succeeded in escaping to America, and he was a man of great courage, energy, and power of will. Among his first converts was Jeremiah Donovan, a young Skibereen man, who soon afterward improved his name by the prefix O' and the affix Rossa. O'Donovan Rossa was in those days a dashing, popular, enthusiastic youth, and soon induced ninety of the hundred members of the Skibereen club to join this secret society, whose secrecy was so tremendous that its existence was known everywhere, and it was denounced from almost every Catholic altar in the kingdom and in the pages of the *Nation*. The combined action of the priesthood and the press checked the growth of the society; but on December 3d a viceregal proclamation was issued stating that a public danger existed, and a few days later the members of the dying conspiracy were immortalized by arrest. Owing to the unhappy association of law with oppression in Ireland, to arrest a man is to secure him the sympathy of the people, and the Phœnix conspirators, hitherto denounced or ignored, were now the popular heroes. But the affair ended tamely enough; the prisoners pleaded guilty and were released, and there was an end of the Phœnix conspiracy. Meanwhile, under the name of the Irish Revolutionary Brotherhood, the society was growing quickly among the American Irish— the outcasts of the famine clearances; but in Ireland it had two great enemies to contend with; the open policy party were dead against it, and the priesthood used every means in their power to crush it, and had it not been for the M'Manus funeral it might perhaps never have taken root.

M'Manus was one of the '48 leaders who had been convicted and transported to Van Diemen's Land whence he had escaped to San Francisco in 1851, where ten years later he died. He had been by no means one of the most influential of his party in Ireland, but was much beloved in America, and after he had been buried it was resolved to take his body home and lay it in his native earth, and this project was carried out in the autumn of '62. The funeral preparations were made on a scale which surprised every one, and along the whole line from San Francisco to Dublin formed one of the most impressive demonstrations ever seen. The Fenians had managed to get the affair into their hands, and they utilized the funeral, and the feelings and memories it aroused, to the utmost. Till then they had been unable to obtain a firm footing in Ireland, but during the three weeks occupied by the obsequies they established the organization, and swore in great numbers of Fenians. A year later, at a meeting of Irishmen in Chicago, the existence of this society for establishing the independence of Ireland by force of arms was publicly announced, and at the same time a Fenian journal, the *Irish People*, was established in Ireland, under the management of John O'Leary, Thomas Clark Luby, and Charles James Kickham, all men of rare intellectual gifts and high moral character. The object of this paper was to inculcate the doctrine of armed resistance, and to warn the people not to trust in constitutional agitation; for two years the work of organization continued, but in

September, 1865, Luby, O'Leary, Rossa, Kickham, and others were arrested, and a month later Stephens was taken at his own house. Ten days later all Europe rang with the news that the Fenian leader had escaped from Richmond gaol through the connivance of his gaolers, who were Fenians too. For some months he remained in Dublin, but, though huge rewards were offered for him, he was never retaken. In November the other prisoners were arraigned on a charge of treason-felony, and the trials revealed the extent of the movement, which had penetrated to almost every part of Ireland; and no less appalling to the loyal mind was the fact that the prisoners, far from being Whiteboy leaders, were men of education, who bore themselves bravely and like gentlemen. They were all found guilty, and sentenced to penal servitude for terms varying from ten to twenty years. But the action of the government and the imprisonment of the leaders did not check the growth of Fenianism, although internal dissension, the Nemesis of rebellion, was weakening the organiaztion. The American war was over, and Irishmen who had gained a knowledge of military tactics in the armies of North and South swelled the number of the Irish Republican Brotherhood. In 1866 the movement was at its height, the loyal Irish were paralyzed with fear, and in February the Habeas Corpus Act was suspended. This checked the movement. Many of the leaders fled, others were arrested; but in the autumn preparations for rebellion were again set on foot, and large quantities of arms were seized by the coastguards. It is noteworthy that in this year the agrarian outrages sank to 87, the lowest number on record. Early in '67 an attempt at insurrection was made in several parts of Ireland, but owing to the disunion of the Fenians themselves, the vigor of the administration, and the treachery of informers, the rebellion was a fiasco. In England things were more serious, and had it not been for the information of traitors the design to seize Chester Castle and its 20,000 stand of arms might have succeeded. Numerous arrests and convictions followed, but as yet the last was not heard of Fenianism.

On the 18th September two Fenian prisoners were being

conveyed from the Manchester police court to the city gaol. On the way the prison van was stopped by a small body of armed men; the horses were shot, the escort dispersed, and the rescuers called to the constable who sat within to unlock the door. The police officer, Charles Brett, gallantly refused and some one in the crowd called to Allen, the leader of the Fenians, to fire the lock off. Unhappily Brett at that moment had approached his eye to the keyhole to see what was going on outside, and the bullet which had been intended for the door gave him a mortal wound. A woman who was within took the keys from the dead man's pocket, and handed them through the ventilator; the doors were opened, the prisoners escaped, but several arrests were made, and five men were tried for the murder of Brett, found guilty, and sentenced to death. One of the prisoners pleaded that he was not a Fenian and had been arrested in mistake, and so slight was the evidence against him that the press reporters who had been present at the trial, signed a memorial praying for his release, and on further investigation, it was found that his arrest had been a blunder, and the finding of the jury a mistake. Another of the prisoners was spared in consideration of his being an American citizen, but the three, Allen, Larkin, and O'Brien were publicly executed on the 23d November. There could be no doubt that the sentence had been terribly severe; the theory at the time was, that an example must be made to deter others from such feats of reckless daring; but in England, after the first horror at the lawlessness of the deed had died out, much sympathy was felt for the rebels, and Mr. Bright, Mr. John Stuart Mill, and Mr. Swinburne strove, but strove vainly, to save their lives. In Ireland the feeling was, and still is, tremendous; the rescue was looked upon as a valiant and patriotic deed; and, in honor of the "Manchester martyrs," commemorative funerals were organized throughout the country: in Dublin, though the day was wet and cold, 150,000 persons took part in the demonstration. In indignation of what was considered the legal murder of these young men, the Home Rulers and Separatists laid aside their difference, and Mr. A. M.

Sullivan, the denouncer of Fenianism, thus described the funerals:—"As the three hearses bearing the names of the executed men passed through the streets, the multitudes that lined the way fell on their knees, every head was bared, and not a sound was heard save the solemn notes of the 'Dead March in Saul,' from the bands, or the sobs that burst occasionally from the crowd." The Nationalist journals of every shade of thought were violent in denunciation of the "judicial murder," and there can be no doubt that, at best, the execution was a very great blunder. The initials A. L. O'B. are to-day a power to conjure up the forces of disaffection in Ireland, and the ballad, "God save Ireland," written by Mr. T. D. Sullivan in commemoration of their death, has been accepted as the national anthem of disaffected Ireland.

Before the close of 1867, a Fenian outrage of a very different character was to electrify society; on December 13th, a Fenian named Barret placed a barrel of gunpowder close to the outer wall of Clerkenwell gaol, and fired it, with the intention of helping a comrade who was within to escape. The most terrible consequences ensued. One man was killed on the spot; three died from their wounds; forty women were prematurely confined, and twenty of the babes died at their birth; two women went mad, and 120 persons were injured. The stupidity of the crime is the only palliation of its atrocity; had Barret possessed the faintest knowledge of the material he was using, he must have known that, had his comrade been near, he, instead of being rescued, must inevitably have been blown to atoms. The Clerkenwell outrage did more than any measures of government to weaken the Fenian organization. The deed, dastardly as it was, was obviously an imitation of the Manchester rescue; a terrible instance of the results of lawless example, and many an honest patriot who had joined the Fenians withdrew from them, seeing with what manner of men those who join secret societies throw in their lot. Another and unexpected result of the Clerkenwell outrage was that it riveted the attention of English statesmen on Ireland, and convinced them that something must be done for the pacification of the country.

CHAPTER XXXIV.
LOPPING THE UPAS TREE.

"THERE are," said Mr. Gladstone, "three branches to the Irish upas tree; the Established Church, the system of land tenure, and the system of national education." The speech is instinct with the spirit of reform, and indeed, while the Fenian movement was agitating Ireland, and filling a large section of the community with vague alarms, the government were considering what steps should be taken for the pacification of the country. The condition of the Established Church in Ireland was an abuse which called loudly for reformation, and motions for its reform were continually brought before the house. The Church Temporalities Act, passed in 1833, had in a measure reduced the expenses of the Establishment, and the Tithe Commutation Act of 1838 had divested the parson of his hated character of tithe-proctor, and averted the downfall of the Establishment. It may be doubted whether the tenantry reaped any money advantage from either the tithe commutation or the disestablishment; rents were raised to include the tithe, and were not lowered again after the disestablishment, but the State support of a Church which had failed so signally in its mission was a very grave abuse. In March, 1865, Mr. Dillwyn moved: "That in the opinion of this house the present position of the Irish Church Establishment is unsatisfactory, and calls for the early attention of her majesty's government." The home secretary, Sir George Grey, stated that no practical grievance existed; and Mr. Gladstone, without attempting to defend the Establishment on its merits, declared that he did not think the time for parliamentary action had arrived. The debate was finally adjourned and never resumed, and in the next year, Sir John Gray revived the subject with a like result. In 1867 it was again brought forward, and finally in 1868 Mr. Gladstone pronounced that, "in order to the settlement of the question of the Irish Church, that Church as a State Church, must cease to exist." No other Church in the world's history ever occupied such a position as did the Established Church in Ireland. "There is nothing like it," said Sydney Smith, "in Europe, in Asia, in the discovered part of Africa, or in all we have heard of Timbuctoo." "The most utterly absurd and indefensible of all the institutions in the civilized world," said Macaulay; while Brougham and Grey stigmatized it as "the foulest practical abuse that ever existed," and "opposed alike to justice, to policy, and to religious principles."

Reformed by the Tudors, the Established Church was enriched by James I. from the confiscated lands of the Irish chiefs, and as time went on the Church property was increased from various sources, and by the payment of tithes which had never been exacted in Ireland by the Roman Church. But though she increased in wealth, the Anglican Church failed signally in her mission. At the accession of James I. not sixty native Irish had embraced the Anglican faith, but after the civil war of 1641 and the plantation of Cromwell, the Protestants of all denominations were as 45 to 120 Catholics. The penal code had a further reforming influence, and between 1730 and 1784 the Protestants of all denominations were as 60 to 120, but at the beginning of the present century they were only 40 to 120; and the census of 1861 shows that there were then only 30 Protestants to 120 Catholics, a lower percentage than there had been since the protectorate, and in 1866 the members of the Established Church were only ten per cent. of the entire population. In the ten years following the disestablishment the number of Anglicans rose to twelve per cent. In many parishes there was not a single Anglican. "I myself," said Mr. George Henry Moore in 1849, "pay tithe in ten parishes; in the whole of these parishes there is not one church, one glebe, or one single resident clergyman. I am not aware that there is one single Protestant in the whole eight parishes, and I do not believe that divine service according to the Protestant ritual has been celebrated in them since the Reformation." In Limerick diocese there were in 1860 twenty-two parishes with no Anglican, and only three parishes claimed fifteen members of the Established Church. The diocese of Dublin, "the capital of the Pale," contained nineteen parishes with no Anglican resident, and only one parish attained the number of twenty-five; and there were in Ireland 199 parishes which did not contain one single member of the Irish Church. Yet all these parishes paid tithe. The annual income of the Irish Church was £600,000, and of this £400,000 consisted of tithe. Such a church had surely forfeited her right to be called the National Church of Ireland, and to the support of the Irish nation.

On the 23d of March Mr. Gladstone moved that the Established Church of Ireland should cease to exist as an Establishment, and on the 16th of June the bill was read for the third time in the Commons, but a fortnight later it was thrown out by the Lords.

In the following November a general election was held, the first under the new Reform Act, which granted household suffrage to the boroughs of Great Britain, and lowered the borough qualification in Ireland to £4. Not for years had there been an election of such great importance; it was a struggle between Liberal and Tory, not merely a question of the disestablishment of the Irish Church. The Liberals were returned with a great majority, and Mr. Gladstone became premier On the first of March he introduced his bill to disestablish and disendow the Irish Church, and to deprive the Presbyterian Church of the *Regium Donum* (the grant made to that body by William III., and amounting to £45,000), and to deprive Maynooth College of the government grant of £26,000, due regard being had to vested interests. The total value of the Church property and of these grants amounted to £16,000,000, and of this sum £10,840,000 was given back to the Church, the surplus being reserved to be applied in the main to the relief of unavoidable calamity in Ireland. The bill did not pass without a struggle; no one attempted to prove that the Church was the Church of the Irish nation, but the disestablishment was denounced as an act of sacrilege, of confiscation, and as a direct violation of the fifth article of union. But on the 26th of July, 1869, the bill received the royal assent, and on January 1st, 1871, it came into operation.

Having felled the first branch of the upas tree, Mr. Gladstone directed his attention to the second. The Land Act of 1860, which secured for the tenant the value of all improvements made *with the consent of the landlord* had been pronounced, "an invitation to the landlord to dissent," and all parties agreed that it had failed. A new scheme had been brought forward by the government six years later, but they abandoned it, and in '67 the Tories had introduced a measure proposing to appoint a "commissioner of improvement," who should decide between the landlord and the tenant. But both landlord and tenant had opposed the measure and it fell through.

In 1870 Mr. Gladstone brought in that Land Act which was intended (1) to legalize the Ulster custom of selling the tenant right and all customs analogous to it outside Ulster; (2) to secure for the evicted tenant compensation for his improvements, and in certain cases for disturbance; and (3) to promote the establishment of a peasant proprietorship. Unfortunately the bill afforded no security against eviction or the arbitrary raising of rents, and the tenants were legally able to contract themselves out of the benefits of the act, and by the threat of eviction the landlord could coerce them into signing almost any contract he chose to force upon them. Its effect upon eviction was *nil*, for during the three years before the act was passed there were 4,253 ejectments, and in the three years following 5,641, and in the three subsequent years the number rose to 8,438; and in the years '79 to '82 there were over ten thousand evictions. The cause for legalizing the sale of tenant right and establishing a peasant proprietorship fared little better; indeed, owing to the determined opposition of the landlords, the bill broke down utterly, though, when it was passed, it was regarded as a final settlement of the Irish land difficulty.

The question of national education seems at first sight a much simpler one than either disestablishment or the passing of such a Land Bill as that of 1870, yet this third branch of the upas tree proved tougher than either of the others, and the effort to hew it down upset the Gladstone ministry. The condition of intermediate and higher education in Ireland was scandalous; the proportion of Irish boys learning dead or living languages was as two to ten or fifteen in England, and what was worse, the tendency was backward instead of forward, for the number of secondary schools fell between '61 and '71 from 729 to 574.

The system of primary education established by Mr. Stanley (afterwards Lord Derby) in 1831 had in great measure provided for the education of the children of the poor, but though the Anglicans had their university and endowed intermediate schools, nothing had been done for the Catholics till 1845. In that year Sir Robert Peel had passed a measure for the creation of three colleges where no denominational instruction was to be given. These were called the Queen's Colleges, and were established at Cork, Belfast, and Galway, and five years later a university in connection with them was chartered and endowed by the state. At first the proposal had been fairly well received, but in the very year of their foundation, O'Connell bestowed on them the nickname of "The Godless Colleges," and in 1851 the Catholic hierarchy condemned the system. Three years later, a Catholic University was founded under the presidency of Dr. Newman, and though, as it was unchartered, it had no legal power of conferring degrees in arts or laws, it was well attended and supported by public subscription. This was the condition of education in Ireland, when, in 1868, Mr. Gladstone became prime minister. In that year, and the next, and again in 1870, Mr. Fawcett brought forward a measure for abolishing all tests in Trinity College, and finally in 1873, all tests were abolished. But this concession did not satisfy the Catholics, who demanded a chartered and endowed Catholic University. This was refused, on the ground that it would lower the national standard of education, but as a compromise Mr. Gladstone, in February 13th, 1873, brought in a bill for the abolition of Queen's University and Dublin University, and the creation of one central university, to which Trinity College, the Catholic University, and other Catholic colleges, and the Queen's Colleges at Belfast and Cork were to be affiliated. Galway Queen's College had collapsed and was to be abandoned. The new foundation was to include no professorial chairs in theology, moral philosophy, or modern history, and a part of the endowments of Trinity College was to be devoted to its support. The proposal satisfied neither Catholics, Anglicans, nor dissenters; and, indeed, a system of education which excluded modern history, moral philosophy and theology, must have been so deficient as to diminish the value of degrees. The bill was thrown out on second reading by a majority of 287 to 284 and the Liberal administration was practically overthrown.

The ministers resigned, but Mr. Disraeli declined to accept office with the existing House of Commons, and the Liberals remained in office till the following January, when Mr. Gladstone dissolved parliament. The Conservatives were then returned by a large majority. We may anticipate matters a little by saying that in 1878 Mr. Disraeli secured £1,000,000 of the surplus fund of the disestablished Church for the benefit of intermediate education in Ireland, and in 1879 he introduced and passed a measure abolishing Queen's University and establishing an Examining Board, with power to confer degrees on approved candidates from any place of education. The Senate of the new establishment was also empowered to create exhibitions, prizes, scholarships, and fellowships, for which the funds were to be supplied by parliament. The foundation of the "Royal University" is the most recent educational measure passed for Ireland. In 1882 1,688 and in 1883 2,095 persons passed through its examinations. But the institution of an Examining Board has not supplied the need for a Catholic University, and it is probable that the last word has yet to be spoken on the subject of education in Ireland.

CHAPTER XXXV.
THE HOME RULE MOVEMENT.

WHILE the Land Act of 1870 was still being debated in the Commons, a meeting of Irishmen of various creeds and shades of political opinion was held in Dublin, for the purpose of forming an organization to promote the cause of local self-government for Ireland. The disestablishment of the Irish Church had removed one of the great objections of Irish Anglicans to repeal of the union, and so it came that many members of "The Home Rule League" were Protestants, and Isaac Butt, a Protestant barrister, became their leader. The movement took hold and increased in popularity, and at the general election of 1874 fifty-one Home Rule members were returned to the imperial parliament, under the leadership of Mr. Butt. The demand of the Home Rule members was very simple; they asked for a local government for local affairs, bearing the same relation to the imperial parliament at Westminister that the senate of each state of the American Union bears to the congress at Washington. The party, however, under the leadershship of Mr. Butt, did not agitate very actively for repeal; once a year they brought forward a Home Rule motion, and once a year they were out-voted, and their energies were chiefly concentrated on the land question. Already in 1871, it had been found that the Land Bill had failed to legalize the Ulster custom, and a short act had been introduced by lord Cairns, providing that in the case of any proceedings in the Landed Estates Court the rights of the tenants under the act of 1870 should remain valid, even in cases where they were not specified or referred to in the conveyance,. The next move came from the landlord party. In 1872 viscount Lifford appealed against the judgment of the Land Court. His appeal was dismissed, and he subsequently moved for a committee to inquire into the working of the bill. The committee deliberated, but no change was made in the working of the act. This brings us down to the general election of 1874. In the following year Mr. Sharman Crawford, son of Mr. Sharman Crawford of tenant-right celebrity, stated, on behalf of the Ulster farmers, that since the passing of the act attempts to destroy the right of free sale had been made by the northern landlords, who had drawn up new office rules and made new agreements, which utterly destroyed the tenant-right and the advantages obtained by the Land Act. As the law then stood, the onus of proof in cases of disputed tenant-right rested with the tenant. He had *primâ facie* to show that the right of selling the goodwill existed on the estate in question; and by his amendment, Mr. Crawford proposed to shift the onus of proof to the landlord. The bill was opposed by the government, and thrown out by a majority of two to one.

The tenants of the south now took up the agitation, and as their representative, Mr. Butt brought in a bill, on the lines now familiar as the "Three F's." On behalf of this measuure, Mr. Butt remarked that the Irish land question could be settled only by measures giving the tenant security of tenure, and that to effect this the landlord must be deprived of the power of arbitrary eviction. "I propose," he continued, "that every tenant shall have permission to claim from the chairman of his county the benefit of his improvements, and if he does that, I propose that a certificate shall be given him protecting him against eviction. That will, in point of time, establish a perpetuity of tenure. The great difficulty in anything of this kind is to get a tribunal which will fairly value the land. I confess it is a difficulty which I have found very hard to meet. The idea of a valued rent seems to be getting largely hold of some of the landlords, and I see that some of them suggest the valuation should be fixed by a government valuer. . . . It is, however, the most difficult thing in the world to find a tribunal to which you can entrust this task. I therefore propose, by this bill, that the landlord and tenant should each select one arbitrator, and the two arbitrators thus appointed shall agree on a third. In cases where the landlord should not appear, I suggest that the rent should be assessed by a jury composed of three special and three common jurors." These, Mr. Butt said, were the main provisions of the bill by which he sought to secure for the tenant fixity of tenure, fair rent, and free sale of tenant right; and it was upon a modification of these lines that the Land Act of 1881 was drawn up, but in '76 the bill was rejected by 290 against 56.

In the preceding year, at the death of Mr. John Martin, a new and very important figure had appeared on the political stage. After the conviction of Mitchel for treason-felony in '48, John Martin had published and edited a seditious newspaper called *The Irish Felon*. In his turn, Martin, too, had been convicted, but had been releasd in '54. Four years later he had returned to Ireland, and in '71 had been elected member for Meath. At the general election, three years later, he was re-elected, but in March, '75, he died, and was succeeded by Mr. Charles Stewart Parnell. At first Mr. Parnell attracted little attention in the House of Commons, but in '77 he led a little band of advanced Home Rulers, who, by a system of ingenious obstruction, tried to prevent the introduction of government measures at late hours of the night. In the meanwhile, the annual Home Rule debate still expressed the protesting acquiescence of the Irish nation in the union, and Mr. Crawford yearly introduced his amendment to the Land Bill, but on each occasion it was withdrawn, out-voted, or talked out. Mr. Butt's programme of the "Three F's" commanded a little more attention; it was brought forward again in '78, and thrown out on the second reading, and immediately after Mr. Butt's death in May, '79, Mr. Shaw, who succeeded him as Home Rule leader, brought it for the last time before the notice of the house.

It was imperative that something should be done for the rural population of Ireland. The two preceding summers had been disastrously cold and wet· the crops had not ripened either in England or Ireland, and even the better class of farmers were terribly pinched, in '77 the potatoe crop alone had fallen from £12,400,000 to £5,200,000, and in '78 it fell to £3,000,000. During the session the subject of Irish distress was frequently brought before the house, and in May Mr. O'Connor Power warned the house that "if parliament did not come forward within a reasonable time with some measure calculated to relieve the depression of the present state of agriculture in Ireland, scenes would arise in Ireland that would be far more dangerous to the rights of property, and to the order and tranquility which should prevail in that country, than any that Ireland had been afflicted with in her long struggle with the ignorance if not the incompetency of the English parliament," and at the same time Mr. Parnell announced that the land question "was one which would have to be taken up by the Irish members in a firm and determined manner."

On the whole, parliament was disposed to take little notice of these representations of the distress in Ireland, which were regarded by the government, and by Mr. James Lowther, the Irish secretary, in particular, as a dishonest attempt to fan the flames of the Home Rule agitation. But the statement of Sir Stafford Northcote that the total value of the principal crop, which in the bad season of '78 had been £32,758,000, had further decreased to £22,743,000, revealed the truth of the Home Rule representations. Meanwhile, the number of evictions for non-payment of rent was increasing rapidly, and the peasantry were resisting them with their old weapons of Whiteboyism and outrage As early as April, '78, the *Times* had declared that there was "a reign of terror on the borders of Mayo, Galway, and Roscommon." Since then another bad season had brought an increase of distress both in England and Ireland. The bad seasons afflicted English landlords and tenants. All over the country the farmers were declaring themselves unable to pay, and the landlords offered abatements, and in many cases forewent their rents altogether. It was impossible to the English farmer to pay, and it was doubly so to the Irish small peasant farmer. Yet many of the large absentee landlords demanded their rents, and ejected those who were unable to pay them; and in June, 1879, Mr. Parnell and Mr. O'Connor Power began a no-rent agitation in Mayo. Mr. Parnell, who had begun as a disciple of the "Three F's," had now adopted a more advanced programme. The principle of the "Three F's" would work well enough in seasons of good or average harvest, but in case of a continuance of bad years it afforded no protection to the tenant, who would be unable to pay what was in ordinary times a fair rent, and who, from the temporary depreciation in the value of land, would in such seasons get little or nothing for his privilege of free sale of the tenant-right. In seasons of distress there are but two securities for the farmer: the one, a landlord who regarded his tenantry as working partners in a business in which he himself is capitalist and sleeping partner, and, as such, liable to bear his share of the loss occasioned by trade depression; the other, that the cultivator should be the owner of the soil. Mr. Parnell adopted the latter as the solution of the land problem.

Meanwhile, an inevitable breach had grown up between the two sections of Home Rulers. The anger of the Irish Anglicans at the disestablishment of the Church had cooled down, and the moderate Home Ruler of 1879 was more moderate than he had been eight years ago; while the advanced party, perceiving that the policy of Mr. Butt and Mr. Shaw had done nothing to advance their cause, resolved on a more active policy, and a series of meetings were announced to promote the cause of Home Rule. The first of these was held at Limerick on the last day of August, and throughout September and October Sunday meetings were held in various parts of the country; and at the end of the latter month the Irish National Land League came very quietly and unobtrusively into existence.

CHAPTER XXXVI.
THE LAND LEAGUE.

During the autumn of '79, Mr. Parnell became the accepted leader of the Irish parliamentary party, and as such he was chosen president of the Land League, but the idea of such a league had originated with the ex-Fenians. "The Fenians," wrote John Devoy in the August of '79, "saw only a green flag, but the men of to-day have discovered that there is such a thing as the land," and it was with Devoy and Michael Davitt, a released Fenian convict, that the idea of a Land League originated. All through the summer of '79, the Home Rule party and Mr. Davitt had been holding separate land meetings, but eventually they combined. To every man, no matter what his views, it was clear that something must be done for the settlement of the land question, and Mr. Parnell was as convinced as Mr. Davitt of the impossibility of an adjustment between the landlords and tenants. "One of them must go," he said some months later," and it is easier to remove the few than the many." He saw, moreover, that the necessity of protecting the interest of the landlord class would prevent the English government granting Home Rule so long as that class existed as a class; it seemed to him that, the land difficulty once settled, the chief obstacle to Home Rule would be removed. In the meantime the distress increased; a wet summer had been followed by a wet autumn; starvation was very near; there was neither money nor food, and funds for the relief of distress were established in Dublin by the duchess of Marlborough, wife of the lord lieutenant, and by the lord mayor; and in New York by Mr. Bennett of the *New York Herald*.

The tenants on many estates were dependent for their daily food on these charities, yet some of the largest landlords exacted their rent, and evicted those who could not pay it. The Land League organized a combination to resist the payment of any rent higher than the tenants felt themselves justly able to pay while the famine continued, and on the 19th of November, Mr. Davitt and two others were arrested for seditious speeches made at a Land League meeting seventeen days earlier. But the great meeting of the year was one convened at Balla, in Mayo, in connection with an eviction. The meeting was organized into a national protest aginst famine ejectments, and thousands of people assembled from all parts of the country. The police assembled to do their work, and the multitude, quivering with indignation and excitement, awaited in the bitter cold the appearance of the evicting officer. Had he come among the people, whose passions were roused, none can tell what might have happened. Happily he did not appear, and the only incident of the Balla meeting was an impassioned address from Mr. Brennan to the Irish constabulary, entreating them to remember that they and the tenantry were united by ties of class, and often of blood, and which resulted in lodging Mr. Brennan in gaol.

The Land League once fairly started, Mr. Parnell resolved on a tour, political and charitable, through the States of America, and accordingly, toward the close of December, he and Mr. John Dillon started as emissaries of the Land League. The absence of these gentlemen in America, of the parliamentary party in London, and the imprisonment of Mr. Davitt and others, had a damping effect on the agitation, and while the Irish members were engaged on the Relief of Distress Bill in Westminister, the evictions were being gone on with and resisted in the old manner. But there was at this time much more threatening than outrage, and though there had been four thousand evictions in '79, Mr. Gladstone was able, at the end of March, 1880, to congratulate the country on its freedom from outrage. But order was maintained by force, and in the six first months of '80 three thousand three hundred police and one hundred and seven officers were employed in protecting process servers in the west riding of Galway alone. On the 8th March lord Beaconsfield announced his intention of appealing to the country, and prominent among the causes which induced him to do so was the condition of Ireland. In his final official letter he vehemently denounced the Home Rule party, and in consequence of this denunciation the Irish vote in England was given exclusively to the Liberals. The result of the election was a Liberal triumph: the Conservatives who, at the last election, had mustered 351, now returned only 243 members, and the Liberals gained 99 seats, their number rising from 250 to 349. The Home Rulers gained nine seats, and numbered 60 in the new parliament. At this change of government the hopes of the Irish party ran high. The

Liberals were known to be in favor of remedial legislation; the Peace Preservation Act was allowed to lapse, and Mr. W. E. Forster, who had always interested himself in the condition of Ireland, and had played a noble part in the Quaker commission during the famine of '49, was appointed chief secretary.

On the opening of the new parliament the Irish members called for immediate legislation on the land question, but Mr. Forster, while admitting the necessity, affirmed that there was no time to deal with the matter during that session. The Irish members then moved for an interim bill to stop evictions until the promised Land Bill should be passed. This was refused, but as a soothing measure a Compensation for Disturbance clause was added to the Relief of Distress Bill. This Compensation for Disturbance Act authorized county court judges in Ireland to allow compensation to tenants evicted for non-payment of rent in cases where the bad seasons could be proved to be the cause of their insolvency. The bill did nothing to prohibit evictions, and therefore did not satisfy the wishes of the Irish party; still, such as it was, they accepted it thankfully. But in England the bill met with the most violent opposition, and when the Lords rejected it by a majority of 203 the government did not move further in the matter. The number of evictions ran up quickly; the landlords fearing some kind of prohibitory clauses in the expected Land Bill made the most of the little time that remained to them; the Land Leaguers begged for some kind of legislation to check the evictions, but none was given, and the distress and disturbance increased. The news of the rejection of the bill produced something like revolt in Ireland; there were riots at evictions; "land grabbers" (tenants who had taken the farms of evicted occupiers) were attacked, their ricks burned and their cattle maimed; in a word, the peasantry were once more having recourse to their old weapon of Whiteboyism. The speeches of the leaders, too, grew much more violent, the people were advised to resist eviction and excessive rents, and to punish eviction and land grabbing by the process now familiar as "boycotting." This terrible weapon was not a Land League manufacture: it is the principle of all exclusive dealing and, in a modified form, has been used in all ages. In justice to the Land League leaders, it must also be admitted that they did not advocate boycotting until the government, by refusing to step in and stop evictions, had thrown the people back on their own resources; and till the peasanty, seeing nothing but outrage to defend them from that sentence of eviction which Mr. Gladstone himself declared to be equivalent to a sentence of death, had once more taken up their old weapon. The number of outrages, and in especial the brutal maiming of cattle increased, and it was at this juncture that Mr. Parnell, in the celebrated Ennis speech, first recommended boycotting—"If you refuse to pay unjust rents, if you refuse to take farms from which others have been evicted, the land question must be settled, and settled in a way that will be satisfactory to you. Now, what are you to do to a tenant who bids for a farm from which another has been evicted? You must shun him on the roadside when you meet him—you must shun him in the shop—you must shun him in the fair green, and in the market place, and in the place of worship; by leaving him severely alone, by putting him in a moral Coventry; by isolating him from the rest of his countrymen as if he were the leper of old, you must show him your detestation of the crime he has committed."

Three days later this sentence was put into execution against the agent of lord Erne, Captain Boycott, who had refused the rent offered by the tenants, and had issued ejectment processes. On September 22d, the process server went forth, but he was forced by the tenantry to retreat, and on the next day Captain Boycott "was left severely alone." Not a stable boy, not a maid servant, not a harvester would remain in his service—not a shopkeeper would sell to him, nor a laundress wash for him; his isolation was complete, and meanwhile his crops stood high and white, and ungathered. In his necessity the Ulster Orangemen took pity on him, and eventually fifty men under an escort of 7,000 military and police saved the crops at a government cost of 1s. for every pound of potatoes and every turnip that was saved; and the harvest over, Captain Boycott and his men went off to Dublin. The affair caused an enormous sensation, the more so because Captain Boycott had always been well liked; and indeed he must have understood that the resentment was not against his person but his action, for he has long since gone back to Lough Mask, and regained his popularity. The success of the experiment encouraged the Leaguers to boycott Mr. Bence Jones, and after this time boycotting became the great instrument of the Land League. But the hopes of its founders that it would supersede agrarian crime were falsified, for while Captain Boycott was isolated, Lord Mountmorres was shot dead; and though the total number of murders throughout the year was only five or six, there was an enormous increase of such outrages as houghing cattle and sending threatening letters; indeed, though the outrages were milder in their nature than in previous outbreaks, the number was enormously greater than in any preceding year, and by December it was known that Mr. Forster had become an advocate of coercion.

There were no two opinions as to the disturbed state of the country; but while the Land Leaguers attributed the disorganization to distress and evictions, the government set down the disorder to the score of the Land League, and in December the principal officials of the League were indicted on a charge of conspiracy to prevent the payment of rents. The trial, which lasted nineteen days, ended in the disagreement of the jury, two being for a conviction and ten for an acquittal; and at the meeting of parliament in January, 1881, Mr. Forster demanded exceptional legislation, as the administration of the law had utterly broken down, and government accordingly signified their intention of passing the Coercion Bill before dealing with the land question. The Coercion Bill was a stringent one. It empowered the Irish government to arrest and imprison, without trial, and for no specified period, any person reasonably suspected of treason, treason-felony, or the commission of crimes of intimidation, or incitement thereto. The act was also retrospective in its action, so that any person who had in the past incited to non-payment of rent, or boycotting, would be liable to its action. It was to be accompanied by an Arms Bill. But it was less the Coercion Act itself than the fact that it obtained priority over the Land Act that incensed the Irish members. There were 40,000 families in Ireland liable to eviction, and if nothing was done to prevent the ejectment of these persons, remedial legislation late in the year would be of little use. The increase in outrages, argued the Land Leaguers, is due, not to the influence of the League, but to the fact that the harvest has been reaped, and the people, in their desperate necessity, are determined to keep it. To the charge that the League might have checked the number of outrages, the Leaguers answered, with some show of reason, that if government, with 25,000 soldiers and 14,000 police, had failed to do so, it was not in a position to twit the Land League with a similar failure. With regard to the houghing of cattle, the Leaguers represented that this abominable outrage had been practiced for centuries, and against this, night visiting, and the cowardly practice of sending threatening letters, the League had exerted its influence to the utmost, and the organization claimed for itself that it had in a measure superseded them by the system of boycotting. The real aim of the Coercion Act, said the Land Leaguers, is not to put down outrages, but to destroy the power of the League, and the League, and the League only, has kept the roof-tree over many families. The action of the organization has made evictions almost impossible west of the Shannon, and it is only by staying evictions that order can be maintained in Ireland. If the Coercion Act succeeds in breaking the power of the League, the effect will be, not to decrease the number of outrages, but to increase them tenfold. The position of the government is, said the Land Leaguers, untenable. Mr. Forster himself had admitted in the preceding spring that evictions, even for the non-payment of rent, must not be left to the discretion of the landlords, and Mr. Gladstone had said that a sentence of eviction was equivalent to a sentence of death. The Compensation for Disturbance Bill had been an acknowledgment that, in the opinion of government, the tenants needed protection, and now, instead of granting them that protection, the government is attempting to destroy the very organization which alone has protected the tenants from wholesale evictions. Let the government pass an act preventing evictions, and there will be no need of coercion; let them reform the land laws, and the Land League will cease to exist. Had the bill been aimed, not against the League, but against crime, the leaders declared they would have met it in a different spirit; but as matters were, they would feel it their duty to resist the measure to the utmost. What guarantee had they that the proposed Land Bill would be such as they could accept; and, even if it met their views, who could say that it might not meet with the fate of the Compensation for Disturbance Bill?

But if the Irish members felt it their duty to oppose the bill, English members on both sides of the house were no less convinced of the necessity of going on with the measure, and each stage was fought out with intense resistance and bitterness. The obstruction of the Irish members was such that the debate on the address had lasted eleven nights; the debate on the first reading of the bill occupied five nights, and was only closed by the *coup d' état* of the Speaker, who, after a sitting of forty-one hours, declined to call upon any more members to speak, and called on the house to decide at once on the first reading. But the back of the obstruction was not broken. The debate on the second reading occupied four nights; the bill took ten nights to pass through committee, and the third reading occupied two. It finally passed the Commons on February 25th, and on March 2d received the royal assent. Directly the Coercion Act left the Commons, government introduced an Arms Bill, but this went through its stages more rapidly, and became law soon after the Coercion Act.

In the meantime the excitement was increasing in Ireland; Michael Davitt had been arrested early in February for infringing the conditions of his ticket-of-leave, and soon afterward the Ladies' Land League sprang into existence. As soon as the Coercion Acts were passed, Mr. John Dillon returned to Ireland, and continued his work of speech-making and Land League organizing, precisely as though there were no Coercion Act in existence. Early in May he was arrested and imprisoned, and about the same time Father Eugene Sheehy, of Kilmallock, was also arrested, but with these exceptions the government attacked the less important men. Early in April the promised Land Bill was brought in, and as its provisions will occupy a separate chapter, I shall merely state here that it became law on August 22d. The business of the session was now over, and the Irish leaders returned to Ireland to begin an autumn campaign, for the Land Bill, drawn up on the lines of the "Three F's," did not satisfy Mr. Parnell's views. The country was far more disorganized than during the preceding autumn; the Coercion Act had as yet failed to pacify the country. In August Mr. Dillon was released, as his life was endangered by the close confinement; a few weeks later Father Sheehy was also liberated. For a time it seemed as though the government intended abandoning the Coercion Act, but in the beginning of October Mr. Gladstone at Leeds made a hot attack on Mr. Parnell, and on the 13th Mr. Parnell, Mr. Dillon, Mr. Sexton, Mr. O'Kelly, Mr. William O'Brien and Mr. Quinn were arrested and taken to Kilmainham Gaol. Arrest followed arrest, the less important men were conveyed to gaol in batches, and a few days later the imprisoned leaders issued a manifesto calling on the people to retaliate on the government by paying no rent while the leaders were imprisoned. That was the death-blow of the Land League; the mandate was not obeyed, and was universally condemned by the clergy. But to the government the manifesto was an unmixed boon, for it justified them in proclaiming the Land League as an illegal society. Thus was the organization crushed, and government having made a clean sweep of the leaders, set to the task of re-establishing law and order in Ireland.

CHAPTER XXXVII.
THE LAND ACT.

WHEN the general election of 1880 brought the Liberals into power, the failure of the Land Bill of 1870 had long been an acknowledged fact, and one of the first acts of the new government was to appoint a royal commission to inquire into the working of the Land Act. The report of the commission was to the effect that the Land Bill had failed to effect any reform in the system of land tenure; it had not checked the unreasonable increase of rent, nor lessened evictions; and by a rise of rent immediately before a sale, the landlord had been able to render the tenant right worthless. "Some landlords," wrote the commissioners, "who previously were content to take low rents, appear to have began a system of rack-renting when the Land Act was passed, either because they judged that their former forbearance was not suitable to the new relations which legislation had established between themselves and their tenants, or because the profits of agriculture were just then high, or because the high price fetched by the tenant right, under the stimulus of the satisfaction engendered by the passing of the act, made them think that they had hitherto been mistaken in letting the lands so cheaply. . . . On some estates, and particularly on some recently acquired, rents have been increased, both before and since the Land Act, to an extensive degree, not only as compared with the value of the land, but so as to absorb the tenant's own improvements. A thorough and very general change," continued the report, "in the system of land tenure is imperatively required—such a change as shall bring home to the tenants a sense of security, shall guard them against undue increase of rent, and shall render them no longer liable to the apprehension of arbitrary disturbance, and shall give them full security for their improvements." This was, in fact, a recommendation to the government to take up Mr. Butt's rejected programme of the "Three F's," and to grant what the tenants had demanded ten years earlier. The Land Bill of '70 had reserved to the landlord the power to fix and raise rents at his own discretion, to evict his tenants under any circumstances, subject to a fine for arbitrary disturbance, and to absorb the tenants' improvements by paying damages for so doing. The fundamental principle of the Land Act of 1881 was the creation of a Land Court by which all disputes between landlord and tenant might be decided. Appeal to this court was to be optional; any tenant could go before the court and demand to have his rent fixed, and this judicial rent was to last for fifteen years, during which no rise of rent was possible, and no eviction save for non-payment of rent or other breach of contract could take place. In case of the tenant wishing to sell the good-will of his holding, he could do so, but to the landlord was reserved the privilege of preëmption at the price fixed by the court as the value of the tenant. The court which was also to perform the functions of a land commission, was to consist of three members, of whom one was always to be a judge or ex-judge of the supreme court: it was also empowered to appoint sub-commissioners to hear applications and fix fair rents. The action of the act was to be retrospective in cases where ejectment proceedings had been begun but not completed, and by an amendment it was subsequently empowered to quash leases drawn up since '70, in which the aims of the bill had been defeated. But the events which had produced so great a change in English public opinion as to render it even possible that such a bill as this could become law, had produced a corresponding advance in Irish demands, and the Land Bill, which ten years earlier would have satisfied the utmost claims of the Home Rule party, now received only their very cold approval. Mr. Parnell had already announced as his opinion that the land should belong to the cultivators, and that he intended to get it for them at as small a price as possible. "If we could get it for noth-

THE LAND ACT. 193

ing at all," he had continued, "the price the farmers have been paying for it for generations would be ample compensation," and it was well known that Messrs. Davitt and Dillon were also in favor of a project for buying out the landlords.

The Nationalists therefore accepted the bill only as a half measure; they never pretended to think it would satisfy the demands of the Irish farmer, nor did they themselves consider it a final adjustment of the land question; indeed, while it was in progress, Mr. Parnell described it as a "bill brought forward by the government in order to prop up for a few years longer the expiring system of landlordism." But though the Nationalists accepted the bill without enthusiasm or gratitude, they desired to render it as useful as possible, and Mr. T. M. Healy distinguished himself by his mastery of the details of the measure, and the construction of the famous "Healy Clause," by which the valuation of improvements made by the tenants are excluded in estimating the amount to be fixed as a judicial fair rent. But if the bill was too moderate to satisfy the representatives of the tenant class, its socialistic tendency laid it open to the denunciations of the landlords, by whom it was stigmatized as revolutionary, a measure of communism, of robbery, and an infringement of the rights of property. The bill, in fact, was a compromise. By depriving the landlord of the power of fixing the value of his own property, of ejecting his tenant, and by acknowledging that some part of the value of the property was the just possession of the tenant, the bill practically conceded that, in the opinion of the government, the Irish landlords had exceeded their rights; that land was not an ordinary article of commerce; that the tenant was joint proprietor; and that the tenantry needed some effectual protection against the rapacity of the landlords. The bill was also opposed on the score of dangerous precedent, and it was argued that the farmers of Great Britain would shortly clamor for the measure of land reform that had been granted to the Irish tenantry. The plain answer to this was that the conditions and system of tenure in Ireland were utterly distinct from those of Great Britain, even admitting that land reform was greatly needed in the larger island. In spite, however, of all opposition, the bill passed through the Commons on July 29th, but after its sojourn in the Lords it was sent back, amended out of all likeness to its original self. The Commons restored its essential provisions, but once more the Lords returned it with the objectionable alterations. Once more the Commons reconsidered the measure and sent it back to the Lords, who now finally accepted the bill as it was, and on August 22d it became law, and came into immediate operation.

There was a tremendous rush of tenantry into the courts, and between August, 1881, and August, 1882, there were 75,807 applications to have a fair rent fixed. The court was blocked; during the year it had only disposed of 15,676 cases, and had still 60,131 applications to consider. Besides these cases there were nearly 1,500 applications in the county courts, and in other cases rents were fixed by mutual agreement between landlord and tenant, resulting in a reduction of about 20 per cent. all round. "Altogether," says Mr. Barry O'Brien, "during the three years ending August 21st, 1884, fair rents were fixed by the Land Court in 70,127 cases, the rental having been reduced, in round numbers, from £1,407,465 to £1,133,174. or 19.4 per cent. Within the same period fair rents were fixed by the county courts in 6,387 cases, the rental having been reduced from £96,121 to £75,849, or 21 per cent. Besides these there were 66,815 cases in which rents were fixed between landlord and tenant under the authority of the land courts, the rental having been reduced from £1,139,453 to £994,451, or 17.1 per cent.; 5,759 cases in which rents were fixed in the same way under the authority of the county courts, the rental having been reduced from £97,316 to £80,319, or 19.4 per cent.; 339 cases in which rents were fixed by valuers under the land courts, the rental having been reduced from £9,033 to £8,091, or 10.4 per cent.; and 12 cases in which rents were fixed by arbitration, the rental having been reduced from £908 to £660, or 27.2 per cent."

No stronger case for the justice of the tenants' claim

could be made out, for in the cases submitted to it, the court decided that the rents averaged 20 per cent. above what was fair. Still the Irish farmer does not accept even these reductions as final. In the present depressed state of agriculture the fair rent of 1881 is excessive rent in the winter of '85-'86. The English landlord is offering reductions of 20, 25, and in some cases even 40 or 50 per cent. off rents which have always been acknowledged by the tenant to be fair. The Irish landlord has in many cases refused any abatement. Ejectment notices have been served in great numbers: on one single day 500 were posted on the door of one country church. At Killarney quarter sessions 250 ejectment notices were disposed of on the 7th January, 1886. "The judge said it was the most painful day he ever experienced in giving so many ejectment decrees, and he hoped that such a state of things would not exist long." And although the weather was the most severe that had been known for years, and snow covered the ground to the depth of several inches, many evictions were carried out. With whomsoever the fault may lie, the land question cannot be considered settled when eviction, boycotting, and outrage are matters of daily occurrence. The Land Bill of 1881 has no more settled thel and question than did its predecessors of 1860 and 1870, and on this subject the last word has yet to be spoken.

CHAPTER XXXVIII.
IRELAND UNDER THE CRIMES ACT.

FIVE months after the suppression of the Land League, the government resolved on a change of policy, and turned its attention once more toward healing measures. The Coercion Act was the most stringent that had been passed since the union; it had destroyed liberty of the press, freedom of speech, and had imprisoned 918 persons without trial, and in many cases without even letting them know the offences with which they were charged. But these drastic measures, far from pacifying the country, had brought it to the very verge of civil war, and outrages increased in number and atrocity. The imprisonment of the "constitutional" agitators had given the country over to secret societies, and though Mr. Forster knew it not, a band of assassins dogged his steps, and his life was preserved only by a series of accidents little short of miraculous. The condition of the country throughout the winter of 1881-82 was truly appalling; there were no inflammatory speeches, no seditious prints, yet lawlessness increased and was only equalled by the wide-spread distress. The landlords, hard [pressed for money, and many of them with heavy mortgage interests to pay, clamored for their rent; the tenants, unable to pay, abandoned by government, deprived of the advice and support of their leaders, took desperate revenge on land grabbers, process servers, and evicting landlords. These outrages steeled the hearts of the landlords, and so throughout the miserable winter the old story of "brutal repression followed by savage retaliation" was told in a hundred different ways. Early in the year, Mr. Parnell drafted an Arrears Bill and sent it out of prison to Mr. John Redmond. This bill proposed to wipe out the inevitable arrears of rent which had accumulated during the bad summers of 1878 and 1879, and which entangled the smaller farmers in a mesh of hopeless difficulty. The measure was favorably criticised by Mr. Gladstone, and it soon became evident that a milder policy was about to be adopted toward Ireland. On the 30th of April a letter from Mr. Parnell to Captain O'Shea was shown by that officer to Mr. Forster and other members of the government, and in consequence of the opinions stated in it the ministry determined on releasing Mr. Parnell and his colleagues. It is this letter which forms the basis of the famous Kilmainham Treaty, and the important passages are as follows:—"I desire to impress upon you the absolute necessity of a settlement of the arrears question which will leave no recurring sore connected with it behind, and which will enable us to show the smaller tenantry that they have been treated with justice and some generosity. . . . If the arrears question be settled upon the line indicated by us, I have every confidence—a confidence shared by my colleagues—that the exertions which we should be able to make, strenuously and unremittingly, would be effective in stopping outrages and intimidation of all kinds. As regards permanent legislation of an ameliorating character, I may say that the views which you always shared with me as to the admission of leaseholders to the fair rent clauses of the act are more confirmed than ever. So long as the flower of the Irish peasantry are kept outside the act there cannot be the permanent settlement of the land question which we all so much desire. I should also strongly hope that some compromise might be arrived at this session with regard to the amendment of the tenure clauses of the Land Act. It is unnecessary for me to dwell upon the enormous advantages to be derived from the full extension of the purchase clauses, which now seem practically to have been adopted by all parties. The accomplishment of the programme I have sketched out to you would, in my judgment, be regarded by the contry as a practical settlement of the land question, and would, I feel sure, enable us to co-operate cordially for the future with the Liberal party in forwarding Liberal principles; and I believe that the government, at the end of the session, would from the state of the country feel themselves thoroughly justified in dispensing with future coercive measures."

Immediately on the receipt of this letter the suspects were released. Lord Cowper and Mr. Forster resigned, and were replaced by lord Spencer and lord Frederick Cavendish; and on May 6th Mr. Davitt was released from Portland prison, but on that very day lord Frederick Cavendish and the under secretary, Mr. Burke, were murdered in Phœnix Park. Never since the murder of Mr. Percival in the lobby of the House of Commons had any event caused so great horror. The motive of the crime was not known, but it seemed a direct answer to the proclamation of a policy of conciliation. Eventually it was discovered that Mr. Burke, who was a permanent official, had been marked out as a victim by the assassination society which had so long dogged the steps of Mr. Forster, and that lord Frederick Cavendish had been killed only because he did not desert his comrade. But the immediate effect of the Phœnix Park murder was to bring the policy of conciliation to a close before it was a week old, and another Coercion Bill was introduced at once. This bill was even more stringent than its forerunner. Its main provisions were to allow trial by three judges without jury, to legalize the right of search by day or night in a proclaimed district, to sanction the arrest without warrant of any person found prowling about after dark, to revive the Alien Act giving power to arrest and remove from the country foreigners who might be considered dangerous to the public peace, to punish intimidation with summary imprisonment, to empower the government to seize newspapers inciting to crime, and to authorize the viceroy to deal with unlawful assemblies by a court of summary jurisdiction consisting of two resident magistrates. The bill was resisted by the Parnellites as passionately as its forerunner had been, but it eventually became law, though some of its most stringent provisions remained a dead letter.

The Arrears Bill ran through the House at the same time as the Crimes Act, and adopted as its basis the principle of compulsion or gift. Its operation was limited to holdings under the value of £30 (Griffith's valuation), and only to such tenants as could show that their rent had been paid between November, 1880, and November, 1881. The tenant, moreover, would have to give good proof before the land commission court or the county court of his inability to pay before his demand on the landlord or State could be entertained. The benefits of the bill were alike open to landlord and tenant, and they provided that the tenant having paid his one year's arrears, the State would pay one half the arrears, or one year's rent, and the landlord would remit the remainder. The bill must undoubtedly have saved many tenants from eviction, but at the same time it was a measure of relief as much to the landlord as the tenant, for the State made compensation for a bad debt which under other circumstances could never have been repaid.

The autumn was marked in Ireland by an attempt to resuscitate Irish trade and industry. An exhibition of

Irish manufactures was held in Dublin, and efforts were made in various ways to encourage home industry. Later in the year the Ladies' Land League was supplanted by a new organization—the National League—in which women took no part, but several members of the Ladies' Land League were empowered by the new society to found industries among the evicted tenantry of the west. These ladies went unprotected and alone to the wildest districts; in some of these places there were no houses for them to live in, and the League provided huts similar to those it was in the habit of erecting for evicted tenants. In these solitary huts the ladies held classes, teaching the women to knit, crochet, and sew; and by their instrumentality many were able to earn the bread they must otherwise have begged. Meanwhile it was found that the new Coercion Act was of no more efficiency than its forerunner in governing the country. The practice of boycotting was put down, but outrages were of daily occurrence, and there were many horrible murders; and in November the life of Mr. Justice Lawson was attempted in the Dublin streets. On the next evening a juryman, named Field, was attacked also in Dublin, and these daring attempts within the city filled society with grave alarms. Further steps were taken to silence seditious speakers, and early in January '83, Messers. Davitt, Healy, and Quinn were charged, not under the Coercion Act, but under a law which had not been put in force since Wentworth's administration in the days of Charles I. Judgment was given against them; they were charged to give surety for good behavior, or in default to six month's imprisonment; they chose the latter alternative, and were committed to gaol early in February. At the same time an action for libel on lord Spencer was proceeding against Mr. William O'Brien, the editor of *United Ireland*, who during the trial was elected member for Mallow. But the great interest of this period was the discovery of the *Invincible* Society, by whose members lord F. Cavendish and Mr. Burke had been murdered, and who had made the attacks on Mr. Justice Lawson and Mr. Field. It was in connection with these latter offences that the arrests were made, and it was not till the beginning of

February that evidence connected the Invincibles with the Phœnix Park murders. Ultimately five of the Invincibles were hanged, others sentenced to various terms of imprisonment, and James Carey, the founder and instigator of the society, turned queen's evidence, and received a free pardon. He did not long live to enjoy the reward of his treachery. Later in the year he and his family emigrated, but he was tracked on board ship, and shot by a man named O'Donnell. O'Donnell was tried in England, but even here much sympathy was felt for him; once the jury disagreed, and at the second trial the jurors asked to bring in a verdict of manslaughter, but he was eventually hanged, and his execution created much less stir than had been anticipated. Meanwhile a new and infinitely terrible society was appearing in Irish-American politics; in March there was an attempt to blow up the offices of the Local Government Board and of the *Times* with dynamite; and in November two explosions occurred on the underground railway. In February, '84, a terrible explosion shattered a great part of the Victoria station, and on the next day infernal machines were discovered at Ludgate Hill, Charing Cross, and Paddington; and in May simultaneous explosions occurred in St. James Square and the Junior Carlton Club. In November there was an explosion in Oldham, and in December one under London Bridge, and a case of two cwt. of dynamite was discovered at Dover custom-house. But the climax was reached in January, 1885, when serious damage was done to St. Stephen's Hall, Westminster, and to the Tower of London. That was the last serious explosion, but the "dynamite party" continued to receive fuds for their abominable outrages till the lapse of the Coercion Act, when the fund suddenly ran down, and was closed for want of support.

The spring session of 1884 was chiefly occupied in passing a Reform Bill conferring the franchise on all householders. The desirability of inculding Ireland in the benefits of act was hotly debated, and lord Claud Hamilton moved as an amendment, that the words Great Britain be substituted for the United Kingdom, but the ministers refused to consider the measure in a mutilated form, and eventually the bill passed the Commons. It was, however, thrown out by the Lords, on the plea that it was worse than useless unless accompanied by a Redistribution Bill, and an autumn session was devoted to passing this measure. The Redistribution Bill was much needed in Ireland. Many of the small boroughs, such as Portarlington, Mallow, New Ross, were thoroughly rotten, and in reducing the number of borough members, and increasing the representatives of the counties, the bill did good work.

That was the last measure of importance passed by the Gladstone ministry for Ireland. Throughout the winter, Egypt, not Ireland, occupied the public mind, and in the spring the Russian difficulty was the center of interest. But Ireland took care that she was not forgotten, and, in April, the prince of Wales made a conciliatory visit to Ireland, taking with him the princess and his young son. A levée and drawing-room were held, and the royal party were well received in Dublin, but in the provinces they met with a less cordial reception. Meanwhile ministers were debating whether to renew the whole or any part of the Crimes Act, which would expire in July. But the Conservatives were destined to decide this question, for on June 8th the Conservatives and Nationalists obtained a majority of twelve over the ministry on a budget question. Mr. Gladstone immediately resigned, and when lord Salisbury became premier he decided on the experiment of governing Ireland without exceptional powers.

CHAPTER XXXIX.

THE ELECTIONS OF 1885.

THE events of the autumn of '85 are too recent for us to be able to see them in their proper proportions, and the facts are too fresh in our memories to require any detailed survey. The early part of the autumn was spent by politicians of the three kingdoms in an election campaign, and in a diligent revision of the voting register.

No sooner were the Liberals out of office than Messrs.

Chamberlain and Dilke formed the project of a tour in Ireland; both had voted for what a Conservative contemporary terms "Cromwellian Coercion Acts," but the failure of these had produced a sudden conversion, and as early as June 17th Mr. Chamberlain was denouncing a system "founded on 30,000 soldiers encamped permanently in a hostile country," and declared that "an alien board of foreign officials" must be removed in favor "of a genuine Irish administration for purely Irish business." But this change of policy within five months of a general election, and while the Irish vote was yet unpromised, was mistrusted by the Nationalists; the proposal of the ex-ministerial tour was coldly received, and for various reasons the project was abandoned. Soon it became known that the Irish vote in England would be given to the Conservatives, partly as a protest against the government that had come in to further a policy of conciliation and had passed the most stringent Coercion Acts of the century, and partly to equalize the English parties, and thus leave the balance of power with Mr. Parnell. The Parnellites in Ireland were thoroughly organizing the country; mass meetings were held in every district, and in October a series of conventions assembled to elect the Nationalist candidates for the various constituencies. The Unionists, seeing the preparations of the Home Rulers, made common cause, and, sinking the old animosities of Whig and Tory, agreed to run only one Loyalist candidate in constituencies that were contested by Nationalists, and in order to determine the true state of public feeling they resolved to contest every constituency in the three southern provinces. This part of the programme was not strictly adhered to, for it was felt that the Unionists would obtain no support in some of the Connaught divisions, and in many that they contested they polled very few votes—30 in East Kerry, 75 in South Mayo, and only just over the hundred in several others, against Nationalist polls averaging four thousand. The Unionists attributed this want of support to the intimidation of the Nationalists, and it is possible that the dread of boycotting, which revived very much during the autumn, may have kept some voters from the poll; but, on the other hand, fear of eviction must have caused many Nationalist farmers, who were backward with their rent, to abstain from voting. But the percentage from either cause cannot have been very high, for there must be always a certain number of voters who, through sickness, stress of business, or distance, are unable to go to the poll, and the total poll of Ireland was 75 per cent of the voters, whereas the percentage in the London boroughs was only 74.

The three southern provinces returned a solid phalanx of Nationalists, and it was in Ulster that the real conflict took place. Twelve Ulster constituencies were so well known to be Unionist that the Nationalists did not contest them. These all fell to Conservatives, and in four contests the Nationalissts were beaten by Conservatives. Thus sixteen of the Ulster seats returned Conservatives, and seventeen Nationalists: Dublin University returned two Conservatives without a contest, so that the representation of Ireland stood—Nationalists, 86; Conservatives, 18; Liberals, 0. The Irish vote in England succeeded in turning the scale in twenty-five boroughs, and thus the casting vote is secured to the Home Rulers, the balance of parties being —Liberals, 333; Conservatives, 251; Home Rulers, 86. Majority of Home Rulers and Conservatives over Liberals, 4; of Liberals and Home Rulers over Conservatives, 148.

The elections were barely over, when Mr. Gladstone let it be known in a semi-official manner that he would be prepared to deal with the Home Rule question on the following lines:—The maintenance of the unity of the empire, the authority of the crown and the supremacy of the imperial parliament to be assured. The creation of an Irish parliament, to be intrusted with the entire management of all legislative and administrative affairs, securities being taken for the representation of minorities, and for an equitable partition of all imperial charges. At the announcement all England, Liberal and Conservative, was in an uproar, and very bitter accusations were made against Mr. Gladstone and his sudden conversion, but it is only just to remember that in February, 1882, while he was pursuing a policy of coercion, Mr. Gladstone already admitted on two occasions that the Home Rule question was one which might be dealt with in parliament. The tone of the English press since the Hawarden utterance, no less than the words of the queen's speech at the opening of parliament on the 21st of January, show that the feeling of the country is antagonistic to repeal of the union. "I have seen with deep sorrow," said her majesty, "the renewal, since I last addressed you, of the attempt to excite the people of Ireland to hostility against the legislative union between that country and Great Britain. I am resolutely opposed to any disturbance of that fundamental law, and in resisting it I am convinced that I shall be heartily supported by my parliament and my people."

But now, at the opening of the first parliament representing the householders of the three kingdoms, let us pause and ask ourselves whither our Irish policy is leading us. During 74 of the 85 years of legislative union we have attempted to govern Ireland by what, in direct contradiction of fact, we still call exceptional legislation, and yet, even with powers more stringent than martial law, we, with a force of forty thousand military and police, are unable to uphold the law among an adult male population of 500,000 persons. Under our government, three-eighths of the population has in one generation disappeared by famine, and the majority of the remainder are worse housed, worse clothed, worse fed than in any other country under heaven pretending to civilization. The lands of Connaught are in many places not worth twopence an acre without the value of the tenants' labor; lay them down in grass or plough them, and in a few years they will return to their pristine bog—only by spade culture can they be kept in cultivation. Yet from such lands as these in the famine year of '78 one man alone drew £27,000, while those who paid him were dependent for very food on charity. By repeated concessions to the tenants we have acknowledged that we know the system of land tenure in Ireland to be wrong; by their spiritless acquiescence in the curtailment of their power the landlords have admitted that they know themselves to have exceeded their rights. The land question of Ireland will never be settled till the cultivator is the possessor of the soil. A long system of wrong has engendered wrong; the landlords of to-day are the victims of their position and of the extravagance of their forefathers. One of three things we must do: we must suppress as best we can by force the expression of discontent born of cold, and misery, and hunger; we must throw the landlords overboard, or we must buy them out. Redress is due to the peasantry, but redress without compensation means wrong to thousands of innocent persons who have grown up under existing laws. We have tried expensive coercion; we have tried cheap conciliation; let us for once and the first time try the experiment of expensive justice to Ireland. Let us realize that peace at home is as well worth a rise of income tax as war abroad, and let the Irish landlords be bought out and compensated as were the slave owners of the West Indies. They must lose something by the transaction, and so must we; but if the tenant buys at ten years' purchase, and the landlord receives fifteen, the generosity of the English taxpayer will cost him no dearer than a few years of coercive policy.

There is another matter that we shall do well to decide calmly and without bitterness. Can we, or can we not, entertain the project of Home Rule? The law of self-preservation is first among nations, as among individuals. A great power cannot sacrifice herself for a small island, and the empire is justified in refusing any demand that endangers the empire. The nearness of Ireland to our coasts, and her richness in natural harbors, compels us to deal with any demand for separation in a high-handed manner. No project for Home Rule could be entertained which would involve the loss of naval or military power in Ireland; the ports, the army, and the forts must be under imperial control. But at this moment there is no real demand for separation. Ireland knows that she gains much in safety and in other ways from the connection, and practical politicians are aware that the day of small States is gone by. The concession of Home Rule would probably kill any wish that now exists for separation; but in our wealth, our army, our population of six to one, we have every security, for we could annihilate Ireland in a week.

A difficulty of another kind is the demand of the Nationalists for the right to protect Irish manufactures, and on this subject the Irish leaders have spoken definitely. "We should insist," says Mr. Parnell, "upon a parliament that shall have the power to protect Irish manufactures. if it be the wish of that parliament, and of the Irish people, that they should be protected. No parliament will work satisfactorily which has not free powers to raise revenues for the purposes of government in Ireland in such a way as shall seem fit and best to it. I am of the opinion—an opinion which I have expressed before now—that it would be well to protect certain industries, at all events for a time."

That this policy would be fatal to what little there is of Irish trade, is a generally received impression in England. But the trade of Ireland is moribund, it cannot be ruined; and if its bad case were made worse by protection the mistake could be remedied in a single day. We do not withhold the right of protection from our colonies. Firmly convinced of the benefits of free trade, we receive the products of Australia and Canada, and let those colonies levy duty on ours. Why should we treat Ireland in a less liberal manner? The empire would not be endangered by a duty on English woolens and calicoes; the Irish consumption is not so great that our trade would be impoverished. At least, before the new parliament forces a fresh coercive measure on Ireland, let us pause and consider the fruits of the repressive policy of the last government. When Mr. Gladstone came into power Ireland was, as now, undergoing a season of agricultural depression. Bad weather had brought bad crops, the tenants could not pay, and the landlords punished poverty with eviction. The Irish members—the representatives of the farming class—warned us that if nothing were done to stay evictions, disturbances would ensue. Nothing was done, the warning was construed as a threat, and was disregarded, the disturbances came, and we met them with coercion; we silenced the mouthpieces of the people, we threw them in gaol, we turned them out of parliament. we checked the expression of discontent, and drove the county into the old paths of outrage We introduced a Land Bill that satisfied our ideas of the needs of Ireland, but the men who knew the country told us that it was insufficient. Again we turned a deaf ear to their warning, and when the event proved the truth of their opinion, we met the difficulty with another Coercian Bill more stringent than the last. By this we forced the agitators from the field; some retired, others took a secondary part to which we had consigned them, but not the law but the outrage-monger and dynamiter played the leading *rôle*. "Men in the extremity of suffering," said Landor, "lose sooner the sense of fear than the excitability to indignation. Cruelty is no more the cure of crimes than it is the cure of suffering; compassion, in the first instance, is good for both. I have known it to bring compunction when nothing else would. Let us try, then, rather to remove the ills of Ireland than to persuade those who undergo them that there are none. For if they could be thus persuaded we should have brutalized them first to such a degree as would render them more dangerous than they were in the reigns of Elizabeth or Charles. There will never be a want of money or a want of confidence in any well-governed State that has been long at peace, and without the danger of its interruption. But a want of the necessaries of life, in peasants or artisans, when the seasons have been favorable, is a certain sign of defect in the constitution, or of criminality in the administration. It may not be advisable or safe to tell every one this truth, yet it is needful to inculcate it on the minds of governors, and to repeat it until they find out the remedy, else the people, one day or other, will send those out to look for it who may trample down more in the search than suits good husbandry."

A TABLE OF DATES.

A.D.
281. Overthrow of the Fenian Power.
378. Accession of Niall Mōr.
432. The Mission of St. Patrick.
465. The Death of St. Patrick.
521. Birth of St. Columba.
563. Mission of St. Columba to the Northern Picts.
795. First Danish Invasion.
980. Brian Boru succeeds to the Throne of Munster.
1014. Defeat of the Danes at Clontarf.
1166. Accession of Rory O'Connor, last Ard-Righ of Erin.
1169. The Norman Barons invade Leinster.
1171. Invasion under Henry II.
1174. Battle of Thurles.
1193. Death of Rory O'Connor.
1216. Henry III., on his accession, extends the privileges of Magna Charta to his Irish subjects.
1367. Statute of Kilkenny.
1478. Gerald Fitzgerald, Earl of Kildare, created Lord Deputy.
1487. Lambert Simnel crowned King of Ireland.
1490. Arrival of Perkin Warbeck in Cork.
1494. Poyning's Law is passed.
1496. Kildare arrested for rebellion, and reinstated Lord Deputy.
1497. Battle of Knocktow.
1513. Death of Kildare—Succeeded by his son Gerald.
1534. Kildare is imprisoned in the Tower—Rebellion of his son, Thomas Fitzgerald.
1537. Execution of Thomas Fitzgerald and his five uncles.
1540. Henry VIII. distributes the Church Lands.
1541. The title of King of Ireland conferred on the English King.
1548. O'More and O'Connor, chieftains of Leix and Offally, imprisoned in England.
1552. Dispute between Matthew and Shane O'Neill.
1558. The plantation of Leix and Offally.
1559. Shane O'Neill succeeds to the title of The O'Neill.
1561. O'Neill visits Queen Elizabeth.
1563. O'Neill signs a peace with Elizabeth and massacres the Scottish settlers of Antrim.

TABLE OF DATES.

A.D.
1567. O'Neill and his retinue take refuge with the Scots and are murdered. Sidney arrests the Earl of Desm)nd and John Fitzgerald and sends them to the Tower.
1568. Rising of Sir James Fitzmaurice Fitzgerald.
1569. Elizabeth confiscates the territory of the O'Neills.
1570. Sir Thomas Smith murdered while attempting to plant County Down.
1572. Sir James Fitzmaurice Fitzgerald surrenders.
1574. Escape of the Earl of Desmond.
1576. Drury and Malby appointed Presidents of Munster and Connaught.
1577. Massacre of Mullaghmast.
1579. The Desmond Rebellion—Death of Sir James Fitzmaurice—The Earl of Desmond joins the rebels.
1582. Death of Sir John and Sir James Geraldine—Suppression of the rebellion.
1583. Death of the Earl of Desmond.
1586. The Plantation of Munster—Perrot seizes Red Hugh O'Donnell.
1589. Confiscation of Monaghan.
1592. Escape of Red Hugh O'Donnell.
1595. Hugh, Earl of Tyrone, elected The O'Neill.
1599. Campaign of Essex in Munster.
1600. Mountjoy commands the English forces.
1603. Surrender of Hugh—Death of Elizabeth.
1607. Flight of Tyrone and Tyrconnel.
1608. Confiscation of six Ulster Counties.
1611. Plantation of Ulster
1612. Plantation of Wexford.
1619. Plantation of Longford and Westmeath.
1622. Plantation of Leitrim and part of Leix and Offally.
1625. Accession of Charles.
1626. The "graces" promised.
1633. Wentworth appointed Lord Deputy.
1635. Commission of Defective Titles in Connaught.
1640. Wentworth becomes Lord Strafford and Lord Lieutenant of Ireland.
1641. Outbreak of the Rebellion.
1642. Owen Roe O'Neill and Colonel Preston land in Ireland—Confederation of Kilkenny
1646. Battle of Benburb.
1649. Peace signed between the King and the Confederates—The Execution of Charles—Cromwell arrives in Ireland—Death of Owen Roe.
1652. End of the Civil War.
1653. Cromwell begins his Plantation.
1658. Death of Cromwell.
1660. Charles II. declared King.

A.D.
1662. The Act of Settlement.
1663. The Court of Claims opens in Dublin.
1685. Accession of James II.
1688. William III. lands in Torbay.
1689. Talbot raises Rapparees for James—Siege of Derry and Enniskillen—James lands at Cork—Convenes Parliament in Dublin—Derry is delivered.
1690. Arrival of William—Battle of the Boyne—Flight of James—First Siege of Limerick—Marlborough captures Cork and Kinsale.
1691. Battle of Aughrim—Siege and Treaty of Limerick.
1692. Emigration of Catholics—Catholics excluded from the Irish Parliament.
1696. Act for disarming Catholics and rendering foreign education penal.
1698. Penal Acts against mixed marriages—Banishment of the Romish Clergy.
1699. Prohibitive tariff on the export of Irish wool.
1701. Roman Catholic Solicitors disqualified.
1702. Accession of Anne.
1704. Penal Acts against Catholics.
1706. Further Acts against Solicitors.
1710. Penal Act against Catholics.
1711. Persecution of Presbyterians.
1713. Swift becomes Dean of St. Patrick's.
1714. Accession of George I.
1719. The English Parliament empowered to make Laws to bind the Irish people—The Irish House of Lords deprived of right to affirm or reverse judgment.
1723. Wood's Patent granted—Cancelled two years later—Potato Famine.
1727. Accession of George II.—Roman Catholics Disfranchised.
1734. Stringent Act against Catholic Solicitors—Berkeley consecrated Bishop of Cloyne.
1744. Chesterfield made Viceroy.
1745. Lucas enters Parliament—Battles of Fontenoy and Prestonpans.
1746. Terrible Potato Famine—Battle of Culloden.
1759. Riots in Dublin on the Rumor of Union.
1760. Accession of George III.—Denis Daly, Hussy Burgh, and Henry Flood enter Parliament.
1761. Whiteboy Insurrection.
1762. Oakboy Insurrection.
1767. Octennial Act.
1768. Rising of the Steelboys.
1773. Irish National Debt reaches the figure of £1,000,000.
1775. Outbreak of the War of American Independence — Grattan enters Parliament—Troops sent from Ireland against the Colonists—Flood becomes Vice-Treasurer.

TABLE OF DATES. 211

A.D.
1776. Embargo on Exports to America.
1778. First Roman Catholic Relief Bill.
1779. Formation of the Irish Volunteers.
1780. Freedom of Trade with the Colonies granted to Ireland.
1782. Grattan's Parliaments.
1783. The Volunteer Convention — Rejection of Flood's Reform Bill.
1784. Agrarian feuds of Orangemen and Defenders.
1786. Anti-Tithe disturbances in Munster.
1789. The Regency difficulty—Outbreak of the French Revolution.
1791. Agitation for Catholic Emancipation—Formation of the Society of United Irishmen.
1792. The Legal Profession opened to Catholics—Restrictions on Catholic Education removed — The House of Commons destroyed by fire.
1793. Catholics allowed to vote at Elections—Enfranchisement of 40s. Freeholders—Execution of Louis XVI.—War declared by France against England—The Pension List revised—Public Debt of Ireland £2,400,000.
1794. Suppression of the Society of United Irishman—Lord Fitzwilliam appointed Viceroy.
1795. Maynooth College founded and endowed by Parliament—Viceroyalty of Lord Fitzwilliam—Recall of Fitzwilliam Rejection of Reform Bill—Reconstruction of United Irish Society—Tone goes to America.
1796. The Insurrection Act—Extension of United Irish Society—French Fleet appears in Bantry Bay.
1797. Martial Law in Ulster—Reform Bill rejected—Execution of William Orr—National Debt of Ireland £4,000,000.
1798. Abercrombie commands the English Forces—Is succeeded by Lake—Arrest of the Directory of the United Irish Society—The Rebellion—French Expedition to Killala and Lough Swilly—Death of Tone—Execution of Rebels—Proposal of Union.
1799. Resistance to Union.
1800. The Union is passed.
1801. Jan. 1., the Union comes into operation—Irish National Debt, £26,841,219—Act for suspending the Habeas Corpus and empowering the Viceroy to proclaim Martial Law.
*1802. Peace of Amiens—United Irishmen released from Fort George—Robert Emmet arrives in Dublin.
*1803. The French War resumed—Emmet's rebellion.
1804. Pitt resumes office—Napoleon crowned Emperor—National Debt of Ireland, £43,000,000.

The years, since the Union, during which Ireland has been governed by ordinary law are marked with a star (*).

A D.
- *1805. Catholic Petition presented by Grenville and Fox—The Veto is first hinted at—National Debt of Ireland, £52,000,000.
- *1806. Death of Pitt—Grenville-Fox ministry—Death of Fox.
- 1807. No Popery ministry—Wellesley becomes Chief Secretary—Revival of Whiteboyism—Insurrection Act.
- 1808. Catholic Petition, with Veto, presented by Grattan—The Roman Catholic Prelates protest against the Veto.
- 1809. Continuation of Catholic agitation—Growth of Orangeism.
- 1810. Veto and payment of Catholic clergy proposed—Rejected by Irish Catholics — O'Connell becomes Chairman of the Catholic Association—Agitation for Repeal.
- *1811. Peel becomes Chief Secretary—Insurrection Act expires.
- *1813. Grattan moves for Catholic Emancipation with Veto.
- 1814. The Catholic Board is suppressed—Insurrection Act.
- 1815. Peace of Waterloo—The population of Ireland, 6,000,000—Act passed facilitating Evictions.
- 1817. Famine and disturbance—Martial law—Military force in Ireland, 126,000—The Irish National Debt, amounting to £112,704,773, incorporated with that of Great Britain.
- *1818. Insurrection Act expires.
- *1819. The six Acts.
- *1820. Accession of George IV.—Death of Grattan.
- *1821. Plunket brings in Emancipation Bill—The King visits Ireland—Population, 6,801,827.
- 1822. Famine—Insurrection Act—Habeas Corpus suspended.
- 1823. The Catholic Association formed by O'Connell and Shiel.
- 1824. The "Catholic rent" represents half-a-million associates.
- 1825. The Association is suppressed and reconstructed—Government brings in a Bill for Emancipation with "wings"—Bill rejected by Lords
- 1826. Exports of grain and Cattle to England worth nearly £8,000,000.
- 1827. Death of Canning.
- 1828. Wellington-Peel ministry—Repeal of Test Act and Corporation Act—O'Connell elected for Clare.
- 1829. Catholic Emancipation—Disfranchisement of the 40s. freeholders.
- *1830. Accession of William IV.
- 1831. Stanley's Bill for National Education—Tithe War—Arms Act—Population of Ireland, 7,734,365; of England and Wales, 13,894,574; of Scotland, 2,365,807.
- 1832. Tithe War.
- 1833. Grey's Coercion Act—Church Temporalities Act.
- 1834. O'Connell takes up the Repeal Question seriously.
- 1835. Lord Lieutenant empowered to issue Special Commissions to try offenders—Thomas Drummond becomes Chief Secretary.
- 1836. Municipal Reform Bill.
- 1837. Accession of Queen Victoria.

TABLE OF DATES. 213

A.D.
1838. Poor Law—Tithe Commutation Act—Father Mathew joins the teetotal movement.
1839. The Precursor Society.
1841. The Peel Ministry—The Repeal Association—Population of Ireland, 8,175,124; of England and Wales, 15,906,741; of Scotland, 2,620,184.
*1842. Foundation of the Young Ireland Party.
1843. The Repeal Year—Arrest of O'Connell and others—The State Trials begin—Value of export provisions to England, £16,000,000—Arms Act.
1844. The Traversers are convicted—Judgment reversed by the House of Lords—The Devon Commission.
1845. The Government Grant to Maynooth increased—Foundation of the Queen's Colleges—Death of Davis—Patato blight.
*1846. Commencement of the Famine—Repeal of Corn Laws—£100,000 voted for relief of distress—The embargo on the importation of Indian corn is raised—Smith O'Brien imprisoned in the Clock Tower—The Young Irelanders secede from the Repeal Association—300,000 persons perish from want and typhus.
1847. Famine—Crime and Outrage Act—Deaths by famine and fever, 500,000; Emigration, 200,000; Value of Agricultural produce, £44,958,120.
1848. The French Revolution—The Abortive Rising.
1849. Encumbered Estates Act.
1850. The Irish Tenant League—Electoral Reform Bill.
1851. Population of Ireland, 6,552,385, of England and Wales, 17,927,609; of Scotland, 2,888,724; Emigratian from Ireland 257,372.
1852. General Election—Many Tenant Leaguers returned—Emigration, 368,764.
1854. Foundation of the Catholic University.
1855. Formation of the Palmerston Ministry.
1860. The Land Bill.
1861. Population of Ireland, 5,764,543; of England and Wales, 20,061,725; of Scotland, 3,061,329.
1862. The M'Manus funeral.
1863. The *Irish People* newspaper founded.
*1864.
1865. Close of the American War—Arrest of the Fenian Leaders —Escape of Stephens—Peace Preservation (Continuance) Act.
1866. Formation of the Derby Ministry.
1867. Fenian Risings—The Manchester Rescue—The Clerkenwell Explosion.
1868. Disraeli becomes Prime Minister—The Reform Bill—Mr. Gladstone declares for Disestablishment of the Irish Church—Dissolution of Parliament.

A.D.
1869. The Liberal Government—The Disestablishment Bill passes.
1870. The Land Act—The Home Rule League.
1871. The Disestablishment Bill comes into operation—Number of Anglicans in Ireland, 600,000 ;—Population, 5,412,407 ; of England and Wales, 22,704,108 ; of Scotland, 3,858,613.
1872.
1873. The Government defeated on the Catholic University Bill—All Tests in Trinity College abolished.
1874. The General Election—Ireland returns 60 Home Rule members.
1875. Lord Hartington succeeds Mr. Gladstone as Leader of the Opposition—Mr. Parnell enters Parliament.
1877. Failure of the Potato Crop—Mr. Parnell leads the Advanced Home Rulers.
1878. Failure of the potato crop—Agrarian disturbances.
1879. Death of Mr. Butt—Mr. Shaw leads the Home Rulers—Disastrous tfailure of crops—Famine—The Land League is founded.
1880. General Election—62 Home Rulers returned to new Parliament—The Peace Preservation Act lapses—Terrible distress and increase of agrarian disturbances—State Trial of the officers of the Land League.
1881. Mr. Forster's Coercion Act—Imprisonment of Messrs. Davitt and Dillon—The Land Bill—Imprisonment of 918 Suspects without trial—The Land League declared illegal—Population of Ireland, 5,159,849 ; of England and Wales, 24,608,391 ; of Scotland, 3,734,370.
1882. Agrarian disturbances—Release of the Leaders—Murder of Lord F. Cavendish and Mr. Burke—The Crimes Act—The Arrears Act—Imprisonment of Mr. Gray—Continued disturbances—The National League founded.
1883. Arrest of the Invincibles—Imprisonment of Messrs. Davitt, Healy and Quin—Dynamite outrages—The Parnell Testimonial.
1884. Parliamentary Reform Bill—Mr. Trevelyan resigns—Redistribution Bill.
1885. Resignation of Liberal Ministry—Lord Carnarvon succeeds Lord Spencer—Crimes Act expires in July—General Election: 86 Nationalists and 18 Conservatives returned to Parliament—Agricultural Depression.

LIST OF AUTHORITIES

Alison, Life of Castlereagh.
Annual Register, various volumes.

Barrington, Personal Recollections.
Barry, (Stephen), A Plan of Tenure Reform for Ireland.
Baldwin Brown, Historical Account of the Laws against the Catholics.
Butler, Hist. Memoirs of the English, Scotch, and Irish Catholics.

Cairnes Political Essays.
Castlereagh, Correspondence.
Cloncurry, Personal Recollections.
Chronicum Scotorum.
Coote, History of the Union.
Cornwallis, Correspondence.
Curran, Memoirs of Curran.
Curry, Review of the Civil Wars.
Curry, The State of the Catholics in the 18th Century.
Cusack, Miss M. F., History of Ireland.
Cusack, Miss M. F., Student's Manual of Irish History.

Daunt, J. O'Neill, Ireland and her Agitators.
Daunt, J. O'Neill, The Financial Grievances of Ireland.
Daunt, J. O'Neill, Personal Recollections of O'Connell.
Davis, Life of Curran.
Davis, Articles in the *Nation*.

Dillon, J. B., Articles in the *Nation*.
Dillon, William. The Dismal Science.
Disraeli, Life of Lord George Bentinck.
Duffy' Sir C. G. Young Ireland.
Duffy, Sir C. G., Four Years of Irish History.

Emerson, Life of Gladstone.

Forman, Courage of the Irish Nation.
Froude, History of England.
Froude, The English in Ireland.
Ferguson, The Irish before the Conquest.

Gardiner, The first two Stuarts and the Puritan Revolution.
George, the Irish Land Question.
Godkin, The Irish Land War.
Gordon, History of the Irish Rebellion.
Grattan, Life and Times of Henry Grattan.
Green, History of the English People.

Hansard, Debates.
Haverty, History of Ireland.
Hitchman, Life of Beaconsfield.

Ireland's case briefly stated by a true lover of his King and Country.
Irish Poor Laws, past and present.

LIST OF AUTHORITIES.

Joyce, Old Celtic Romances.

Keating, History of Ireland.

Landor, Imaginary Conversations.
Lecky, The History of England in the 18th Century.
Lecky, Leaders of Public Opinion in Ireland.
Lingard, History of England.

Macauley, History of England.
M'Carthy, History of our own Times.
M'Carthy, The Four Georges, Vol. I.
M'Carthy, J. H., An Outline of Irish History.
M'Carthy, J. H., England under Gladstone.
M'Gee, James, Sketches of Irish Soldiers in every land.
M'Gee, James, the Men of '48.
M'Gee, T. D'A., Popular History of Ireland.
M'Gee, T. D'A., History of the Irish Settlers in North America.
M'Geoghegan, History of Ireland.
M'Nevin, Confiscation of Ulster.
M'Nevin, The Irish Volunteers.

Madden, History of the Penal Laws.
Madden, Lives and Times of the United Irishmen.
Maddyn, Ireland and her Rulers.
Maddyn, Leaders of Parties.
Maguire, Life of Father Mathew.
Meehan, Life of the Geraldines.
Meehan, Life of Hugh O'Neill.
Memoirs of Ireland, by the author of the Secret History of Europe.
Mill, J. S., The Irish Land Question.
Mitchel, Life and Times of Hugh O'Neill.

Mitchel, Jail Journal.
Mitchel, History of Ireland.
Mitchel, Last Conquest of Ireland (perhaps).
Moore, Life of Lord Edward Fitzgerald.
Mountmorres, Impartial Reflections upon the present Crisis.
Musgrave, Select Passages from the History of the Irish Rebellion.

Narrative of Visits in '46 and '47 by Members of the Society of Friends.

O'Brien, Barry, Fifty Years of Concessions to Ireland.
O'Brien, W. Smith, Principles of Government.
O'Brien, W. Smith, On the Causes of Discontent.
O'Callaghan, History of the Irish Brigade.
O'Callaghan, The Green Book.
O'Connell, John, Life of D. O'Connell.
O'Connell, John, Commercial Injustices.
O'Conor, Military History of the Irish Nation.
O'Curry, The Manners and Customs of the Ancient Irish.
O'Curry, Lectures on Irish History.
O'Donovan, Annals of the Four Masters.
O'Driscoll, History to the Treaty of Limerick.
O'Grady, History of Ireland—Scientific and Philosophical.
O'Grady, History of the Heroic Period.

Parliamentary Register.
Phillips, Life of Curran.
Plowden, History of Ireland.
Plowden, From the Union to the year 1810.

LIST OF AUTHORITIES. 217

Real wants of the Irish People.
Report of the Commissioners for administering the Poor Law.

Spencer, View of the state of Ireland.
Stephen, Leslie, Life of Swift.
Sullivan, New Ireland.
Swift, Tracts and Pamphlets on Ireland.

Temple, The Irish Rebellion.
Times, Reprinted Articles on the Irish Famine.

Tone, Life and Adventures of Wolfe Tone.
Trevelyan, The Irish Crisis—being an account of the remedial measures for the Relief of the Famine of '46, '47.

Walpole, A Short History of the Kingdom of Ireland.
Warner, The Rebellion in Ireland.
Warner, History of Ireland.
Wright, History of Ireland.

Young, Tour in Ireland.

Sundry Articles in the Quarterly; Nineteenth Century; Fortnightly Dublin and Saturday Reviews; and in the daily papers.

www.ingramcontent.com/pod-product-compliance
Lightning Source LLC
Chambersburg PA
CBHW031829230426
43669CB00009B/1274